SIXTH EDITION
GRAMMAR 1
IN CONTEXT

SANDRA N. ELBAUM

 NATIONAL GEOGRAPHIC LEARNING

 CENGAGE Learning

Australia • Brazil • Mexico • Singapore • United Kingdom • United States

Grammar in Context 1, Sixth Edition
Student Book
Sandra N. Elbaum

Publisher: Sherrise Roehr

Executive Editor: Laura Le Dréan

Managing Editor: Jennifer Monaghan

Development Editor: Claudi Mimó

Executive Marketing Manager: Ben Rivera

Product Marketing Manager: Dalia Bravo

Senior Director, Production: Michael Burggren

Content Project Manager: Mark Rzeszutek

Manufacturing Planner: Mary Beth Hennebury

Interior Design: Brenda Carmichael

Compositor: SPi Global

Cover Design: Brenda Carmichael

Cover Photo: Canyonlands National Park,
Colorado Plateau, Utah

For permission to use material from this text or product, submit all requests online at www.cengage.com/permissions

Further permissions questions can be emailed to
permissionrequest@cengage.com

ISBN 13: 978-1-305-07537-5

National Geographic Learning
20 Channel Center Street
Boston, Massachusetts 02210
USA

Cengage Learning is a leading provider of customized learning solutions with office locations around the globe, including Singapore, the United Kingdom, Australia, Mexico, Brazil, and Japan. Locate our local office at international.cengage.com/region

Cengage Learning products are represented in Canada by Nelson Education, Ltd.

Visit National Geographic Learning online at **ngl.cengage.com**
Visit our corporate website at **www.cengage.com**

Printed in the United States of America
Print Number: 01   Print Year: 2016

CONTENTS

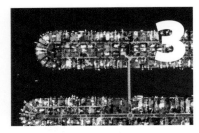

GRAMMAR **Singular and Plural Nouns**
There Is/There Are
Articles
CONTEXT **Housing**

GRAMMAR **Possession**
Object Pronouns
Questions About the Subject
CONTEXT **Families and Names**

5

GRAMMAR **The Present Continuous**
CONTEXT **Planet in Danger**

6

GRAMMAR **The Future**
CONTEXT **Our Future**

GRAMMAR **Count and Noncount Nouns**
Quantity Words and Phrases
CONTEXT **Healthy Living**

GRAMMAR **Adjectives and Adverbs**
Noun Modifiers
Too/Very/Enough
CONTEXT **Great Women**

GRAMMAR   **Comparatives and Superlatives**
  CONTEXT   **American Experiences**

GRAMMAR   **Verb Review**
                Auxiliary Verbs with *Too* and *Either*
                Auxiliary Verbs in Tag Questions
  CONTEXT   **People on the Move**

APPENDICES

GLOSSARY OF GRAMMATICAL TERMS

INDEX

I am grateful to the team at National Geographic Learning/Cengage Learning for showing their faith in the *Grammar in Context* series by putting their best resources and talent into it. I would especially like to thank Laura Le Dréan for driving this series into an exciting, new direction. Her overall vision of this new edition has been a guiding light. I would also like to thank my development editor, Claudi Mimó, for managing the difficult day-to-day task of polishing and refining the manuscript toward its finished product. I thank Development Editor Yeny Kim for her keen eye for detail and invaluable suggestions. I would like to thank Dennis Hogan, Sherrise Roehr, and John McHugh for their ongoing support of *Grammar in Context* through its many editions.

I wish to acknowledge the immigrants, refugees, and international students I have known, both as a teacher and as a volunteer with refugee agencies. These people have increased my understanding of my own language and taught me to see life from another point of view. By sharing their observations, questions, and life stories, they have enriched my life enormously.

This new edition is dedicated to the millions of displaced people in the world. The United States is the new home of many refugees, who survived unspeakable hardships in Burundi, Rwanda, Iraq, Sudan, Burma, Bhutan, and other countries. Their resiliency in starting a new life and learning a new language is a tribute to the human spirit.
—*Sandra N. Elbaum*

The author and publisher would like to thank the following people for their contributions:

Pamela Ardizzone, Rhode Island College;

Dorothy S. Avondstoudt, Miami Dade College—Wolfson Campus;

Patricia Bennett, Grossmont College;

Mariusz Bojarczuk, Bunker Hill Community College;

Rodney Borr, Glendale Community College;

Nancy Boyer, Golden West College;

Charles Brooks, Norwalk Community College;

Gabriela Cambiasso, Harold Washington College;

Julie Condon, St. Cloud State University;

Anne Damiecka, Lone Star College — CyFair;

Mohammed Debbagh, Virginia Commonwealth University;

Frank DeLeo, Broward College;

Jeffrey DiIuglio, Boston University Center for English Language and Orientation Programs;

Monique Dobbertin Cleveland, Los Angeles Pierce College;

Lindsey Donigan, Fullerton College;

Jennifer J. Evans, University of Washington;

Norm Evans, Brigham Young University—Hawaii;

David Gillham, Moraine Valley Community College;

Martin Guerra, Mountain View College;

Eric Herrera, Universidad Técnica Nacional;

Cora Higgins, Bunker Hill Community College;

Barbara Inerfeld, Rutgers University;

Barbara Jonckheere, California State University, Long Beach;

Gursharan Kandola, University of Houston;

Roni Lebrauer, Saddleback College;

Dr. Miriam Moore, Lord Fairfax Community College;

Karen Newbrun Einstein, Santa Rosa Junior College;

Stephanie Ngom, Boston University Center for English Language and Orientation Programs;

Charl Norloff, International English Center, University of Colorado Boulder;

Gabriella Nuttall, Sacramento City College;

Fernanda Ortiz, University of Arizona;

Dilcia Perez, Los Angeles City College;

Stephen Peridore, College of Southern Nevada;

Tiffany Probasco, Bunker Hill Community College;

Natalia Schroeder, Long Beach City College;

Elizabeth Seabury, Bunker Hill Community College;

Maria Spelleri, State College of Florida, Manatee-Sarasota;

Susan Stern, Irvine Valley College;

Vincent Tran, University of Houston;

Karen Vlaskamp, Northern Virginia Community College—Annandale;

Christie Ward, Intensive English Language Program, Central Connecticut State University;

Colin Ward, Lone Star College—North Harris;

Laurie A. Weinberg, J. Sargeant Reynolds Community College

My parents immigrated to the United States from Poland and learned English as a second language as adults. My sisters and I were born in the United States. My parents spoke Yiddish to us; we answered in English. In that process, my parents' English improved immeasurably. Such is the case with many immigrant parents whose children are fluent in English. They usually learn English much faster than others; they hear the language in natural ways, in the context of daily life.

Learning a language in context, whether it be from the home, from work, or from a textbook, cannot be overestimated. The challenge for me has been to find a variety of high-interest topics to engage the adult language learner. I was thrilled to work on this new edition of *Grammar in Context* for National Geographic Learning. In so doing, I have been able to combine exciting new readings with captivating photos to exemplify the grammar.

I have given more than 100 workshops at ESL programs and professional conferences around the United States, where I have gotten feedback from users of previous editions of *Grammar in Context*. Some teachers have expressed concern about trying to cover long grammar lessons within a limited time. While ESL is not taught in a uniform number of hours per week, I have heeded my audiences and streamlined the series so that the grammar and practice covered is more manageable. And in response to the needs of most ESL programs, I have expanded and enriched the writing component.

Whether you are a new user of *Grammar in Context* or have used this series before, I welcome you to this new edition.

Sandra N. Elbaum

For my loves

Gentille, Chimene, Joseph, and Joy

Grammar in Context presents grammar in interesting contexts that are relevant to students' lives and then recycles the language and context throughout every activity. Learners gain knowledge and skills in both grammar structures and topic areas.

New To This Edition

NATIONAL GEOGRAPHIC PHOTOGRAPHS introduce unit themes and draw learners into the context.

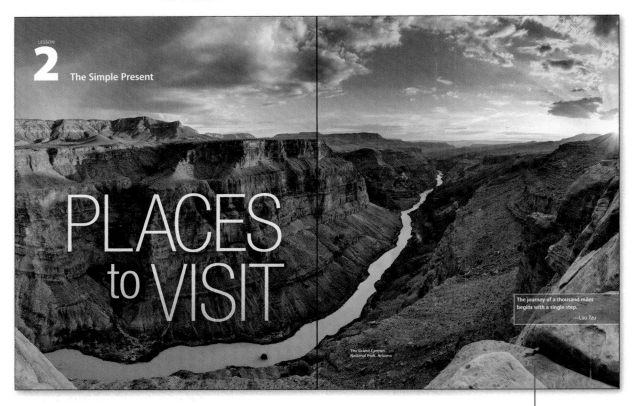

LESSON

2

The Simple Present

PLACES to VISIT

The journey of a thousand miles begins with a single step.
—Lao Tzu

The Grand Canyon
National Park, Arizona

New To This Edition

EVERY LESSON OPENER includes a quote from an artist, scientist, author, or thinker that helps students connect to the theme.

NEW AND UPDATED READINGS,
many with National Geographic content, introduce the target grammar in context and provide the springboard for practice.

NEW LISTENING EXERCISES
reinforce the grammar through natural spoken English.

TIMES SQUARE

🎧 Read the following essay. Pay special attention to the words in bold.

I live in New York City. New York has so many things to see and do. I especially love Times Square. Times Square is a top tourist attraction in the United States. Times Square is **always** a busy place. More than 300,000 pedestrians⁶ pass through Times Square every day. It has hotels, restaurants, theaters, and shopping. **Every night** visitors come to see an amazing display of electronic billboards.⁷

New Year's Eve is especially wonderful at Times Square. **Every year** New Yorkers and tourists come together at Times Square to count down to the new year. About a million people wait for the Waterford Crystal ball to drop, marking the beginning of the new year. The ball **always** drops at exactly midnight.

I **usually** go to Times Square with my friends to see the ball drop. I **never** drive there because parking is so expensive. We **always** take the subway. **Sometimes** it's very cold on New Year's Eve. If the temperature is below 10 degrees, I **usually** stay home and watch the ball drop on TV with my friends.

Times Square is also near the theater district in New York. I **hardly ever** go to the theater because it's so expensive. Some theater tickets cost more than $200! It's **often** hard to get a ticket for the popular shows. The tickets are **almost always** sold out.⁸

I love New York City. Tourists from all over the world love it, too.

―――――――
⁶ *pedestrian:* a person on foot
⁷ *billboard:* a large outdoor sign
⁸ *sold out:* all gone

The Simple Present **53**

A: Does your aunt (*ever/never*) come to New York to see you here?
　　8.

B: No, she (*ever/never*) does. She says it's too cold here.
　　9.

A: But it's not cold in the summer.

B: She (*always says/says always*) it's too crowded here. What about you? Do you travel a lot?
　　10.

A: No. I like to travel, but my husband doesn't. So we do things here in New York.

B: Do you (*ever go/go ever*) to Times Square on New Year's Eve?
　　11.

A: No, we never (*do/don't*). (*It's always/Always it's*) so crowded. We
　　12.　　　　13.
(*get together often/often get together*) with friends on New Year's Eve.
　　14.

2.13 Prepositions of Time

Preposition	Examples	Explanation
in	Times Square isn't crowded **in the morning**. We visit museums **in the afternoon**. Theaters are crowded **in the evening**.	We use *in* with general times of day: *the morning, the afternoon, the evening.*
	We elect a U.S. president every four years: **in 2016**, **in 2020**, **in 2024**, and so on.	We use *in* with years.
	We like to travel **in the summer**. People go to Times Square even **in the winter**.	We use *in* with seasons: *the summer, the fall, the winter, the spring.*
	New York is cold **in December**.	We use *in* with months.
on	Many people go to Times Square **on New Year's Eve**. We watch the ball drop **on December 31**.	We use *on* with specific dates and days, such as holidays.
	I like to relax **on the weekend**.	We use *on* with *the weekend.*
at	Let's go to Times Square **at 10 o'clock**. The ball in Times Square drops **at midnight**.	We use *at* with specific times of day: *2 o'clock, noon, midnight.*
	There are many people in Times Square **at night**.	We use *at* with *night.*
from...to from...until	The national parks are crowded **from May to October**. The subway in Washington runs **from 5 a.m. until midnight** on weekdays.	We use *from … to/until* with a beginning time and an ending time.

Language Note:
In informal English, we sometimes say *from … till* instead of *from … until.*
　　The museum is open **from 9 till 4 o'clock**.

58 Lesson: 2

NEW REDESIGNED
GRAMMAR CHARTS offer
straightforward explanations and provide contextualized, clear examples of the structure.

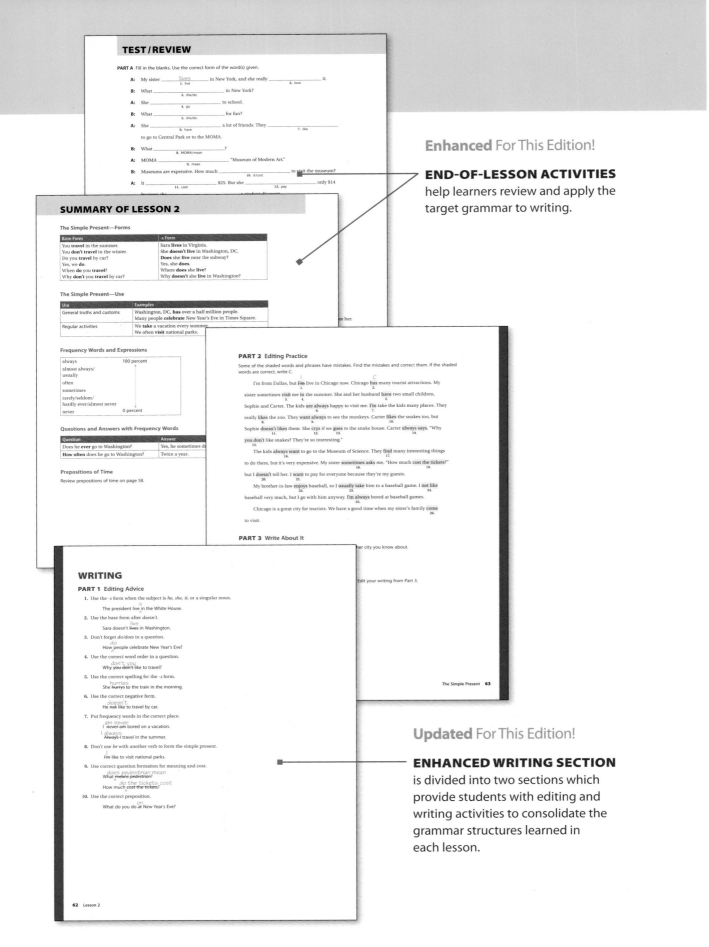

TEST / REVIEW

PART A Fill in the blanks. Use the correct form of the word(s) given.

A: My sister ___lives___ in New York, and she really ___ it.
　　　　　　1. live　　　　　　　　　　　　　　　2. love

B: What ___ in New York?
　　　　3. she/do

A: She ___ to school.
　　　　4. go

B: What ___ for fun?
　　　　5. she/do

A: She ___ a lot of friends. They ___
　　　　6. have　　　　　　　　　　　7. like
to go to Central Park or to the MOMA.

B: What ___?
　　　　8. MOMA/mean

A: MOMA ___ "Museum of Modern Art."
　　　　9. mean

B: Museums are expensive. How much ___ to visit the museum?
　　　　　　　　　　　　　　　10. it/cost

A: It ___ $25. But she ___ only $14
　　　　11. cost　　　　　　　　12. pay

SUMMARY OF LESSON 2

The Simple Present—Forms

Base Form	-s Form
You **travel** in the summer.	Sara **lives** in Virginia.
You **don't travel** in the winter.	She **doesn't live** in Washington, DC.
Do you **travel** by car?	**Does** she **live** near the subway?
Yes, we **do.**	Yes, she **does.**
When **do** you **travel?**	Where **does** she **live?**
Why **don't** you **travel** by car?	Why **doesn't** she **live** in Washington?

The Simple Present—Use

Use	Examples
General truths and customs	Washington, DC, **has** over a half million people.
	Many people **celebrate** New Year's Eve in Times Square.
Regular activities	We **take** a vacation every summer.
	We often **visit** national parks.

Frequency Words and Expressions

always	100 percent
almost always/ usually	
often	
sometimes	
rarely/seldom/ hardly ever/almost never	
never	0 percent

Questions and Answers with Frequency Words

Question	Answer
Does he **ever** go to Washington?	Yes, he sometimes d...
How often does he go to Washington?	Twice a year.

Prepositions of Time

Review prepositions of time on page 58.

PART 2 Editing Practice

Some of the shaded words and phrases have mistakes. Find the mistakes and correct them. If the shaded words are correct, write C.

　　　　　　　　　　　　　　　　　　C
I'm from Dallas, but I'm live in Chicago now. Chicago has many tourist attractions. My
　　　　　　　1.　　　　　　　　　　　2.
sister sometimes visit me in the summer. She and her husband have two small children,
　　　　　3.　　4.　　　　　　　　　　　　　5.
Sophie and Carter. The kids are always happy to visit me. I'm take the kids many places. They
　　　　　　　　　　　　6.　　　　　　　7.
really likes the zoo. They want always to see the monkeys. Carter likes the snakes too, but
　　　8.　　　　　9.　　　　　　　　　　　10.
Sophie doesn't likes them. She crys if we goes to the snake house. Carter always says, "Why
　　　11.　　　　　12.　　　13.　　　　　　　14.
you don't like snakes? They're so interesting."
15.
　　The kids always want to go to the Museum of Science. They find many interesting things
　　　　　16.　　　　　　　　　　　　　　　　17.
to do there, but it's very expensive. My sister sometimes asks me, "How much cost the tickets?"
　　　　　　　　　　　　　　18.　　　　　　　　　19.
but I doesn't tell her. I want to pay for everyone because they're my guests.
20.　　21.
　　My brother-in-law enjoys baseball, so I usually take him to a baseball game. I not like
　　　　　　　　　22.　　　　　23.　　　　　　　　24.
baseball very much, but I go with him anyway. I'm always bored at baseball games.
　　　　　　　　　　　　　　　25.
　　Chicago is a great city for tourists. We have a good time when my sister's family come
　　　　　　　　　　　　　　　　　　　　　　　　26.
to visit.

PART 3 Write About It

... her city you know about.

... Edit your writing from Part 3.

WRITING

PART 1 Editing Advice

1. Use the -s form when the subject is *he, she, it,* or a singular noun.
　　　　　　　　　s
　　The president live in the White House.
　　　　　　　　　　　　^

2. Use the base form after *doesn't.*
　　　　　　　live
　　Sara doesn't lives in Washington.

3. Don't forget *do/does* in a question.
　　　　do
　　How people celebrate New Year's Eve?
　　　　^

4. Use the correct word order in a question.
　　　don't you
　　Why you don't like to travel?

5. Use the correct spelling for the -s form.
　　　hurries
　　She hurrys to the train in the morning.

6. Use the correct negative form.
　　　doesn't
　　He not like to travel by car.
　　　^

7. Put frequency words in the correct place.
　　　am never
　　I never am bored on a vacation.
　　I always
　　Always I travel in the summer.

8. Don't use *be* with another verb to form the simple present.
　　I'm like to visit national parks.

9. Use correct question formation for meaning and cost.
　　　does pedestrian mean
　　What means pedestrian?
　　　　do the tickets cost
　　How much cost the tickets?

10. Use the correct preposition.
　　　　　　　　on
　　What do you do at New Year's Eve?

Enhanced For This Edition!

END-OF-LESSON ACTIVITIES
help learners review and apply the target grammar to writing.

Updated For This Edition!

ENHANCED WRITING SECTION
is divided into two sections which provide students with editing and writing activities to consolidate the grammar structures learned in each lesson.

ADDITIONAL RESOURCES FOR EACH LEVEL

Updated For This Edition!

ONLINE WORKBOOK

powered by MyELT provides students with additional practice of the target grammar and greater flexibility for independent study.

- Engages students and supports classroom materials by providing a variety of interactive grammar activities.
- Tracks course completion through student progress bars, giving learners a sense of personal achievement.
- Supports instructors by maximizing valuable learning time through course management resources, including scheduling and grade reporting tools.

Go to NGL.Cengage.com/MyELT

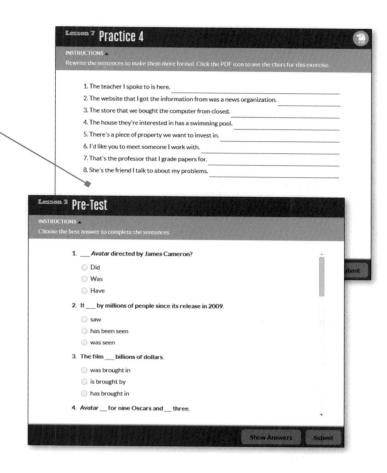

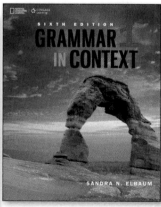

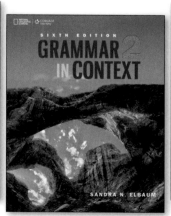

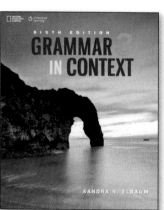

LESSON

1

Be: Present

Library at the University
of Chicago, Illinois

STUDENT LIFE

Education is the most powerful weapon which you can use to change the world.

— Nelson Mandela

Truman College

 Read the following article. Pay special attention to the words in bold.

CD 1
TR 2

Truman College **is** a community college. It **is** in Chicago, Illinois. It **is** one of the seven city colleges of Chicago. Truman students **are** from 160 different countries and 90 different language groups. About half the students **are** Latino. ESL classes **are** very popular at Truman College. About half the students **are** in ESL classes.

The college **is** convenient[1] for students because it **is** near public transportation—buses and trains. For students with a car, parking **is** free. Professors **are** usually friendly. Classes **are** small. (In universities some classes **are** very large.)

Adult education classes **are** free. College credit classes **are** not free. Most of the students **are** residents[2] of the city. Tuition[3] for city residents **is** low. Some of the students **are** international students. Tuition **is** high for these students.

A typical class **is** very interesting. There **are** young students, older students, married students, students with children, full-time students, and part-time students.

Truman **is** very proud[4] of its nursing program. It **is** the oldest and most successful nursing program in Illinois. Truman **is** also proud of its biotechnology program. It **is** the only one in the state of Illinois.

---

1. *convenient*: easy to get to
2. *resident*: a person who lives in a particular area
3. *tuition*: the cost of going to college
4. *proud*: pleased because you have or did something good

COMPREHENSION CHECK Based on the reading, tell if the statement is true (**T**) or false (**F**).

1. The nursing program at Truman College is very successful.

2. Classes at Truman College are very large.

3. About 160 students are in ESL classes at Truman College.

1.1 *Be*—Present Forms

The verb *be* has three forms in the present: *am, is,* and *are.*

Subject	Form of *Be*	
I	**am**	a professor.
My teacher	**is**	American.
She		from Chicago.
My professor		excellent.
He		from the Philippines.
The college		convenient.
It		near public transportation.
We	**are**	ESL students.
You		a good teacher.
The professors		friendly.
They		nice.

Language Notes:

1. The subject is a noun (*professor, college,* etc.) or a pronoun (*I, you, he, she, it, we, they*).

2. We begin sentences with the subject.

The **teacher is intelligent**. (NOT: *Is intelligent* the *teacher.*)

EXERCISE 1 Listen to a student talking about his classes. Fill in the blanks with the words you hear.

My name _____is_____ Rolando Lopez. I _____ from Guatemala.
                    1.   **2.**

I _____ a student at Truman College. My major _____
         3.   **4.**

engineering. My engineering classes _____ at night, and my English class
                                              5.

_____ on Saturdays. I _____ married. My wife, Susana,
      6.   **7.**

_____ a student here, too. Susana _____ in the nursing program.
      8.   **9.**

Susana's classes _____ in the morning. Our children _____ in
                          10.   **11.**

school in the day, and Susana _____ home with them in the evening.
                                        12.

The teachers here _____ friendly and helpful. The students in my ESL class
                          13.

continued

_____ from nine different countries. Some students _____ in
      14.   **15.**

their forties, fifties, or sixties. Some students _____ in their twenties. I
                                          16.

_____ in the middle. I _____ 35 years old.
    17.   **18.**

I _____ happy to be in the United States. I _____ unhappy
   19.   **20.**

about one thing: Chicago _____ cold in the winter.
                                    21.

1.2 *Be*—Uses

Examples	Explanation
Evening classes are **convenient**. The tuition is **low**.	We use a form of *be* with a description of the subject.
Chicago is **a city**. Illinois is **a state**.	We use a form of *be* with a classification or definition of the subject.
Truman College is **in Chicago**. The college is **near public transportation**.	We use a form of *be* with the location of the subject.
I am **from Guatemala**. My wife is **from Mexico**.	We use a form of *be* with the place of origin of the subject.
Rolando is **35 years old**.	We use a form of *be* with the age of the subject.
It is **cold** in Chicago in the winter.	We use *is* with weather. The subject for weather is *it*.
It is **6 o'clock** now.	We use *is* with time. The subject for time is *it*.

EXERCISE 2 Fill in the blanks with a form of *be*.

1. My name _____is_____ Rolando Lopez.

2. I _____ from Guatemala.

3. My wife _____ from Guatemala, too.

4. My wife and I _____ students.

5. Truman College _____ a two-year college.

6. My classmates _____ from nine different countries.

7. We _____ immigrants.

8. You _____ interested in nursing.

9. My major _____ engineering.

10. It _____ warm in Guatemala all year.

11. My native language _____ Spanish.

EXERCISE 3 Match each subject with the correct phrase. Then write a sentence using each subject and phrase with the correct form of *be*.

1. Trains and buses ___d___
2. The University of Illinois _____
3. Some adult education classes _____
4. Truman College students _____
5. Tuition _____
6. I _____
7. Truman College _____
8. Rolando and Susana Lopez _____
9. Spanish _____
10. It _____

a. a state university.
b. the cost of college courses.
c. from many different countries.
d. forms of transportation.
e. an ESL student.
f. hot in Guatemala in the summer.
g. the language of Mexico.
h. from Guatemala.
i. a community college.
j. free.

1. _Trains and buses are forms of transportation._
2. _____
3. _____
4. _____
5. _____
6. _____
7. _____
8. _____
9. _____
10. _____

EXERCISE 4 Fill in the blanks to make true statements.

1. My classroom is on _the second floor_____.
   _{location}
2. Chicago and Los Angeles are _____.
   _{classification}
3. The school is in _____.
   _{location}
4. The teacher is about _____ years old.
   _{age}
5. The teacher is from _____.
   _{place}

continued

6. It is _____ now.

time

7. It is _____ today.

weather

8. My school is _____ .

description

1.3 Subject Pronouns and Nouns

Examples	Explanation
You are a good student. **I** am in the United States. **It** is Monday.	The subject pronouns are *I, you, he, she, it, we,* and *they*.
Chicago is very big. **It** is in Illinois. **My wife** is a student. **She** is from Mexico. **My parents** are in Guatemala. **They** are happy.	Subject pronouns (*it, she, they*) can take the place of subject nouns (*Chicago, wife, parents*).
My classmates are from many countries. **They** are immigrants. **English and math** are my favorite subjects. **They** are useful subjects.	We use *they* for plural people and things.
You are a good teacher. **You** are good students.	*You* can be a singular or plural subject pronoun.
My wife and I are in the United States. **We** are in Chicago.	When the subject is another person and *I*, we put the other person before *I*.

Language Note:

In conversation, you sometimes hear "me and my wife" in the subject position. This is common but incorrect.

EXERCISE 5 Fill in the blanks with the correct subject pronoun.

1. Nicaragua and Guatemala are countries. _____They_____ are in Central America.

2. My wife and I are students. _____ are students at Truman College.

3. Guatemala is a small country. _____ is south of Mexico.

4. _____ is warm in Guatemala all year.

5. Some students are international students. _____ are from China, Japan, and Spain.

6. _____ am an ESL student.

7. English is a useful language. _____ is necessary in the United States.

8. Adult classes at my college are free. _____ are for ESL students.

9. My book is new. _____ is *Grammar in Context.*

10. I am a student. _____ are the teacher.

11. My teacher is a nice woman. _____ is from Boston.

12. My classmates and I are interested in American life. _____ are new here.

EXERCISE 6 Put the words in the correct order to make a statement. Use a capital letter at the beginning and a period at the end.

1. a two-year college/my college/is

   My college is a two-year college.

2. am/I/a student

   _____

3. my parents/in Guatemala/are

   _____

4. high/is/tuition at a four-year college

   _____

5. is/convenient for me/my college

   _____

6. my teacher/is/40 years old

   _____

7. is/from New York/my teacher

   _____

8. eight weeks long/the summer semester/is

   _____

9. Rolando/married/is

   _____

10. cold/it/is/in the winter

   _____

1.4 Contractions with *Be*

Examples		Explanation
I am You are She is He is It is We are They are	**I'm** in Minneapolis. **You're** a student. **She's** a young teacher. **He's** 74 years old. **It's** cold in winter. **We're** busy. **They're** big.	We can make a contraction with a subject pronoun + *am, is,* or *are.* We put an apostrophe (') in place of the missing letter. We usually use contractions when we speak. We sometimes use contractions in informal writing.
Rolando is Guatemala is	**Rolando's** from Guatemala. **Guatemala's** in Central America.	We can make a contraction with most nouns + *is.*
Here is	**Here's** a class schedule.	We can make a contraction with *here is.*
My cla<u>ss</u> **is** big. Beli<u>ze</u> **is** in Central America. Engli<u>sh</u> **is** the language of the United States. Mit<u>ch</u> **is** my English teacher. Colle<u>ge</u> **is** different here.		We don't make a contraction with *is* if the subject noun ends in *s, se, z, ze, ge, ce, sh, ch,* or *x.*
Textbooks **are** expensive. The classrooms **are** big.		We don't make a contraction with a plural noun and *are.*

EXERCISE 7 Complete the conversation between a new student (A) and a teacher (B). Use contractions with a form of *be* and the subject nouns or pronouns.

A: I 'm _____ late.
      1.

B: That _____ OK.
       2.

A: I _____ sorry.
      3.

B: No problem. It _____ the first day of class.
                        4.

A: The parking lot _____ very crowded.
                        5.

B: Yes, it _____ a problem.
             6.

A: My friend _____ late, too. He _____ in the parking lot.
                7.   8.

B: Don't worry. The first day _____ always hard.
                                9.

A: I _____ so sorry.
       10.

B: It _____ OK. Really.
        11.

A: You _____ very kind. Oh. Here _____ my friend now.
            12.   13.

B: Good. We _____ ready to begin.
               14.

EXERCISE 8 Complete the paragraph with the correct forms of *be*. Use contractions when possible.

OK, class. It 's _____ time to begin. You _____ all here now.
      1.   **2.**

My name _____ Peter Lang. Call me Peter. English _____ my
              3.   **4.**

native language. I _____ happy to be your teacher. Here _____ a
              5.   **6.**

paper with information about the school, the class, and the textbook. The

information _____ on my class website, too. My office _____ on
              7.   **8.**

the second floor, Room 2030. The textbook for the course _____ *Grammar in*
                                                    9.

Context. The bookstore _____ on Broadway Avenue. The
                             10.

address _____ 4545 North Broadway.
              11.

EXERCISE 9 Complete the paragraph with the correct forms of *be*. Use contractions when possible.

I 'm _____ a student of English at Truman College. I _____
      1.   **2.**

happy in the United States. My teacher _____ American.
                               3.

His name _____ Charles Madison. Charles _____ a good teacher.
              4.   **5.**

He _____ patient with foreign students.
     6.

My class _____ big. All the students _____ immigrants, but
              7.   **8.**

we _____ from different countries. Five students _____ from
   9.   **10.**

Asia. One woman _____ from Poland. She _____ from Warsaw,
                  11.   **12.**

the capital of Poland. Many students _____ from Mexico.
                             13.

We _____ ready to learn English, but English _____ a hard
     14.   **15.**

language for me.

1.5 *Be* with Descriptions

Examples				Explanation
Subject	***Be***	**(*Very*)**	**Adjective**	
My teacher The desks The college I	is are is am	very	kind. small. interesting. tired.	After a form of *be*, we can use a word that describes the subject. Descriptive words are adjectives. *Very* can come before an adjective.
I'm **thirsty**. We're **afraid**.				We use a form of *be* with physical or mental conditions: *hungry, thirsty, cold, hot, tired, happy, afraid*, etc.

Language Note:

Some adjectives end with *-ed* or *–ing*:

  married, divorced, worried, tired, crowded, confused, interested, bored, confusing, interesting, boring

EXERCISE 10 About You Fill in the blanks with a singular or plural subject and the correct form of *be* to make sentences about your school. Use contractions when possible. Then compare your answers with a partner.

1. _____ My teachers are _____ intelligent.

2. _____ expensive.

3. _____ cheap.

4. _____ new.

5. _____ big.

6. _____ friendly.

7. _____ hard.

8. _____ interesting.

EXERCISE 11 Find a partner. Fill in the blanks with the correct form of *be*. Add an adjective to describe each subject.

1. The classroom _is clean_____.

2. The college _____.

3. The school library _____.

4. The school cafeteria _____.

5. The textbook for the course _____.

6. The parking lot _____ .

7. The tuition at the school _____ .

8. American students _____ .

9. Schools in the United States _____ .

10. Students in the United States _____ .

1.6 *Be* with Definitions and Classifications

Singular Subject	Be	A/An	Adjective	Singular Noun
Harvard	is	a		university.
I	am	an	international	student.
You	are	a	great	teacher.
Guatemala	is	a	small	country.

Plural Subject	Be		Adjective	Plural Noun
You and I	are		new	students.
They	are		good	friends.

Language Notes:

1. We use the articles *a* and *an* for singular nouns. We don't use *a* or *an* for plural nouns.

2. We use *a* before a consonant sound. We use *an* before a vowel sound. The vowels are *a, e, i, o,* and *u.*

3. We use *a* when a beginning *u* is not a vowel sound.

      English is **a useful** language.

EXERCISE 12 Fill in the blanks with the correct form of *be*. Add *a* or *an* when necessary.

1. Nursing and technology _____*are*_____ popular college programs.

2. The University of Illinois _____ state university.

3. It _____ old university.

4. Chicago _____ interesting city.

5. Truman College and Washington College _____ city colleges of Chicago.

6. You _____ teacher.

7. I _____ immigrant.

8. Some students _____ international students.

9. My dictionary _____ useful book.

EXERCISE 13 Find a partner. Fill in the blanks to make true statements about your college or school. Use the correct form of *be* and *a* or *an* when necessary.

1. _____Math 101 is an_____ easy course.

2. _____ hard courses.

3. _____ useful website.

4. _____ heavy book.

5. _____ noisy places.

6. _____ quiet place.

7. _____ American teachers.

8. _____ good students.

9. _____ crowded place.

1.7 Negative Statements with *Be*

Examples	Explanation
I **am not** married. Rolando **is not** from Mexico. We **are not** Americans.	We put *not* after a form of *be* to make a negative statement.

Contractions in Negative Statements with *Be*

	Contraction with subject pronoun and *be*	Contraction with *be* and *not*
I **am not**	I**'m not**	—
you **are not**	you**'re not**	you **aren't**
he **is not**	he**'s not**	he **isn't**
she **is not**	she**'s not**	she **isn't**
it **is not**	it**'s not**	it **isn't**
we **are not**	we**'re not**	we **aren't**
they **are not**	they**'re not**	they **aren't**

Language Notes:

1. We cannot make a contraction with *am + not*. (NOT: I *amn't*)

2. We can make contractions with most nouns:

   Rolando is not Mexican. = Rolando's not Mexican. = Rolando isn't Mexican.

3. Remember: We cannot make a contraction with certain words + *is*. (See Chart 1.4.)

   English is not my native language. = English isn't my native language. (NOT: *English's* not)

EXERCISE 14 Fill in the blanks with a subject pronoun and a negative form of *be*. Use both ways of making contractions when possible.

1. The classroom is clean and big.

   _____It isn't_____ dirty. _____It's not_____ small.

2. We're in the classroom.

   _____ in the library. _____ in the cafeteria.

3. Today's a weekday.

   _____ Saturday. _____ Sunday.

4. I'm a student.

   _____ a teacher.

5. The students are busy.

   _____ lazy. _____ tired.

6. You're on time.

   _____ early. _____ late.

7. My classmates and I are in an English class.

   _____ in the cafeteria. _____ in the library.

EXERCISE 15 About You Write if the statement is true (**T**) or false (**F**). If it's false, make the statement negative and write a true statement. Use pronouns and contractions. Share your answers with a partner.

1. Today is the first day of class. _____F_____

   Today's not the first day of class. It's the third day of class.

2. All of the students in this class are immigrants. _____

   _____

3. I'm an immigrant. _____

   _____

4. I'm married. _____

   _____

5. The school is convenient for me. _____

   _____

continued

6. My parents are proud of me. _____

_____

7. The parking lot is free here. _____

_____

8. The school is near public transportation. _____

_____

9. The semester is eight weeks long. _____

_____

10. Spanish is my native language. _____

_____

Public School FAQs

Read the following questions and answers about education in the United States. Pay special attention to the words in bold.

Are you interested in American education? **Are** you confused about some things? Here **are** some frequently asked questions (FAQs):

Q: **Is** education in the United States free?

A: Yes, it **is**. It**'s** free in public schools.

Q: **Are** all children in public schools?

A: No, they **aren't**. Eighty-eight percent of children **are** in public schools. Nine percent **are** in private schools.

Q: What about the other three percent?

A: Three percent **are** homeschooled. The parents **are** the child's teachers.

Q: How many months a year **are** students in school?

A: They**'re** in school for ten months a year.

Q: What**'s** a freshman?

A: A freshman **is** a student in the first year of high school or college. A sophomore **is** a student in the second year. A junior **is** a student in the third year. A senior **is** a student in the fourth year.

Q: How many years **are** students in school?

A: Most students **are** in school for twelve years. It depends on the state.

Q: **Are** rules different from state to state?

A: Yes, they **are**.

The chart below shows the different possibilities for a twelve-year education in the United States.

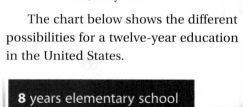

8 years elementary school
4 years high school

6 years elementary school
2 years middle school
4 years high school

6 years elementary school
3 years middle school
3 years high school

COMPREHENSION CHECK Based on the reading, tell if the statement is true (**T**) or false (**F**).

1. Middle school is always three years in the United States.

2. All students in the United States are in public schools.

3. A freshman is a first-year student in high school or college.

1.8 *Yes/No* Questions and Short Answers with *Be*

Statement	*Yes/No* Question	Short Answer
I am a student.	**Am I** a good student?	Yes, you are.
You are in college.	**Are you** at a state university?	No, I'm not.
He is a teacher.	**Is he** a good teacher?	Yes, he is.
She is in high school.	**Is she** a junior?	No, she isn't.
It is June.	**Is it** vacation time?	Yes, it is.
We are in high school.	**Are we** freshmen?	Yes, we are.
They are students.	**Are they** in public school?	No, they aren't.
Education is free in public schools.	**Is education** free in college?	No, it isn't.

Language Notes:

1. We use a contraction for a short *no* answer. We don't use a contraction for a short *yes* answer.

> Is the school open on December 25? No, **it isn't.**
>
> Is a *C* a passing grade? Yes, **it is.** (NOT: Yes, *it's.*)

2. We use a pronoun in a short answer.

> Is Rolando a freshman? Yes, **he** is.

EXERCISE 16 Complete the conversation between two students. Use contractions when possible.

A: Hi. My name 's _____ Hector. I _____ new here.
                                  1.   **2.**

B: Hi. My name _____ Eduardo.
                             3.

A: I'm from Mexico. _____ from Mexico, too?
                                     4.

B: No, _____ . I'm from Brazil.
                    5.

A: I'm a sophomore. _____ a sophomore, too?
                                   6.

B: Yes, _____ .
               7.

A: _____ in the same ESL class?
            8.

B: Yes, we _____ .
                  9.

A: _____ the teacher American?
            10.

B: No, _____ . She's Canadian.
              11.

A: _____ time for class now?
            12.

B: Yes, it _____ . _____ almost 10 o'clock. Let's go.
                    13.   14.

EXERCISE 17 Find a partner. Ask and answer *yes/no* questions about your school and this class. Use the words given and the correct form of *be*. Use contractions in your answers when possible.

1. the school / big
   A: *Is the school big?*
   B: *Yes, it is.*

2. it / near public transportation

3. the cafeteria / on the first floor

4. it / open now

5. the library / closed now

6. the course / free

7. the textbooks / free

8. the teacher / American

9. the classroom / clean

10. it / big

11. you / a freshman

1.9 *Wh-* Questions with *Be*

Statement	*Wh-* Question
I am late.	How late **am I**?
You are from South America.	What country **are you** from?
He is a teacher.	Who **is he**?
She is a freshman.	Where **is she** a freshman?
It is late.	What time **is it**?
We are lost.	Where **are we**?
They are here once a week.	When **are they** here?
The teacher isn't here today.	Why **isn't the teacher** here today?

Language Notes:

1. We can make a contraction with a *wh-* word + *is*: who's, what's, when's, where's, how's, why's.
2. After *what*, we can use a noun:
   what kind, what nationality, what country, what time
3. *How* can ask about health or an opinion.
   How are you? I'm fine.
   How is your English class? It's hard.
4. After *how*, we can use an adjective or an adverb:
   how long, how hard, how old, how big, how much, how many

EXERCISE 18 Complete the conversation between two students. Use contractions when possible.

A: You're in my math class, right?

B: Yes, I am. _____What's_____ your name?
<u> </u> **1.**

A: Ricardo Gomez.

B: Nice to meet you. I'm Maya Levina.

A: _____ your English teacher?
2.

B: Peter Lang.

A: He's my teacher, too! Are we in the same class?

B: _____ your class?
3.

A: It's on Mondays and Wednesdays at 10 a.m.

B: My class is on Tuesdays and Thursdays at 9 a.m.

A: _____ nationality is Mr. Lang?
4.

B: He's Canadian, I think. I'm from Russia. _____ you from?
5.

A: I'm from Costa Rica.

B: _____ Costa Rica?
6.

A: It's in Central America.

B: _____ your native language?
7.

A: It's Spanish. Mr. Lang speaks Spanish, too.

B: Mr. Lang isn't here today.

A: _____ here today? Is he sick?
8.

B: No, he isn't. His daughter is in a play.

A: How old _____ ?
9.

B: She's six years old.

EXERCISE 19 Choose the correct word(s) to complete the phone conversation between a student in the United States (A) and his brother back home (B).

A: Hello?

B: Hi, Sayed. It's Ali. How are you?

A: I'm fine.

B: Where (*are you*/*you are*) now?
1.

A: I'm in my dorm. (*Are you*/*You are*) at home?
2.

B: Yes, (*I am*/*I'm*). It's 4:15 p.m. here. (*What time is it*/*What time it is*) there?
3.　　　　　　　　　　　　　　　　　　4.

A: It's 1:15 a.m. here. It's late but I'm not tired.

B: Why (*aren't you*/*you aren't*) tired?
5.

A: I'm nervous about my test tomorrow.

B: (*How's*/*What's*) college life in the United States? (*It is*/*Is it*) very different from here?
6.　　　　　　　　　　　　　　　　　　　　　　7.

A: Yes, (*is it*/*it is*). My new classmates are so interesting. (*They're*/*Are they*) from many countries
8.　　　　　　　　　　　　　　　　　　　　　　9.

and are all ages. One man in my class is very old.

B: (*How old is he*/*How is he old*)?
10.

A: He's 75.

B: Really? (*Where he is*/*Where's he*) from?
11.

A: Korea. (*Where are Mom and Dad*/*Where Mom and Dad are*) now?
12.

B: At work. (*They're*/*They*) worried about you.
13.

A: Why (*they are*/*are they*) worried about me?
14.

B: Because you're alone in the United States.

A: (*It's*/*Is*) not a problem for me. I'm on the dean's list.
15.

B: (*What's*/*Who's*) the dean's list?
16.

A: It's a list of students with high grades.

B: (*I'm*/*I*) proud of you.
17.

EXERCISE 20 [About You] Fill in the blanks to make true statements. Then use the words given to write questions. Use contractions when possible.

1. I'm from _____Bosnia_____.

    where _Where are you from?_____

2. My name is _____.

    what _____

3. I'm from _____.

    where _____

4. The president/prime minister of my country is _____.

    who _____

5. The flag from my country is _____.

    what color _____

6. My country is in _____.

    where _____

7. I'm _____ feet, _____ inches tall.

    how tall _____

8. My birthday is in _____.

    when _____

9. My favorite subject in school is _____.

    what _____

10. It's _____ in my hometown.

    what time _____

Find a partner (from a different country, if possible). Ask and answer your questions.

    A: *I'm from Bosnia. Where are you from?*

    B: *I'm from Taiwan.*

EXERCISE 21 Complete the phone conversation between two friends.

A: Hello?

B: Hi, Cindy. This is Maria.

A: Hi, Maria. How _____are you_____?
1.

B: I'm fine.

A: _____ your first day of class?
2.

B: Yes, it _____. I'm at school now, but I'm not in class.
3.

A: Why _____ in class?
4.

B: Because it's break time now.

A: How _____ the break?
5.

B: It's 10 minutes long.

A: How _____?
6.

B: My English class is great. My classmates are very interesting.

A: Where _____ from?
7.

B: They're from all over the world.

A: _____ your teacher American?
8.

B: Yes, she _____. She's from California. _____?
9. 10.

A: It's 3:35.

B: Oh, I'm late.

A: Let's get together soon. _____ free this weekend?
11.

B: Yes, I am. I'm free on Saturday afternoon.

A: I have a class on Saturday.

B: When _____ free?
12.

A: On Sunday afternoon.

B: Sunday's fine, after 1 o'clock. Talk to you later.

1.10 Prepositions of Place

We use prepositions to show location and origin.

Preposition	Examples	
on	The book is **on** the table. The cafeteria is **on** the first floor.	
at	I am **at** school. My brother is **at** home. My parents are **at** work.	
in	The students are **in** the classroom. The wastebasket is **in** the corner.	
in front of	The chalkboard is **in front of** the students.	
in back of/behind	The teacher is **in back of** the desk. The chalkboard is **behind** the teacher.	
between	The empty desk is **between** the students.	
over/above	The exit sign is **over** the door. The clock is **above** the exit sign.	
below/under	The green textbook is **below** the desk. The red dictionary is **under** the textbook.	
by/near/close to	The pencil sharpener is **by** the window. The pencil sharpener is **near** the window. The pencil sharpener is **close to** the window.	

next to	The light switch is **next to** the door.	
across from	Room 202 is **across from** Room 203.	
far from	Los Angeles is **far from** New York.	
in (a city)	Truman College is **in** Chicago.	
on (a street)	Truman College is **on** Wilson Avenue.	
at (an address)	Truman College is **at** 1145 West Wilson Avenue.	
from (a place)	Rolando is **from** Guatemala.	

Language Notes:

1. We use *at* for a general area. We use *in* for a completely or partially closed area.

    Compare:

    I'm **at** school.

    I'm **in** the library.

2. A preposition can come at the end of a question.

    Where is Rolando's wife **from**?

    What street is the college bookstore **on**?

EXERCISE 22 About You Fill in the blanks to make true statements about the location of things or people. Use the correct form of *be* and a preposition.

1. My dictionary _____ is in my book bag _____.

2. My classroom _____.

3. I _____.

4. The library _____.

5. The cafeteria _____.

6. The teacher _____.

7. We _____.

8. My books _____.

9. The parking lot _____.

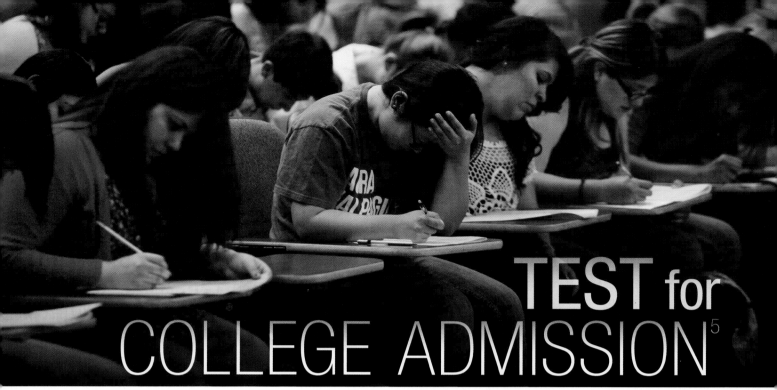

TEST for COLLEGE ADMISSION[5]

Students take a test at the University of California, Riverside.

CD 1
TR 5

Read the following conversation between a mother and her teenage son. Pay special attention to the words in bold.

A: What's **this**? Is it an application for college?

B: No, it isn't. It's an application for the SAT.

A: SAT? What's **that**?

B: It's a test for college admission.

A: What are **those** dates?

B: They're the dates of the test. The test is only a few times a year.

A: What's **that** book?

B: It's a practice book. The questions are similar to the questions on the SAT.

A: What kind of questions are **these**?

B: They're multiple-choice questions.

A: Are all the questions multiple choice?

B: No. Look here. **These** are essay[6] questions for the writing part.

A: Is **this** a test for all subjects?

B: The main test is for reading, math, and writing.

A: What about other subjects, like history and science?

B: Tests for **those** subjects are separate.

A: What are all **these** prices?

B: **This** price is for the main test. **These** prices are for the subject tests.

---

5 *admission*: permission to enter college
6 *essay*: a piece of writing by a student on a topic

COMPREHENSION CHECK Based on the reading, tell if the statement is true (**T**) or false (**F**).

1. The SAT is a college admissions test.

2. The SAT has only multiple-choice questions.

3. The SAT has questions about science and history.

1.11 *This, That, These, Those*

Examples		Explanation
Singular	**This** is my application. **That** is my professor.	We use *this* (near) and *that* (not near) to identify singular objects and people.
Plural	**These** are the prices. **Those** are the dates.	We use *these* (near) and *those* (not near) to identify plural objects and people.
This question is hard. **Those dates** are convenient.		A noun can follow *this, that, these,* and *those*.

Language Notes:

1. Only *that is* can form a contraction (*that's*).

   That's my professor.

2. When the question contains *this* or *that*, the answer uses *it*.

   Is **that** your math teacher? No. **It**'s my English teacher.

3. When the question contains *these* or *those*, the answer uses *they*.

   What are **those** papers? **They**'re applications.

EXERCISE 23 Choose the correct word(s) to complete the conversation between a father and his son.

A: What's (~~this~~/these)?
       1.

B: (*Its/It's*) my application for a scholarship.
       2.

A: What are (*that/those*)?
       3.

B: (*They/They're*) applications for different colleges. (*This/These*) college is nearby. (*That/Those*)
       4.   5.   6.

   colleges are in different states. (*It's/They're*) more expensive. Colleges (*are/is*) more expensive
                                      7.   8.

   for out-of-state students. (*That's/Those*) the way it is here.
                               9.

A: What's (*that/these*) price? (*It is/Is it*) the price of a college course?
               10.   11.

B: No. (*That's/They're*) the price of the test.
           12.

A: Oh. (*It's/Is*) expensive! College, books, tests—(*they're/it's*) all so expensive.
           13.   14.

B: That's why (*is/it's*) important for me to get a scholarship.
                   15.

A: Yes, it is. (*This is/This's*) very important.
                    16.

SUMMARY OF LESSON 1

Forms of *Be: Am, Is, Are*

AFFIRMATIVE STATEMENT	She **is** a senior.	You **are** late.
NEGATIVE STATEMENT	She **isn't** a junior.	You **aren't** on time.
YES/NO QUESTION	**Is** she a senior in college?	**Are** you OK?
SHORT ANSWER	No, she **isn't**.	Yes, I **am**.
WH- QUESTION	Where **is** she a senior?	Why **are** you late?
NEGATIVE WH- QUESTION	Why **isn't** she in college?	Why **aren't** you on time?

Uses of *Be*

Use	Examples
DESCRIPTION	Chicago **is** big.
CLASSIFICATION	Chicago **is** a city.
LOCATION	Chicago **is** in Illinois.
PLACE OF ORIGIN	The teacher **is** from Chicago.
AGE	I **am** 25 (years old).
TIME	It **is** 6 p.m.
WEATHER	It **is** warm today.
IDENTIFICATION	Those **are** college applications.

Subject Pronouns

I	you	he	she	it	we	they

Contractions with *Be*

Use	Examples
With pronouns	I'm, you're, he's, she's, it's, we're, they're
With nouns	the teacher's, Rolando's
With *that*	that's
With question words	what's, when's, where's, why's, how's, who's
With *not*	isn't, aren't

Articles *A/An*

A (before a consonant sound)	*An* (before a vowel sound)
The University of Iowa is **a** big college.	I'm **an** international student.
English is **a** useful language.	The test is in **an** hour.

This/That/These/Those

	Singular	Plural
Near	**This** is a college application.	**These** are multiple-choice questions.
Not near	**That**'s a test application.	**Those** are essay questions.

Choose the correct word(s) to complete the conversation between two students. If both answers are correct, circle both choices.

A: Hi, Sofia. How's your English class?

B: Hi, Danuta. (*It's*/*She's*) wonderful. (*I*/*I'm*) very happy with it.
                    1.   **2.**

A: What level (*you are*/*are you*) in?
                    3.

B: Level 2. My English teacher (*is*/*'s*) Kathy Lee.
                              4.

A: (*Is she*/*She's*) American?
        5.

B: Yes, (*she's*/*she is*). She's (*from*/*of*) New York. (*She's*/*She is*) a very good teacher.
       6.   **7.**   **8.**

      (*Who's your teacher*/*Who your teacher is*)?
                    9.

A: Bob Sanchez. He's (*a teacher very good*/*a very good teacher*). But (*I'm not*/*I amn't*) happy
                              10.   **11.**

      with my class.

B: Why (*you aren't*/*aren't you*) happy with your class?
              12.

A: The classroom's (*on*/*in*) the third floor. It's (*next*/*next to*) the cafeteria, so it's noisy.
                        13.   **14.**

B: (*How big is your class*/*How is your class big*)?
                      15.

A: Thirty-five students.

B: (*Those*/*That's*) a big class. My (*class's not*/*class isn't*) big—only fifteen students.
       16.   **17.**

      The students (*in*/*on*) my class (*'re*/*are*) from seven different countries.
                      18.   **19.**

A: Where (*are the students from*/*are from the students*)?
                  20.

B: They're from Mexico, Russia, India, Peru, Iraq, Poland, and Vietnam.

A: (*That's*/*This's*) an interesting group. In my class, we (*'re*/*are*) all from Mexico.
       21.   **22.**

B: (*Is American Mr. Sanchez*/*Is Mr. Sanchez American*)?
                    23.

A: No, (*he's not*/*he isn't*). He's from Mexico. (*English's not*/*English isn't*) his native language.
            24.   **25.**

      But (*that's not*/*that isn't*) a problem. His English (*'s*/*is*) very good.
               26.   **27.**

B: (*Ms. Lee's*/*Ms. Lee is*) about 55 years old. How (*is Mr. Sanchez old*/*old is Mr. Sanchez*)?
        28.   **29.**

A: (*He's a young man*/*He's young man*). He's about 25.
        30.

WRITING

PART 1 Editing Advice

1. Don't repeat the subject noun with a pronoun.

   My teacher ~~he~~ is from Los Angeles.

2. Use the correct word order.

   My class is small   is your teacher
   ~~Is small my class.~~   Where ~~your teacher~~ is from?

3. Every sentence has a subject. For time and weather, the subject is *it*.

   It's   It's
   ~~Is~~ 6 o'clock now.   ~~Is~~ very cold today.

4. Don't confuse *this* and *these*.

   This   These
   ~~These~~ is my book bag.   ~~This~~ are my books.

5. Don't use a contraction for *am not*.

   I'm not
   ~~I amn't~~ an American.

6. Put the apostrophe in place of the missing letter.

   It's   isn't
   ~~Its~~ late.   The teacher ~~is'nt~~ here.

7. Use *a* or *an* before a singular noun. Don't use *a* or *an* before a plural noun.

             an
   Biology is ^ interesting subject.

   Mr. Sanchez and Ms. Lee are ~~a~~ good teachers.

8. For age, use a number only or a number + *years old*.

             old
   He's 12 years ^. OR He's 12.

9. Don't use a contraction for a short *yes* answer.

              I am
   Are you from Mexico? Yes, ~~I'm.~~

10. Don't make a contraction with *is* after *s, se, z, ze, ge, ce, sh, ch,* or *x*.

    This is
    ~~This's~~ an easy test.

PART 2 Editing Practice

Some of the shaded words and phrases have mistakes. Find the mistakes and correct them. If the shaded words are correct, write *C*.

           C   I'm
A: Hi. My name is Leo. ~~I~~ from Latvia. What's your name?
          1.   **2.**   **3.**

B: My name's Diane.
        4.

A: Nice to meet you, Diane. Where you are from?
                      5.

B: I from Rwanda.
    6.

A: Where Rwanda is?
        7.

B: Its in Central Africa. Rwanda is a country very small. Is a city or a country Latvia?
    8.   9.   10.

A: Latvia is country. Is in Europe. Tell me more about Rwanda. What's the language of Rwanda?
         11.   12.

B: My native language is Kinyarwanda. French's also a language in Rwanda. Whats your native
              13.   14.   15.
language?

A: Latvian. Russian's also a language in Latvia. You are married?
          16.   17.

B: Yes, I'm. My husband is'nt from Rwanda. He's from the Congo. Are you married?
    18.   19.   20.   21.

A: No, I amn't. I'm only 18. I'm in the United States with my parents and sister.
      22.   23.

B: How your sister is old?
          24.

A: She's 16.
    25.

B: Is in high school your sister?
          26.

A: Yes, she is. She's a junior.
      27.

B: This are pictures of my kids, Jimmy and Lance.
      28.

A: Are they a twins?
      29.

B: No. Jimmy's 8 and Lance's 7.
    30.   31.

A: The teacher he's here. Is time for class.
      32.   33.

PART 3 Write About It

Fill in the blanks with affirmative or negative forms of *be*. Then rewrite the paragraphs with an affirmative statement after each negative statement.

My name ____is____ _____ . I _____ from an English-speaking
              1.   your name   2.

country. I _____ a student at a community college. My classmates _____ all
            3.   4.

very young. We _____ all from the same country. We _____ all immigrants.
              5.   6.

I _____ a freshman. This _____ my first course here. The school
          7.   8.

_____ convenient for me. My teacher _____ American. She/He
   9.   10.

_____ very young. The classroom _____ very nice. It _____ clean.
   11.   12.   13.

I _____ in my English class now. My class _____ big. I _____
  14.   15.   16.

happy with my college.

PART 4 Edit Your Writing

Reread the Summary of Lesson 1 and the editing advice. Edit your writing from Part 3.

PLACES to VISIT

The journey of a thousand miles begins with a single step.

—Lao Tzu

The Grand Canyon
National Park, Arizona

The Washington Monument, Washington, DC

WASHINGTON, DC

CD 1
TR 6

Read the following article. Pay special attention to the words in bold.

Tourists from all over the world **visit** Washington, DC, the capital of the United States. Is DC a state? No, it isn't. What, exactly, is DC? *DC* **means** District of Columbia. The District of Columbia **is** a special government district. More than a half million people **live** in Washington.

Washington **doesn't have** factories. Government and tourism **are** the main businesses of Washington. Washington **doesn't have** tall buildings like other big cities.

Many Washington workers **don't live** in Washington. They **live** in nearby states: Virginia and Maryland. Washington **has** a good subway system. It **connects** Washington to nearby cities in Virginia and Maryland.

Tourists **come** to see the White House, where the president **lives**. They also **want** to see the Capitol. The Capitol, the building where Congress **meets**, **is** on a hill. Senators and representatives from each state **work** on Capitol Hill. They **make** the country's laws.

Besides government buildings, Washington also **has** many interesting museums and monuments. The Smithsonian Institution **has** nineteen museums. Tourists **don't pay** to see government buildings and museums. But people **need** tickets to see many places because they **are** crowded.

A trip to Washington **is** an enjoyable and educational experience.

COMPREHENSION CHECK Based on the reading, tell if the statement is true (**T**) or false (**F**).

1. It's expensive to visit government buildings in Washington, DC.

2. The president works in the Capitol Building on Capitol Hill.

3. The District of Columbia isn't a state.

2.1 The Simple Present—Affirmative Statements

A simple present verb has two forms: the base form and the *-s* form.

Examples			Explanation
Subject	**Base Form**		We use the base form when the subject is *I, you, we, they,* or a plural noun.
I You We They My friends	**live**	in Washington.	
Subject	**-s Form**		We use the *-s* form when the subject is *he, she, it,* or a singular noun. *Family* is a singular noun.
He She It The president My family	**lives**	in Washington.	
I **have** friends in Washington, DC. Washington **has** many museums.			*Have* is an irregular verb. The *-s* form is *has.*

EXERCISE 1 Listen to a student essay about museums in Washington, DC. Fill in the blanks with the words you hear.

For my vacation next month, I _____plan_____ to go to Washington, DC, with my
_{1.}

family. Washington _____ many interesting museums and government
_{2.}

buildings. We _____ to visit the National Museum of the American Indian.
_{3.}

My son _____ a school project. He _____ to know more
_{4.} _{5.}

about American Indian culture and history. The museum _____ big. It
_{6.}

_____ four levels. We _____ about 3 or 4 hours to see everything.
_{7.} _{8.}

We also _____ to visit the Air and Space Museum. I _____
_{9.} _{10.}

some information about this museum. It's the most popular museum in the world! About

seven million people _____ each year. The museum _____ the
_{11.} _{12.}

history of space exploration.

continued

We also _____ to visit the zoo. The zoo _____ giant pandas.
                      13.   14.

My daughter _____ pandas.
                          15.

   We only _____ five days for vacation. We _____ to see a lot
                      16.   17.

in five days.

2.2 The Simple Present—Use

Examples	Explanation
The president **lives** in the White House. The president **meets** with leaders of other countries.	We use the simple present with general truths or customs.
We **take** a vacation every summer. We sometimes **go** to Washington.	We use the simple present with regular activities or repeated actions.
I **come** from New York. He **comes** from California.	We use the simple present with a place of origin.

Language Notes:

1. For a place of origin, we can use *come from* or *be from*.

    He **comes from** California. = He **is from** California.

2. We can follow some verbs with an infinitive (*to* + the base form).

    Tourists **like to see** the White House.

EXERCISE 2 Choose the correct form of the verb to complete each statement.

1. Visitors (*like* / *likes*) the museums.

2. The president (*live* / *lives*) in the White House.

3. Many people in Washington (*work* / *works*) for the government.

4. Washington (*have* / *has*) many beautiful museums.

5. Millions of tourists (*visit* / *visits*) Washington every year.

6. The subway (*connect* / *connects*) Washington to nearby cities.

7. You (*need* / *needs*) a ticket for some museums.

8. *DC* (*mean* / *means*) "District of Columbia."

9. I (*want* / *wants*) to visit Washington.

EXERCISE 3 About You Fill in the blanks to make true statements about yourself. Use the correct form of the verb given. Then share your statements with a partner.

1. I _come from Colombia_ .
   come

2. In my native city, I especially _____ .
   like

3. My family _____ .
   live

4. The capital of my country _____ .
   have

5. Most people in my country _____ .
   speak

6. Tourists in my country _____ .
   visit

7. My native city _____ .
   have

8. The president _____ .
   work

9. Many people in my country _____ .
   want

10. My country _____ .
    need

11. For transportation, most people _____ .
    use

2.3 Spelling of the -s Form

Rule	Base Form	-s Form
We add -s to most verbs to make the -s form.	hope eat	hope**s** eat**s**
When the base form ends in *ss, sh, ch, z,* or *x,* we add -es.	miss wash catch buzz mix	miss**es** wash**es** catch**es** buzz**es** mix**es**
When the base form ends in a consonant + *y,* we change the *y* to *i* and add -es.	carry worry	carr**ies** worr**ies**
When the base form ends in a vowel + *y,* we add -s. We do not change the *y.*	pay enjoy	pay**s** enjoy**s**
We add -es to *go* and *do.*	go do	goe**s** doe**s**
Have is irregular. The -s form is *has.*	have	**has**

EXERCISE 4 Write the -s form of each verb.

1. eat _____ *eats* _____
2. study _____ *studies* _____
3. watch _____
4. try _____
5. play _____
6. have _____
7. go _____
8. worry _____
9. want _____
10. do _____
11. push _____

12. enjoy _____
13. think _____
14. say _____
15. change _____
16. brush _____
17. like _____
18. reach _____
19. fix _____
20. raise _____
21. charge _____
22. see _____

2.4 Pronunciation of the -s Form

Pronunciation	Rule	Examples	
/s/	We pronounce the -s as /s/ after voiceless sounds: /p, t, k, f/.	hope—hopes eat—eats	pick—picks laugh—laughs
/z/	We pronounce the -s as /z/ after voiced sounds: /b, d, g, v, m, n, ŋ, l, r/ and all vowel sounds.	grab—grabs read—reads hug—hugs live—lives hum—hums run—runs	sing—sings fall—falls hear—hears see—sees go—goes play—plays
/əz/	We pronounce the -s as /əz/ after these sounds: /s, z, ʃ, tʃ, dʒ/.	miss—misses dance—dances fix—fixes use—uses	buzz—buzzes wash—washes watch—watches change—changes

Pronunciation Notes:

1. The -s forms of the following verbs have a change in the vowel sound.

   do /du/—does /dʌz/

   say /seɪ/—says /sɛz/

2. See Appendix A on page AP1 for a list of vowel and consonant sounds in English.

EXERCISE 5 Find a partner. Take turns saying the base form and the -s form of each verb in Exercise 4.

EXERCISE 6 Fill in the blanks with the correct form of each underlined verb.

1. I <u>like</u> to visit big cities. My wife _____ likes _____ to sit by a pool and read.

2. She <u>wants</u> to visit Miami. I _____ to visit Washington, DC.

3. I <u>enjoy</u> museums. She _____ swimming.

4. She <u>prefers</u> a relaxing vacation. I _____ an active vacation.

5. I <u>want</u> to use public transportation. She _____ to rent a car.

6. She <u>gets</u> up late. I _____ up early.

7. I <u>take</u> one small suitcase. She _____ two big suitcases.

EXERCISE 7 Write three sentences about the current U.S. president or the leader of a country you know. Use the simple present. Then find a partner and share your answers.

1. _____

2. _____

3. _____

2.5 The Simple Present—Negative Statements

Examples	Explanation
The president **lives** in the White House. The vice president **does not live** in the White House. Washington **has** many government buildings. It **doesn't have** tall buildings.	We use *does not* + the base form when the subject is *he, she, it,* or a singular noun. *Doesn't* is the contraction for *does not*.
Visitors **pay** to enter most museums. They **do not pay** to enter Smithsonian museums. We **live** in Maryland. We **don't live** in Washington.	We use *do not* + the base form when the subject is *I, you, we, they,* or a plural noun. *Don't* is the contraction for *do not*.

Language Note:

Compare the negative form with *be* and other simple present verbs.

Washington, DC, **isn't** a big city.

It **doesn't have** tall buildings.

EXERCISE 8 Fill in the blanks with the negative form of each underlined verb.

1. You <u>need</u> tickets for some museums. You _____*don't need*_____ money for the

   Smithsonian museums.

2. Washington <u>has</u> monuments. It _____ factories.

3. The subway <u>runs</u> all day. It _____ after midnight on weeknights.

4. You <u>need</u> a car in many cities. You _____ a car in Washington.

5. Washington <u>has</u> a subway system. Miami _____ a subway system.

6. My friend <u>lives</u> in Virginia. He _____ in Washington.

7. I <u>like</u> American history. I _____ geography.

8. The president <u>lives</u> in Washington. He _____ in New York.

9. The president <u>serves</u> a four-year term. He _____ a six-year term.

10. We <u>have</u> a president. We _____ a prime minister.

11. The U.S. Congress <u>makes</u> the laws. The president _____ the laws.

EXERCISE 9 About You Write affirmative or negative statements about your hometown. Use the words given with the correct form of the verb. Then find a partner and share your answers.

1. have a zoo

   My hometown has a zoo.

2. get a lot of rain

   My hometown doesn't get a lot of rain.

3. be modern

   _____

4. have very tall buildings

   _____

5. have more than a million people

   _____

6. be the capital of my country

   _____

7. have government buildings

_____

8. attract a lot of tourists

_____

9. have a subway

_____

10. have an airport

_____

EXERCISE 10 Complete the paragraphs with the correct form of the verbs given. When *not* is given, make a contraction with *does* or *do*.

Sara Harris _____*is*_____ a 30-year-old woman. She
      1. be

_____ in Arlington, Virginia. She _____
  2. live   **3.** work

in Washington, but she _____ there because it's too expensive. Rent
           4. not/live

is cheaper in Arlington. Sara _____ a car, but she
              5. have

_____ it to go to work. She _____ the
  6. not/use   **7.** take

subway to work.

Sara _____ for the government. She _____ a
      8. not/work   **9.** be

tour guide. She _____ groups on tours of the Capitol. Tourists
         10. lead

_____ to pay to enter the Capitol, but they
  11. not/need

_____ a reservation.
  12. need

Sara _____ two roommates. They _____
      13. have   **14.** work

in government offices. Sara and her roommates _____ very busy, so
                          15. be

they _____ much free time.
    16. not/have

The Smokies

Read the following article. Pay special attention to the words in bold.

What **do** you **like** to do on vacation? **Do** you **like** to visit big cities? Or **do** you **prefer** to be out in nature? Many American families enjoy visiting national parks.

The most popular national park in the United States is the Great Smoky Mountain National Park in Tennessee. Sometimes we call the Smoky Mountains "The Smokies." Here are some frequently asked questions (FAQs) about the park.

Q: How many visitors **does** this park **receive** a year?

A: It receives more than 9 million visitors a year.

Q: What **do** visitors **do** in the park?

A: Some people like to drive through the Smokies to see the natural beauty. Some people prefer to get out of the car and hike.[1] This park has 800 miles of hiking trails.

Q: **Does** the park **have** many plants and animals?

A: Yes, it **does**. The park is home to 100 different native species[2] of trees. There are 1,600 species of flowering plants in the park. The park has 60 species of mammals and 200 species of birds.

Q: **Do** bears **live** in the park?

A: Yes. The park has about 1,500 black bears.

Q: **Does** the park **have** educational programs?

A: Yes, it **does**. It has programs to teach young people about conservation.

Q: What **does** *conservation* **mean**?

A: It means protection. The park protects plants and animals.

Q: Why **do** the mountains **have** the name *Smoky Mountains*?

A: The plants release[3] chemicals. These chemicals produce vapor.[4] The vapor looks like smoke.

Q: Where **do** visitors to the park **stay**?

A: The park has a lodge[5] and campgrounds. Most visitors prefer to stay in the lodge.

Q: How much **does** it **cost** to enter Smoky Mountain National Park?

A: Entrance to the park is free. If you want to camp, you have to pay.

---

[1] *to hike*: to walk in nature for exercise
[2] *species*: a grouping of living things
[3] *to release*: to let something go

[4] *vapor*: a gas
[5] *lodge*: a small country house, often that you use on vacation

COMPREHENSION CHECK Based on the reading, tell if the statement is true (**T**) or false (**F**).

1. Smoky Mountain National Park produces smoke from fires.

2. Smoky Mountain National Park has educational programs.

3. It is free to camp at Smoky Mountain National Park.

2.6 The Simple Present—*Yes/No* Questions and Short Answers

Compare statements and *yes/no* questions.

Statement	Yes/No Question	Short Answer
The park **has** hiking trails.	**Does** the park **have** campgrounds?	Yes, it **does.**
The park **charges** money for camping.	**Does** the park **charge** an entrance fee?	No, it **doesn't.**
Birds **live** in the park.	**Do** bears **live** in the park?	Yes, they **do.**
Parks **get** a lot of visitors in the summer.	**Do** the parks **get** a lot of visitors in the winter?	No, they **don't.**

Language Notes:

1. For *yes/no* questions with *he, she, it,* and singular subjects, we use:

    Does + subject + base form . . . ?

    For a short answer, we use:

    Yes, + subject pronoun + *does.*

    No, + subject pronoun + *doesn't.*

2. For *yes/no* questions with *I, we, you, they,* and plural subjects, we use:

    Do + subject + base form . . . ?

    For a short answer, we use:

    Yes, + subject pronoun + *do.*

    No, + subject pronoun + *don't.*

3. Compare *yes/no* questions and short answers with *be* and with other simple present verbs:

    Is the park free? Yes, it **is.**

    Is the park **crowded** in winter? No, it **isn't.**

    Does the park **have** a campground? Yes, it **does.**

    Do you **like** to camp? No, I **don't.**

EXERCISE 11 Reread Exercise 10 on page 41. Then answer the questions with a short answer. Use a subject pronoun in your answers.

1. Does Sara work in Washington, DC? _____ *Yes, she does.* _____

2. Does Sara live in Washington, DC? _____

3. Does Sara work for the government? _____

4. Does Sara have a car? _____

continued

5. Does Sara need a car to go to work? _____

6. Do Sara's roommates work for the government? _____

7. Do Sara and her roommates have a lot of free time? _____

8. Do tourists need to pay to enter the Capitol? _____

EXERCISE 12 Complete the conversation with the words given. Use *does* or *do* when necessary.

A: <u>Does the United States have</u> a lot of national parks?
                      1. the United States/have

B: Yes, it _____ . _____ fifty-nine parks. Grand
              2.   3. it/have

Canyon National Park is very popular.

A: _____ near Smoky Mountain National Park?
          4. Grand Canyon National Park/be

B: No, it _____ . The Grand Canyon is in Arizona. Smoky Mountain
          5. is/not

National Park is in Tennessee.

A: _____ the Grand Canyon each year?
          6. a lot of people/visit

B: Yes. About five million tourists visit each year.

A: _____ a lot of time to visit the Grand Canyon?
          7. I/need

B: No, you _____ . Many visitors just go to the edge of the
          8.

canyon for the day.

A: _____ crowded in the summer?
          9. it/be

B: Yes, it _____ .
          10.

A: _____ a tour guide to see the park?
          11. we/need

B: No, you _____ . You can use your smartphone for a self-guided tour.
          12.

A: _____ an entrance fee?
          13. this park/charge

B: Yes, it _____ . It charges $30 per car.
          14.

A: _____ into the park?
          15. buses/go

B: Yes, they _____ . Passengers pay $15.
          16.

A: _____ into the canyon?
          17. people/go

B: Most people don't go into the canyon. Some people take a helicopter tour.

A: _____ over the canyon?
          18. the helicopter/go

B: Yes, it _____ .
      19.

A: _____ expensive to take a helicopter tour?
      20. it/be

B: Yes, it _____ . It's over $300 for a 45-minute ride.
      21.

EXERCISE 13 Look at the information about two popular national parks. Then read each sentence about one of the parks. Use the words in the statement to write a *yes/no* question about the other park. Answer with a short answer.

Yosemite National Park, California

- gets about 4 million visitors a year
- has black bears
- giant sequoia trees grow here
- has waterfalls
- entrance fee is $30 per car
- has bicycle trails
- part of the National Park Service

Grand Canyon National Park, Arizona

- gets about 5 million visitors a year
- has black bears
- no giant sequoia trees grow here
- has waterfalls
- entrance fee is $25 per car
- has no bicycle trails
- part of the National Park Service

1. Yosemite National Park is in California.

   Is Grand Canyon National Park in California? _____

   No, it isn't. _____

2. Grand Canyon National Park gets about 5 million visitors a year.

   _____

   _____

3. Yosemite National Park has black bears.

   _____

   _____

4. Giant sequoia trees grow in Yosemite National Park.

   _____

   _____

continued

5. Grand Canyon National Park has waterfalls.

_____

_____

6. The entrance fee for Yosemite National Park is $30 per car.

_____

_____

7. Yosemite National Park has bicycle trails.

_____

_____

8. Yosemite National Park is part of the National Park Service.

_____

_____

EXERCISE 14 Fill in the blanks to complete each conversation.

1. **A:** Most big cities have tall buildings. _____Does Washington have_____ tall buildings?
   a.

   B: No, it _____doesn't_____. Washington doesn't have tall buildings.
   b.

2. **A:** The trains run all day. _____ 24 hours a day?
   a.

   B: No, they _____. On weekdays they run from early morning to midnight.
   b.

3. **A:** In my city, all passengers pay the same fare on the subway. _____ the
   a.

   same fare on the subway in Washington?

   B: No, they _____.
   b.

4. **A:** You need a ticket to enter museums in my hometown. _____ a ticket to
   a.

   enter museums in Washington?

   B: Yes, you _____.
   b.

5. **A:** The Washington Monument is very tall. _____ an elevator?
   a.

   B: Yes, it _____. It has an elevator.
   b.

6. **A:** The president works in Washington. _____ on Capitol Hill?
   a.

   B: No, he _____.
   b.

7. A: _____ the laws?
   a.

   B: No, he _____ . The president doesn't make the laws. Congress does.
   b.

8. A: The president lives in the White House. _____ in the White House?
   a.

   B: No, he _____ . The vice president doesn't live in the White House.
   b.

9. A: Washington, DC, is on the East Coast. _____ on the East Coast?
   a.

   B: No, it _____ . Washington State is on the West Coast.
   b.

10. A: Many museums in Washington, DC, are free. _____ free?
   a.

   B: Yes, it _____ . The zoo is free.
   b.

2.7 The Simple Present—*Wh-* Questions

Compare statements and *wh-* questions.

Statement	*Wh-* Question
The park **receives** many visitors.	How many visitors **does** the park **receive** each year?
The park **has** bears.	What kind of bears **does** the park **have**?
You **prefer** a vacation in nature.	Where **do** you **prefer** to go?
Visitors **do** many things in the park.	What **do** visitors **do** in the park?
The park **doesn't charge** an entrance fee.	Why **doesn't** the park **charge** an entrance fee?
I **don't like** to camp.	Why **don't** you **like** to camp?

Language Notes:

1. For *wh-* questions with *he, she, it,* or a singular subject, we use:

   Wh- word + *does* + subject + base form ...?

2. For *wh-* questions with *I, we, you, they,* or a plural subject, we use:

   Wh- word + *do* + subject + base form ...?

3. For negative *wh-* questions, we use:

   Wh- word + *don't* or *doesn't* + subject + base form ...?

4. In informal English, we usually put the preposition at the end of a *wh-* question.
   We use *whom*, not *who*, after a preposition.

   INFORMAL: Who do you travel **with**?

   FORMAL: **With** whom do you travel?

5. Compare *wh-* questions with *be* and with other simple present verbs:

   What kind of vacation **are** you interested in?

   Why **aren't** you interested in tour groups?

   What kind of places **do** you **like** to visit?

   Why **don't** you **like** museums?

EXERCISE 15 Listen to the conversation. Fill in the blanks with the words that you hear.

A: _____ to go on your next vacation?
1.

B: We want to go to Washington, DC.

A: _____ to see and do there?
2.

B: We want to visit the government buildings, of course, and the museums. We plan to go to the

National Museum of the American Indian.

A: What kind of exhibits _____ there?
3.

B: Some exhibits show the history of the American Indian. Others show their life and culture.

They also _____ a theater.
4.

A: _____ in the theater?
5.

B: Different things like the storytelling, dance, and music of American Indians.

A: It sounds like a big museum. _____?
6.

B: It has four levels.

A: Wow! That's big. _____ to see everything?
7.

B: At least 2 hours.

A: _____?
8.

B: It's free.

A: Really? Nothing's free! All the museums in this city charge a lot of money.

_____ any money in Washington museums?
9.

B: We _____ with our taxes.
10.

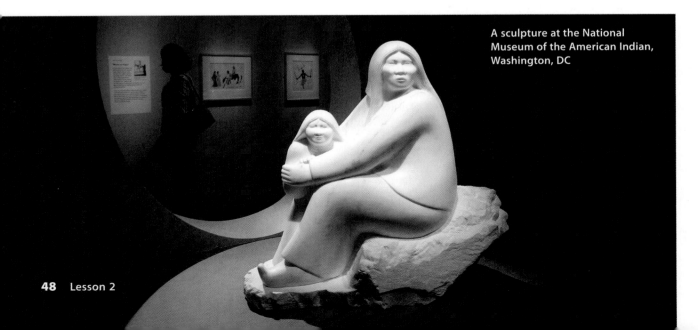

A sculpture at the National Museum of the American Indian, Washington, DC

EXERCISE 16 Complete the conversation between two friends. Use the underlined verbs to help you form each question.

A: I <u>plan</u> to visit a national park next summer.

B: Which park _____*do you plan*_____ to visit?
                                 1.

A: I <u>plan</u> to visit Yosemite National Park.

B: What month _____ to go there?
                            2.

A: I <u>want</u> to go in July.

B: It's crowded in July. It <u>gets</u> a lot of visitors.

A: How many visitors _____ ?
                                   3.

B: Let's look on the park website. Maybe we can find the answer there.

A: It doesn't matter. That's the time my wife <u>has</u> vacation.

B: How many weeks of vacation _____ ?
                                           4.

A: She has two weeks of vacation.

B: Do you plan to camp?

A: My wife <u>doesn't like</u> to camp.

B: Why _____ to camp?
                  5.

A: She <u>likes</u> to sleep in a bed, not on the ground.

B: Where _____ to sleep?
                   6.

A: I <u>like</u> to sleep in a tent under the stars.

EXERCISE 17 Write questions with the words given. Use the underlined verbs to help you.

1. The museum <u>has</u> several floors. (how many floors)

    _How many floors does it have?_____

2. We <u>don't pay</u> to go to the museum. (why/not pay to go to the museum)

    _____

3. The museum <u>has</u> programs. (what kind of programs)

    _____

4. The museum <u>opens</u> at 9 a.m. (what time/close)

    _____

continued

5. The Grand Canyon <u>gets</u> a lot of visitors. (how many visitors)

_____

6. Smoky Mountain National Park <u>is</u> in Tennessee. (where/Grand Canyon National Park)

_____

7. Yosemite National Park <u>charges</u> an entrance fee. (how much money)

_____

8. The United States <u>has</u> a lot of national parks. (how many national parks)

_____

EXERCISE 18 Complete the conversation between two friends. Use the underlined verbs to help you.

A: Let's do something fun today.

B: What _____*do you want*_____ to do?
　　　　　　　　　　　　1.

A: I <u>want</u> to go to a museum.

B: I <u>don't like</u> museums.

A: Really? Why _____ museums?
　　　　　　　　　　　　　2.

B: They're boring.

A: No, they're not. You learn a lot when you go to a museum.

B: Which museum _____ to visit?
　　　　　　　　　　　　　　3.

A: I <u>want</u> to visit the history museum. It's free on Fridays.

B: I <u>don't like</u> history.

A: Why _____ history?
　　　　　　　　4.

B: History is boring. I prefer to go to the movies.

A: Come with me to the museum. Please?

B: What kind of exhibits _____ ?
　　　　　　　　　　　　　　5.

A: It <u>has</u> exhibits about American life. Come on, let's go! The museum is free on Fridays.

B: What time _____ today?
　　　　　　　　　　　6.

A: The museum <u>closes</u> at 5 p.m.

B: OK. Let's go to the museum at 3 p.m., and then we can go to a movie, OK?

A: Fine.

EXERCISE 19 About You Find a partner. Ask and answer *yes/no* questions. Use the words given. Then ask an affirmative or negative follow-up *wh-* question.

1. like to travel

   A: *Do you like to travel?*   **A:** *Why don't you like to travel?*

   B: *No, I don't.*   **B:** *I'm afraid to fly and I don't like driving.*

2. like museums

3. like to learn about American history

4. visit parks in the summer

5. plan to take a vacation

2.8 Questions About Meaning, Spelling, Cost, and Time

Wh- Word	*Do/Does*	Subject	Verb	
What	does	*DC*	mean?	
How	do	you	spell	*government*?
How	do	you	say	*government* in your language?
How much	does	it	cost	to enter the park?
How long	does	it	take	to see the museum?

Language Note:

We use *do* and *does* to ask questions about meaning, spelling, cost, and time.

What **does** DC **mean**? (not: *What means* DC?)

EXERCISE 20 Fill in the blanks to complete each conversation.

1. **A:** How much _____ *does it cost* _____ to enter the Air and Space Museum?

   B: It doesn't cost anything to enter the Air and Space Museum. It's free.

2. **A:** How long _____ to see the museum?

   B: It takes at least 2 hours.

3. **A:** How _____ *Yosemite*?

   B: You spell *Yosemite* Y-O-S-E-M-I-T-E.

4. **A:** What _____ ?

   B: *DC* means "District of Columbia."

5. **A:** How much _____ to enter Smoky Mountain National Park?

   B: It doesn't cost anything. It's free to enter.

continued

6. **A:** How _____ *mountain* in Spanish?

   B: In Spanish, you say *montaña*.

EXERCISE 21 Complete the conversation between two students.

A: Are these your children in this photo?

B: Yes, they are.

A: How old _____ are they _____?
   _{1.}

B: Ana's 23 and Marek's 29.

A: Do they live with you?

B: No. Ana lives in New York, and Marek lives in Maryland near Washington, DC.

A: _____ for the government?
   _{2.}

B: Yes, he does. He works at the IRS.

A: What _____?
   _{3.}

B: *IRS* means "Internal Revenue Service." It's the government tax collection agency.

A: How long _____ Marek to get to work

   from Maryland?
   _{4.}

B: It only takes about 45 minutes. He uses the subway.

A: My niece lives in Maryland, too.

B: Where _____ in Maryland?
   _{5.}

A: She lives in Fallston.

B: I don't know that city. How _____ *Fallston*?
   _{6.}

A: *F-A-L-L-S-T-O-N.* My niece loves living there.

B: _____ for the government?
   _{7.}

A: No. She's a teacher.

B: I'm late for an appointment. Bye.

A: How _____ *good-bye* in Polish?
   _{8.}

B: We say *Do widzenia*.

TIMES SQUARE

 CD 1 TR 10

Read the following essay. Pay special attention to the words in bold.

I live in New York City. New York has so many things to see and do. I especially love Times Square. Times Square is a top tourist attraction in the United States. Times Square is **always** a busy place. More than 300,000 pedestrians[6] pass through Times Square every day. It has hotels, restaurants, theaters, and shopping. **Every night** visitors come to see an amazing display of electronic billboards.[7]

New Year's Eve is especially wonderful at Times Square. **Every year** New Yorkers and tourists come together at Times Square to count down to the new year. About a million people wait for the Waterford Crystal ball to drop, marking the beginning of the new year. The ball **always** drops at exactly midnight.

I **usually** go to Times Square with my friends to see the ball drop. I **never** drive there because parking is so expensive. We **always** take the subway. **Sometimes** it's very cold on New Year's Eve. If the temperature is below 10 degrees, I **usually** stay home and watch the ball drop on TV with my friends.

Times Square is also near the theater district in New York. I **hardly ever** go to the theater because it's so expensive. Some theater tickets cost more than $200! It's **often** hard to get a ticket for the popular shows. The tickets are **almost always** sold out.[8]

I love New York City. Tourists from all over the world love it, too.

---

6 *pedestrian*: a person on foot
7 *billboard*: a large outdoor sign
8 *sold out*: all gone

COMPREHENSION CHECK Based on the reading, tell if the statement is true (**T**) or false (**F**).

1. Times Square is only popular at night.

2. The writer always goes to Times Square on New Year's Eve.

3. Theater tickets in New York are very expensive.

2.9 Frequency Words and Expressions with the Simple Present

Frequency Word/Expression	Frequency	Examples
always	100 percent	Times Square is **always** crowded.
almost always/ usually		Popular shows are **almost always** sold out. I **usually** go to Times Square on New Year's Eve.
often		It is **often** hard to get theater tickets.
sometimes		It is **sometimes** very cold on New Year's Eve.
seldom/rarely/ hardly ever/almost never		I **seldom** go to the theater. I **hardly ever** use my car in New York City.
never	0 percent	I **never** drive to Times Square.

Language Note:

Seldom and *rarely* are formal. *Hardly ever* and *almost never* are informal expressions that mean the same thing as *seldom* and *rarely*.

EXERCISE 22 About You Fill in the blanks to make true statements about yourself. Use a frequency word or expression. Then find a partner and compare your answers.

1. I _____ hardly ever _____ go to the zoo.

2. I _____ celebrate New Year's Eve.

3. I _____ go to the theater.

4. I _____ use public transportation.

5. I _____ go to museums.

6. I _____ eat in restaurants.

7. I _____ visit people in other cities.

8. I _____ receive visitors from other cities.

9. I'm _____ interested in visiting other cities.

2.10 Position of Frequency Words and Expressions

Examples	Explanation
Times Square is **always** busy. It is **almost never** quiet in Times Square.	We put the frequency word or expression after the verb *be*.
I **never** drive to Times Square. We **hardly ever** stay home on New Year's Eve.	We put the frequency word or expression before other verbs.
Sometimes it's cold on New Year's Eve. **Often** it's hard to get theater tickets.	We can put *sometimes, usually,* and *often* at the beginning of the sentence.
Every night people visit Times Square. People visit Times Square **every night**.	We can put frequency expressions that start with *each* or *every* at the beginning or at the end of the sentence.

Language Note:

We don't put *always, hardly ever,* or *never* before the subject.

> I **always** celebrate New Year's Eve. (NOT: *Always I celebrate ...*)

EXERCISE 23 Rewrite each sentence. Use the frequency word or expression given. In some cases, more than one correct word order is possible.

1. I travel with my family. (often)

   I often travel with my family.

2. My family and I take a vacation in the summer. (every year)

   _____

3. We are interested in seeing something new. (always)

   _____

4. We visit major cities, like New York and San Francisco. (often)

   _____

5. We visit relatives in other cities. (sometimes)

   _____

6. We travel by car. (usually)

   _____

7. We fly. (hardly ever)

   _____

continued

8. We take a lot of pictures. (always)

_____

9. We are bored. (never)

_____

2.11 Questions and Short Answers with *Ever*

We use *ever* to ask a question about frequency. We begin the question with an auxiliary verb or a form of *be*.

Do/Does	Subject	Ever		Short Answer
Do	you	**ever**	travel in the winter?	Yes, we **sometimes** do.
Does	your brother	**ever**	travel with you?	No, he **rarely** does.
Be	**Subject**	**Ever**		**Short Answer**
Is	Washington	**ever**	hot in the summer?	Yes, it **usually** is.
Is	Times Square	**ever**	crowded?	Yes, it **always** is.

Language Notes:

1. In a short answer, we put the frequency word or expression between the subject and the verb.

2. We don't use a negative verb in a short answer when the frequency word is *never*.

   A: Is the school **ever** open on January 1?

   B: No, it **never** is.

EXERCISE 24 About You Find a partner. Ask and answer each question. Use frequency words or expressions in your answers.

1. Do you ever travel by train in the United States?

   A: *Do you ever travel by train in the United States?*

   B: *No, I never do.*

2. Do you ever travel by car?

3. Do you ever visit museums in this city?

4. Do you ever use the Internet to plan a trip?

5. Do you ever stay with relatives when you travel?

6. Do you ever celebrate New Year's Eve with friends?

7. Do you ever take pictures when you travel?

8. Do you ever use GPS in a car?

2.12 Questions and Answers with *How Often*

We use *how often* to ask a question about frequency. We use an auxiliary verb after *how often*.

Examples	Explanation
How often does your family take a vacation? We take a vacation **once a year**. **How often** do you take the subway? I take the subway **twice a day**.	We answer questions beginning with *how often* with frequency expressions such as *once/twice/three times a week/month/year*.
How often do you drive downtown? I drive downtown **once in a while**.	For a less specific answer, we can use *once in a while*.

Language Note:

When answering a question with *how often*, we can put some frequency expressions at the beginning or at the end of the sentence.

> **Twice a year**, I visit my family.
>
> I visit my family **twice a year**.

EXERCISE 25 About You Find a partner. Ask and answer each question. Use frequency words or expressions in your answers.

1. How often do you travel?

   A: *How often do you travel?*

   B: *I travel about three times a year.*

2. How often do you visit your native country?

3. How often do you go to a museum?

4. How often do you use public transportation?

5. How often do you go to the zoo?

6. How often do you stay in a hotel?

EXERCISE 26 Choose the correct word(s) to complete the conversation.

A: Do (you ever/ever you) travel to other countries?
1.

B: No, I (ever/rarely) do. (One/Once) a year, I go back to my country, but that's all.
2.   3.

A: (What/How) often do you travel in the United States?
4.

B: (Once a while/Once in a while), I go to see my aunt in Miami. But I (ever/never) go there
5.   6.

in the summer because it's too hot.

A: (It's sometimes/It sometimes is) hot in New York, too.
7.

B: Yes, but not like in Miami.

continued

A: Does your aunt (*ever/never*) come to New York to see you here?
    8.

B: No, she (*ever/never*) does. She says it's too cold here.
    9.

A: But it's not cold in the summer.

B: She (*always says/says always*) it's too crowded here. What about you? Do you travel a lot?
    10.

A: No. I like to travel, but my husband doesn't. So we do things here in New York.

B: Do you (*ever go/go ever*) to Times Square on New Year's Eve?
    11.

A: No, we never (*do/don't*). (*It's always/Always it's*) so crowded. We
    12.   **13.**

   (*get together often/often get together*) with friends on New Year's Eve.
    14.

2.13 Prepositions of Time

Preposition	Examples	Explanation
in	Times Square isn't crowded **in the morning.** We visit museums **in the afternoon.** Theaters are crowded **in the evening.**	We use *in* with general times of day: *the morning, the afternoon, the evening.*
	We elect a U.S. president every four years: **in 2016, in 2020, in 2024,** and so on.	We use *in* with years.
	We like to travel **in the summer.** People go to Times Square even **in the winter.**	We use *in* with seasons: *the summer, the fall, the winter, the spring.*
	New York is cold **in December.**	We use *in* with months.
on	Many people go to Times Square **on New Year's Eve.** We watch the ball drop **on December 31.**	We use *on* with specific dates and days, such as holidays.
	I like to relax **on the weekend.**	We use *on* with *the weekend.*
at	Let's go to Times Square **at 10 o'clock.** The ball in Times Square drops **at midnight.**	We use *at* with specific times of day: *2 o'clock, noon, midnight.*
	There are many people in Times Square **at night.**	We use *at* with *night.*
from...to from...until	The national parks are crowded **from May to October.** The subway in Washington runs **from 5 a.m. until midnight** on weekdays.	We use *from ... to/until* with a beginning time and an ending time.

Language Note:

In informal English, we sometimes say *from … till* instead of *from … until.*

The museum is open **from 9 till 4 o'clock.**

EXERCISE 27 About You Fill in the blanks with the correct preposition of time. Then find a partner and ask and answer each question.

1. What do you usually do _____ December 31?

2. Do you like to travel _____ the summer?

3. What do you usually do _____ the morning?

4. What do you usually do _____ Saturday morning?

5. What do you usually do _____ night?

6. What do you like to do _____ your birthday?

7. What do you like to do for fun _____ the weekend?

EXERCISE 28 About You Find a partner. Ask and answer each question. Use prepositions of time in your answers.

1. When do students in your country have vacation?

2. What do kids usually do on vacation?

3. When do you do your homework?

4. What hours are you in school?

5. When is your birthday?

The New York City skyline showing the Empire State Building

SUMMARY OF LESSON 2

The Simple Present—Forms

Base Form	-s Form
You **travel** in the summer.	Sara **lives** in Virginia.
You **don't travel** in the winter.	She **doesn't live** in Washington, DC.
Do you **travel** by car?	**Does** she **live** near the subway?
Yes, we **do**.	Yes, she **does**.
When **do** you **travel**?	Where **does** she **live**?
Why **don't** you **travel** by car?	Why **doesn't** she **live** in Washington?

The Simple Present—Use

Use	Examples
General truths and customs	Washington, DC, **has** over a half million people. Many people **celebrate** New Year's Eve in Times Square.
Regular activities	We **take** a vacation every summer. We often **visit** national parks.

Frequency Words and Expressions

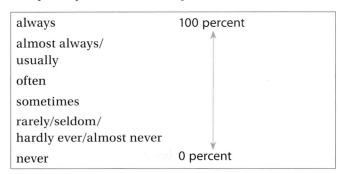

always — 100 percent

almost always/ usually

often

sometimes

rarely/seldom/ hardly ever/almost never

never — 0 percent

Questions and Answers with Frequency Words

Question	Answer
Does he **ever** go to Washington?	Yes, he sometimes does.
How often does he go to Washington?	Twice a year.

Prepositions of Time

Review prepositions of time on page 58.

TEST / REVIEW

PART A Fill in the blanks. Use the correct form of the word(s) given.

A: My sister _____ lives _____ in New York, and she really _____ it.
1. live   2. love

B: What _____ in New York?
3. she/do

A: She _____ to school.
4. go

B: What _____ for fun?
5. she/do

A: She _____ a lot of friends. They _____
6. have   7. like

to go to Central Park or to the MOMA.

B: What _____?
8. MOMA/mean

A: MOMA _____ "Museum of Modern Art."
9. mean

B: Museums are expensive. How much _____ to visit the museum?
10. it/cost

A: It _____ $25. But she _____ only $14
11. cost   12. pay

because she _____ a student discount.
13. get

B: _____ a car?
14. your sister/have

A: No, she doesn't. She _____ the subway.
15. use

PART B Choose the correct word(s) to complete the conversation from above.

B: Do (you ever/ever you) visit your sister?
1.

A: Yes, I (do sometimes/sometimes do). I like to go (in/on) December for winter break.
2.   3.

B: Do you (ever/never) go to Times Square (on/in) New Year's Eve?
4.   5.

A: No, we never (do/don't).
6.

B: Really? Why (don't you/you don't) go to Times Square? It looks like so much fun.
7.

A: My sister doesn't (like/likes) crowds. (Always we/We always) watch Times Square on TV.
8.   9.

B: How (often/ever) does your sister (come/comes) home to visit your family?
10.   11.

A: She (comes usually/usually comes) (in/on) the summer. (I'm always/I always am) happy to see her.
12.   13.   14.

B: New York (have/has) so many museums and theaters. But they're so expensive.
15.

A: Some things (cost/costs) a lot of money, but other things are free. Central Park is beautiful, and
16.

it (doesn't cost/isn't cost) any money. My sister (have/has) a part-time job now, so that helps.
17.   18.

B: What kind of work (she does/does she do)?
19.

A: (She's work/She works) in a coffee shop (on/at) Saturdays.
20.   21.

WRITING

PART 1 Editing Advice

1. Use the *-s* form when the subject is *he, she, it,* or a singular noun.

   The president live in the White House.

^s^

2. Use the base form after *doesn't.*

   Sara doesn't ~~lives~~ *live* in Washington.

3. Don't forget *do/does* in a question.

   How people celebrate New Year's Eve?

^do^

4. Use the correct word order in a question.

   Why ~~you don't~~ *don't you* like to travel?

5. Use the correct spelling for the *-s* form.

   She ~~hurrys~~ *hurries* to the train in the morning.

6. Use the correct negative form.

   He ~~not~~ *doesn't* like to travel by car.

7. Put frequency words in the correct place.

   I ~~never am~~ *am never* bored on a vacation.

   ~~Always I~~ *I always* travel in the summer.

8. Don't use *be* with another verb to form the simple present.

   ~~I'm~~ I like to visit national parks.

9. Use correct question formation for meaning and cost.

   What ~~means pedestrian~~ *does pedestrian mean*?

   How much ~~cost the tickets~~ *do the tickets cost*?

10. Use the correct preposition.

    What do you do ~~at~~ *on* New Year's Eve?

PART 2 Editing Practice

Some of the shaded words and phrases have mistakes. Find the mistakes and correct them. If the shaded words are correct, write *C*.

I'm from Dallas, but ~~I'm~~ live in Chicago now. Chicago has many tourist attractions. My
    1.   2.
sister sometimes visit me in the summer. She and her husband have two small children,
            3.   4.   5.
Sophie and Carter. The kids are always happy to visit me. I'm take the kids many places. They
                        6.   7.
really likes the zoo. They want always to see the monkeys. Carter likes the snakes too, but
    8.   9.   10.
Sophie doesn't likes them. She crys if we goes to the snake house. Carter always says, "Why
        11.   12.   13.   14.
you don't like snakes? They're so interesting."
    15.

The kids always want to go to the Museum of Science. They find many interesting things
            16.   17.
to do there, but it's very expensive. My sister sometimes asks me, "How much cost the tickets?"
                                18.   19.
but I doesn't tell her. I want to pay for everyone because they're my guests.
    20.   21.

My brother-in-law enjoys baseball, so I usually take him to a baseball game. I not like
                    22.   23.   24.
baseball very much, but I go with him anyway. I'm always bored at baseball games.
                                    25.

Chicago is a great city for tourists. We have a good time when my sister's family come
                                                        26.
to visit.

PART 3 Write About It

1. Write about an interesting place in this city or in another city you know about.
2. Write about how you celebrate New Year's Eve.

PART 4 Edit Your Writing

Reread the Summary of Lesson 2 and the editing advice. Edit your writing from Part 3.

LESSON 3

Singular and Plural Nouns
There Is/There Are
Articles

Satellite imagery of Palm Island and
Hibiscus Island in Miami Beach, Florida

HOUSING

Home is the nicest word there is.

—Laura Ingalls Wilder

The HIGH COST of HOUSING

 Read the following article. Pay special attention to the words in bold.

Some **people** live paycheck to paycheck. They spend all their money from one paycheck and need to wait for their next paycheck to pay their **bills**. Who are these people? People with low **incomes**? No. They are often middle-class Americans, people with good salaries.[1] Some of these people are "house rich but cash poor." This means that they put all their **savings** into a house or condo[2] and have nothing left for **emergencies**. About one-third of American **households** live this way. Financial **planners**[3] tell **homeowners** to keep three to six **months** of **expenses** for **emergencies**, but many homeowners don't follow this advice. If they have **illnesses** or lose their **jobs**, they can even lose their **homes**.

Some Americans don't want to own a house. They prefer to rent an apartment because they don't want debt.[4] This is especially true of **millennials**, people born between 1980 and 2000. But renting is often very expensive. Some **cities** have very high rent. Miami, New York City, Los Angeles, San Francisco, and Oakland have the highest rent in the United States.

Some single young adults prefer not to own and not to rent. They live with their parents. Fifty-six percent of young American adults between the ages of 18 and 24 live with their parents. More men than women choose to live with their parents. Of course, when mom and dad pay all the bills and don't charge them rent, it's a very good way to save money on living expenses.

---

[1] *salary*: a regular payment for work done
[2] *condo*: private housing usually in an apartment building
[3] *financial planner*: someone who helps people manage their money
[4] *debt*: money owed to another

COMPREHENSION CHECK Based on the reading, tell if the statement is true (**T**) or false (**F**).

1. Financial planners tell homeowners to keep money for emergencies.

2. Rent in New York City is very expensive.

3. About 50 percent of U.S. households live paycheck to paycheck.

3.1 Singular and Plural Nouns

Examples	Explanation
He lives with his **mother**. He lives with his **parents**.	*Singular* means one. *Plural* means more than one. Plural nouns usually end in -*s*.
Some young **men** and **women** live with their parents. Some **children** live with their grandparents.	Some plural nouns are irregular. They don't end in -*s*.

Language Note:

Some nouns have no singular form: *pajamas, clothes, pants, (eye)glasses, scissors.*

3.2 Regular Plural Nouns—Spelling

Plural nouns usually end in -*s* or -*es*.

Word Ending	Singular Form	Plural Ending	Plural Form
vowel	expense movie	+ -*s*	expense**s** movie**s**
consonant	bill month	+ -*s*	bill**s** month**s**
ss, sh, ch, x	class dish church box	+ -*es*	class**es** dish**es** church**es** box**es**
vowel + *y*	boy day	+ -*s*	boy**s** day**s**
consonant + *y*	lady emergency	~~y~~ + -*ies*	lad**ies** emergenc**ies**
vowel + *o*	patio radio	+ -*s*	patio**s** radio**s**
consonant + *o*	mosquito tomato	+ -*es*	mosquito**es** tomato**es**
Exceptions: *photos, pianos, solos, altos, sopranos, autos, avocados, condos*			
-*f* or -*fe*	leaf knife	~~f~~ + -*ves* ~~fe~~ + -*ves*	lea**ves** kni**ves**
Exceptions: *beliefs, chiefs, roofs, chefs*			

EXERCISE 1 Listen to the report. Fill in the blanks with the words you hear.

   Maybe you rent an apartment now, but in the future you plan to own a house. You

probably have a lot of _____ **1.** . For example, what is better, a house or a condo?

Here are some _____ **2.** to consider:

   Do you want control over all your _____ **3.** ? Then a condo probably isn't for you.

_____ **4.** are part of an association. The association has a lot of _____ **5.** .

For example, some _____ **6.** don't allow _____ **7.** .

   Are you very busy? Do you have time to shovel⁵ the snow in the winter or take care of the

lawn⁶ in the summer? _____ **8.** have a lot of _____ **9.** . If you don't

have time for these _____ **10.** , then home ownership is probably not right for you.

If you own a condo, you pay a maintenance fee⁷ each month. The association pays someone to

do these _____ **11.** .

   Do you have _____ **12.** ? Maybe you want a yard where they can play and a

garage for their _____ **13.** and _____ **14.** . Then a house is a better choice.

EXERCISE 2 Write the plural form of each noun.

1. loaf	_loaves_	**11.**	key	_____
2. toy	_____	**12.**	age	_____
3. brush	_____	**13.**	kiss	_____
4. country	_____	**14.**	potato	_____
5. half	_____	**15.**	rent	_____
6. book	_____	**16.**	watch	_____
7. valley	_____	**17.**	photo	_____
8. life	_____	**18.**	lip	_____
9. story	_____	**19.**	tax	_____
10. sofa	_____	**20.**	video	_____

---

⁵ *to shovel*: to pick up and move away snow
⁶ *lawn*: grass
⁷ *fee*: a charge, cost

21. moth _____

22. studio _____

23. adult _____

24. illness _____

EXERCISE 3 About You Fill in the blanks with the plural form of the nouns given. Then find a partner and tell whether each statement is true (**T**) or false (**F**) in your native countries.

1. _____Houses_____ are very expensive.
   <small>house</small>

2. Most _____ live with their _____.
   <small>a. kid</small>   <small>b. grandparent</small>

3. Most single _____ live with their _____.
   <small>a. adult</small>   <small>b. parent</small>

4. Most _____ live in a house.
   <small>a. family</small>

5. Most _____ stay in the same house all their _____.
   <small>a. family</small>   <small>b. life</small>

6. Most people save money for _____.
   <small>emergency</small>

3.3 Regular Plural Nouns—Pronunciation

	Rule	Examples	
/s/	We pronounce the plural ending as /s/ after the voiceless sounds: /p, t, k, f, ø/.	lip—lips cat—cats rock—rocks	cuff—cuffs month—months
/z/	We pronounce the plural ending as /z/ after all vowels and after the voiced sounds: /b, d, g, v, m, n, ŋ, l, r/.	bee—bees cab—cabs lid—lids bag—bags stove—stoves	sum—sums can—cans thing—things bill—bills car—cars
/əz/	We pronounce the plural ending as /əz/ after the sounds: /s, z, ʃ, tʃ, ʒ, dʒ/.	class—classes place—places tax—taxes cause—causes	dish—dishes beach—beaches garage—garages bridge—bridges

EXERCISE 4 Find a partner. Say the plural form of each word in Exercise 2 on pages 68–69.

3.4 Irregular Plural Nouns

Singular	Plural	Explanation
man woman tooth foot	men women teeth feet	Some plural nouns have a vowel change from the singular form.
sheep fish deer	sheep fish deer	Some plural nouns are the same as the singular form.
child person mouse	children people mice	Some plural nouns have a different word form.

Language Note:

The plural of *person* can also be *persons*, but *people* is more common.

Pronunciation Note:

We hear the difference in pronunciation between *woman* (/wΩmən/) and *women* (/wimən/) in the first syllable.

EXERCISE 5 Write the plural form of each noun.

1. man _____ men _____

2. foot _____

3. woman _____

4. policeman _____

5. child _____

6. fish _____

7. mouse _____

8. sheep _____

9. tooth _____

10. person _____

EXERCISE 6 Fill in the blanks with the plural form of the nouns given.

1. Some ___ houses ___ are very big.
   house

2. The United States has about 320 million _____ .
   person

3. Americans move many _____ .
   time

4. Some young _____ and _____ live with their _____ .
   a. man   b. woman   c. parent

5. _____ are very expensive in some _____ .
   a. home   b. city

6. In many _____ , adult _____ live with their parents.
   a. country   b. child

7. How many square _____ does your house or apartment have?
   foot

8. Some apartments have a problem with _____ .
   mouse

FINDING AN APARTMENT

 Read the following article. Pay special attention to the words in bold.

There are several ways to find an apartment. One way is to look online. **There are** a lot of websites to help you find an apartment. **There are** often pictures of the building and the apartment for rent. **There is** sometimes a map to show you the location of the building.

Another way to find an apartment is to look in the newspaper. **There is** an "Apartments for Rent" section in the back of the newspaper. **There are** many ads[8] for apartments and houses for rent. Many newspapers also put this information online.

You can also find an apartment by looking at buildings in the neighborhood where you want to live. **There are** often "For Rent" signs on the front of the buildings. **There is** usually a phone number on the sign. You can call and ask the owner or manager for information. You can ask:

- How much is the rent?
- Is heat included?
- What floor is the apartment on?
- **Is there** an elevator?

- How many bedrooms **are there** in the apartment?
- How many closets **are there** in the apartment?
- Is the apartment available[9] now?

If an apartment interests you, you can make an appointment to see it. When you go to see the apartment, ask:

- **Is there** a lease?[10] How long is the lease?
- **Is there** a janitor or manager?
- **Is there** a parking space for each tenant?[11] Is it free, or do I have to pay extra?
- **Are there** smoke detectors?[12]
- **Is there** a laundry room in the building? Where is it?

The owner sometimes asks you a few questions, such as:

- How many people **are there** in your family?
- Do you have any pets?

Look at the apartment carefully before you sign the lease. If **there are** some problems, ask the owner to fix them before you move in.

---

[8] *ad*: (advertisement) a notice about products or services
[9] *available*: free and ready to use
[10] *lease*: a contract to pay to use an apartment for a period of time
[11] *tenant*: a person who pays rent for a property
[12] *smoke detector*: a device that senses smoke from a fire

COMPREHENSION CHECK Based on the reading, tell if the statement is true (**T**) or false (**F**).

1. It's not good to ask the owner a lot of questions.

2. Tenants always get a free parking space.

3. Some apartments don't have a lease.

3.5 *There Is/There Are*

We use *there is* or *there are* to introduce a subject, especially with a location or a time.

	There	Is	A/An/One	Singular Subject	Location/Time
Singular (Affirmative)	There	is	an	air conditioner	in the bedroom.
	There	is	one	dryer	in the basement.
	There	is	a	rent increase	this year.
	There	**Isn't**	**A/An**	**Singular Subject**	**Location/Time**
Singular (Negative)	There	isn't	a	back door	in my apartment.
	There	isn't	an	elevator	in the building.
	There	**Is**	**No**	**Singular Subject**	**Location/Time**
	There	is	no	elevator	in the building.
	There	**Are**	**(Plural Word)**	**Plural Subject**	**Location/Time**
Plural (Affirmative)	There	are	—	smoke detectors	near the bedrooms.
	There	are	several	windows	in the bedroom.
	There	are	some	children	in the building.
	There	are	two	closets	in the hall.
	There	**Aren't**	**(Any)**	**Plural Subject**	**Location/Time**
Plural (Negative)	There	aren't	any	new tenants	this month.
	There	**Are**	**No**	**Plural Subject**	**Location/Time**
	There	are	no	parking spaces	on the street.

Language Notes:

1. We can write a contraction with *there is*: *there's*. We don't write a contraction with *there are*.

2. When two nouns follow *there*, we use a singular verb (*is*) if the first noun is singular.

> **There is** one closet in the bedroom and two closets in the hall.
>
> **There is** a washer and dryer in the basement.

We use a plural verb (*are*) if the first noun is plural.

> **There are** two closets in the hall and one closet in the bedroom.

3. Remember: We use *a* before a consonant sound. We use *an* before a vowel sound.

> There's **a** young family in the next apartment.
>
> There's **an** old woman on the third floor.

EXERCISE 7 `About You` Write true statements about your house or apartment. Use *there is* or *there are* and the words given. Then find a partner and compare your answers. (If you live in a dorm, do Exercise 8 instead.)

1. carpet/in the living room

   There's a carpet in the living room.

2. trees/in front of the building

   There are no trees in front of the building.

3. curtains/on the windows

   _____

4. door/in every room

   _____

5. window/in every room

   _____

6. closet/in the living room

   _____

7. number/on the front door

   _____

8. overhead light/in every room

   _____

9. microwave oven/in the kitchen

   _____

10. back door

   _____

11. fireplace

   _____

12. smoke detectors

   _____

curtains

overhead light

fireplace

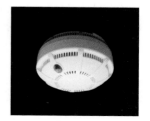
smoke detector

EXERCISE 8 [About You] Write statements about your dorm or dorm room. Use *there is* or *there are* and the words given. Then find a partner and compare your answers. (If you live in an apartment or a house, skip this exercise.)

1. window/in the room

   There's a window in the room.

2. curtains/on the window

   There are no curtains on the window.

3. closet/in the room

   _____

4. two beds/in the room

   _____

5. bathroom/for every room

   _____

6. men and women/in the dorm

   _____

7. cafeteria/in the dorm

   _____

8. snack machines/in the dorm

   _____

9. noisy students/in the dorm

   _____

10. numbers/on the doors

    _____

11. elevator(s)/in the dorm

    _____

12. laundry room/in the dorm

    _____

3.6 Questions and Short Answers with *There*

Compare statements and questions with *there*.

	Statement	Yes/No Question and Short Answer
Singular	**There is** a laundry room in the building. **There is** a smoke detector in the apartment.	A: **Is there** a laundry room in your dorm? B: No, **there isn't.** OR No, **there's not.** A: **Is there** a smoke detector near the bedroom? B: Yes, **there is.**
Plural	**There are** some children in my building. **There are** parking spaces behind the building.	A: **Are there** any children on your floor? B: Yes, **there are.** A: **Are there** parking spaces for all of the tenants? B: No, **there aren't.**

	Statement	*How Many* Question and Short Answer
Plural	**There are** ten apartments in my building.	A: **How many** apartments **are there** in your building? B: (**There are**) twenty-five.

Language Notes:

1. We often use *any* before a plural noun in a question with *there*.
   Are there **any** windows in the kitchen?

2. In a short answer with *no*, we usually make contractions: *No, there isn't.* OR *No, there's not.*
   We don't make a contraction in a short answer with *yes*.

3. In *how many* questions with a location, we sometimes omit *there*.
   How many apartments are (there) in your building?

EXERCISE 9 `About You` Find a partner. Ask and answer questions about your partner's apartment (Column A) or your partner's dorm (Column B). Use *there* and the words given.

1. smoke detectors/in the hall
   A: *Are there any smoke detectors in the hall?*
   B: *Yes, there are.*

A

2. how many closets/in the bedroom
3. children/in your building
4. a dishwasher/in the kitchen
5. a yard/in front of your building
6. trees/in front of your building
7. a basement/in the building
8. a laundry room/in the building
9. noisy neighbors/in the building
10. an elevator/in the building
11. how many closets/in the apartment
12. how many apartments/in your building

B

2. married students/in your dorm
3. a computer room/in your dorm
4. an elevator/in the building
5. graduate students/in your dorm
6. a quiet place to study/in your dorm
7. an air conditioner/in your room
8. a parking lot/near your dorm
9. how many rooms/in your dorm
10. how many floors/in your dorm
11. how many students/in your dorm
12. a bike room/in the building

EXERCISE 10 Complete the phone conversation between a student (A) and an owner (B). Use *there is, there are, is there, are there,* and other related words.

A: I'm calling about an apartment for rent on Grover Street.

B: We have two apartments available. _____There's_____ a two-bedroom apartment on the first
                                                 1.

    floor and a one bedroom apartment on the fourth floor. Which one are you interested in?

A: I prefer the smaller apartment. _____ an elevator in the building?
                                                 2.

B: Yes, there is. How many people _____ in your family?
                                               3.

A: I live alone. I'm a student. Is this a quiet building?

B: Oh, yes. This is a very quiet building. _____ no kids in the building.
                                               4.

A: That's good. I have a car. _____ parking spaces?
                                               5.

B: Yes. _____ twenty spaces in the back of the building.
                     6.

A: How _____ apartments _____ in the building?
                  7.   8.

B: _____ thirty apartments.
       9.

A: Twenty parking spaces for thirty apartments? Then _____ enough spaces for all
                                             10.

    the tenants.

B: Don't worry. Not everyone has a car. And _____ a lot of spaces on the street.
                                          11.

A: _____ a laundry room in the building?
       12.

B: Yes. _____ washers and dryers in the basement.
       13.

A: I hear a dog. Is that your dog?

B: Yes, but don't worry. I don't live in the building. _____ no dogs in the building.
                                          14.

3.7 *There, They,* and Other Pronouns

Examples	Explanation
There's a janitor in the building. **He's** in the basement. **There's** a little girl in the next apartment. **She's** 10 years old. **There's** an empty apartment downstairs. **It's** available now. **There are** two washing machines. **They're** in the basement.	To introduce a new noun, we use *there* + *is/are*. When this noun is the subject of the next sentence, we use the subject pronoun *he, she, it,* or *they.*

Spelling Note:

Don't confuse *there* and *they're*. They have the same pronunciation. *They're* is the contraction
for *they + are.*

    There are dogs in the next apartment. **They're** very friendly.

EXERCISE 11 Fill in the blanks with one of the items from the box. You can use an item more than once.

| there's | there are | it's | she's | is she | are they |
| is there | are there | is it | he's | is he | they're |

1. ___There's___ a small apartment for rent in my building. ___It's___ on the fourth floor.
    a.   b.

2. _____ an old woman in the next apartment. _____ very quiet.
    a.   b.

3. _____ parking spaces in the back of the building. _____ for the tenants.
    a.   b.

4. _____ a young man in the basement. _____ busy with his laundry.
    a.   b.

5. _____ a 5-year-old girl in the next apartment. _____ in school?
    a.   b.

6. _____ a boy in the family? How old _____?
    a.   b.

7. How many apartments _____ in the building? _____ big?
                  a.   b.

8. _____ an elevator in the building? _____ next to the front door?
    a.   b.

9. _____ a janitor in the building. His name is Marco. _____ busy now.
    a.   b.

EXERCISE 12 Complete the conversation between a student (A) and a building manager (B). Use *there, is, are, it, he, they,* or a combination of these words.

A: ___Is there___ a laundry room in the building?
      1.

B: Yes, _____. _____ in the basement.
         2.   3.

A: I need change for the washing machines.

B: _____ a dollar-bill changer in the laundry room.
       4.

A: How many machines _____?
             5.

B: _____ four washers and two dryers.
      6.

A: Only two dryers?

B: Yes. _____ very big.
        7.

A: _____ a manager in the building?
      8.

B: Yes, _____. _____ outside now taking care of the yard.
          9.   10.

Tiny HOUSES

Read the following article. Pay special attention to the words in bold.

Do you have **a** dream to own **a** house? Does **the** house of your dreams have many rooms? **The** typical American home is about 2,600 square feet. **A** big house is expensive. Americans spend one-third to one-half of their salaries on housing costs. Most homeowners have **a** mortgage.[13] They make **a** down payment[14] and then pay **the** mortgage—plus interest—over **a** long period of time. Besides **the** cost of **the** house plus interest, there is insurance, property tax, repairs, and improvements. Over thirty years, **a** $300,000 house can cost over one million dollars!

Not everyone wants to own **a** big house. Some people want to own **a** small house. In fact, some people want to own **a** very tiny house. Who wants to live in **a** tiny house? More and more people do. Most tiny-house owners have middle incomes.

Tiny houses come in all shapes and sizes, but they are usually between 100 and 400 square feet. Why do people want **a** very small house? **The** owners of tiny houses want **a** simple life. **The** average cost of **a** tiny house is $23,000. Sixty-eight percent of tiny-house owners do not have **a** mortgage. They have more savings than other Americans.

There are several websites with pictures of tiny houses. Look at **the** pictures. Is this lifestyle for you?

---

[13] *mortgage*: a long-term loan from a bank for buying property
[14] *down payment*: the first payment at the time of buying something (usually 10–20 percent of the cost)

A 238 square-foot tiny home, Pasadena, Maryland

COMPREHENSION CHECK Based on the reading, tell if the statement is true (**T**) or false (**F**).

1. Most Americans spend more than half of their salaries on housing.

2. Tiny-house owners save more money than other homeowners.

3. The average American home is about 2,600 square feet.

3.8 Definite and Indefinite Articles

Examples	Explanation
We have **a house**. **The house** has three bedrooms. There's **an apartment** for rent in my building. Do you want to see **the picture**?	We introduce a singular noun with the indefinite article *a* or *an*. When we refer to this noun again, we use the definite article *the*.
There are **(some) websites** for tiny-house owners. Do you want to see **the websites**? Does your house need **(any) repairs**? How much do **the repairs** cost?	We introduce a plural noun with *some, any,* or no article. When we refer to this noun again, we use the definite article *the*.
The neighbors on my block are friendly. **The mortgage** for our house is expensive.	We use *the* before a noun to talk about a specific person or thing.

Language Notes:

1. We use *the* before a singular or plural noun if the speaker and listener share an experience and are thinking about the same person or thing.

   (husband to wife) We need to pay **the bills** next week.

2. We use *the* before a singular or plural noun in these expressions: *the next, the first, the second, the last, the only, the same.*

   The mortgage is not **the only expense**.

3. We often use *the* with certain familiar places and people:

the bank	the beach	the bus	the store	the zoo	the post office
the train	the hospital	the park	the doctor	the movies	

EXERCISE 13 Listen to the conversation about problems in an apartment. Fill in the blanks using *a, an,* or *the*.

CD 1
TR 15

A: I have _____*a*_____ problem in my apartment.
                    1.

B: What's _____ problem?
                    2.

A: _____ owner doesn't provide enough heat. I have to wear _____ sweater all the
        3.   4.

time in _____ apartment.
            5.

B: Why don't you talk to _____ building manager? Maybe _____ heat doesn't work.
                                6.   7.

continued

A: Maybe. There's one more problem. I have _____ neighbor who has _____ small

8.
9.

dog. _____ dog makes a lot of noise. We share _____ wall, and I can hear

10.
11.

_____ dog through _____ wall.

12.
13.

B: I don't have problems like that. We have _____ very nice building manager. If there's

14.

_____ problem, I send her _____ e-mail, and she usually takes care of it

15.
16.

right away.

EXERCISE 14 Complete the phone conversation between a student (A) and the manager of an
apartment building (B). Fill in the blanks with *a, an, the, some,* or *any.*

A: Hello? I want to speak with _____ owner.

1.

B: I'm _____ manager of _____ building. Can I help you?

2.
3.

A: I need to find _____ apartment.

4.

B: Where do you live now?

A: I live in _____ big apartment on Wright Street. I have _____

5.
6.

roommate, but he's graduating. I need _____ one-bedroom apartment. Are there

7.

_____ small apartments in your building?

8.

B: There's one.

A: What floor is it on?

B: It's on _____ third floor.

9.

A: Does _____ kitchen have _____ stove and _____

10.
11.
12.

refrigerator?

B: Yes. _____ refrigerator is old, but it works well. _____ stove is new.

13.
14.

A: Can I see _____ apartment?

15.

B: I have _____ questions for you first. Do you have _____ dog?

16.
17.

We don't allow dogs.

A: No, I don't.

B: Do you have _____ pets?

18.

A: I have _____ snake.

19.

B: A snake?

A: Don't worry. My snake doesn't cause _____ problems. It's not

20.

_____ very big snake. I keep _____ snake in _____

21.   22.   23.

glass box.

B: Is _____ box always closed?

24.

A: Yes, it is. I only open it to feed _____ snake. It eats mice.

25.

B: Mice?

A: Yes. When can I see _____ apartment?

26.

B: Uh, I have to speak to _____ landlord. I don't think he wants

27.

_____ snakes or mice in _____ building.

28.   29.

3.9 Making Generalizations

A generalization says that something is true about all members of a group.

Examples	Explanation
A homeowner pays tax. = **Homeowners** pay tax. **An apartment** is expensive. = **Apartments** are expensive.	To make a generalization about the subject, we can use the indefinite article *a* or *an* before the singular form of the subject. We can also use the plural form of the subject with no article.
I like big **rooms**. I'm not interested in tiny **houses**.	To make a generalization about the object, we use the plural form with no article.

EXERCISE 15 Rewrite each generalization with the plural form of each subject. Make any other necessary changes.

1. A homeowner has a lot of expenses.

   Homeowners have a lot of expenses.

2. A house in San Francisco is expensive.

   _____

continued

3. A condo association has a lot of rules.

_____

4. A building manager takes care of buildings.

_____

5. A renter pays rent every month.

_____

6. A yard is good for small children.

_____

EXERCISE 16 Fill in the blanks with a plural subject. Then find a partner and compare your answers.

1. _____ Students _____ need a cheap apartment.

2. _____ don't want to rent to people with pets.

3. _____ sometimes make a lot of noise in an apartment.

4. _____ need an apartment with an elevator.

5. _____ like houses with a garden.

6. _____ need a big apartment.

7. _____ are expensive in the United States.

EXERCISE 17 About You Find a partner. Ask and answer questions about the things he or she likes in the place where he or she lives. Use the plural form of each object noun.

1. rug

   A: _Do you like rugs?_

   B: _No, I don't._

2. white wall

3. curtain on the window

4. picture on the wall

5. plant

6. friendly neighbor

7. bright light

EXERCISE 18 Complete the conversation between two students. Use *a, an, the, some, any*, or Ø for no article. More than one answer may be possible.

A: My new apartment is great. I'm so happy. I don't have _____*any*_____ big problems.
                                                                              1.

Do you have _____ problems with your apartment?
                            2.

B: Yes. I don't like _____ janitor. He's impolite. Also, I want to get
                        3.

_____ dog, but it's not allowed. _____ owner says that
            4.   5.

_____ dogs make a lot of noise.
            6.

A: Can you get _____ cat?
                            7.

B: Yes, but I don't like _____ cats.
                                    8.

A: Is your building quiet?

B: No. There are _____ children in _____ building. When I try to
                            9.   10.

study, I can hear _____ children in the next apartment. They watch TV all
                                11.

the time.

A: What about your roommate? Is this a problem for her, too?

B: I don't have _____ roommate now.
                            12.

A: You need to find _____ apartment in _____ different building.
                                13.   14.

Singular and Plural Nouns

Regular Plurals	Irregular Plurals
boy—boys	man—men
box—boxes	woman—women
story—stories	child—children
tomato—tomatoes	foot—feet
wife—wives	fish—fish

There Is/There Are

Singular	Examples
AFFIRMATIVE STATEMENT	**There's** a laundry room in my building.
NEGATIVE STATEMENT	**There isn't** an elevator in my building.
YES/NO QUESTION	**Is there** a yard behind your building?
SHORT ANSWER	Yes, **there is**.

Plural	Examples
AFFIRMATIVE STATEMENT	**There are** foreign students in my dorm.
NEGATIVE STATEMENT	**There aren't** any graduate students in my dorm.
YES/NO QUESTION	**Are there** any married students in your dorm?
SHORT ANSWER	No, **there aren't**.
HOW MANY QUESTION	How many students **are there** in your dorm?

Articles and *Some/Any*

Use	Singular	Plural
To introduce a new noun	There's **a tree** in front of my house. My house has **a big yard**.	I have **(some) flowers** in my yard. There aren't **(any) trees** in my yard.
To talk about specific people or things	**The janitor** in my building is very helpful.	**The apartments** in my building are small.
To talk about the only one of something	I don't like **the president** of my condo association.	—
To make a generalization	**A dog** is a popular pet.	**Dogs** are popular pets. I like **dogs**.

Choose the correct word(s) to complete the conversation. Circle Ø for no article. Where you see a blank, write the plural form of the word given.

A: My husband and I have (**a**/the/Ø) new condo. It has three ___bedrooms___ and two bathrooms.
    1.   2. bedroom

B: How many square _____ do you have?
                      3. foot

A: About 2,000. (*There are/They are/There's*) thirty _____ in (*a/the/Ø*)
                 4.   5. apartment   6.

    building. There's (*a/an/the*) exercise room. (*There's/It's/There*) not very big, but my husband
                      7.   8.

    likes to use it. There are (*some/any/a*) weight machines. (*There/It's/There's*) also (*a/the/any*)
                             9.   10.   11.

    swimming pool.

B: How often do you use (*a/the/Ø*) pool?
                           12.

A: We use it one or two _____ a week. Our _____ really love it.
                          13. day   14. kid

    (*There are/They're/There*) other _____ with small _____ in the building.
                15.   16. family   17. child

    I like to sit at (*the/a/Ø*) pool with a few _____. We talk and watch (*a/the/Ø*) kids.
                   18.   19. woman   20.

B: Do you ever invite (*a/any/the*) _____ to your pool?
                        21.   22. guest

A: No. (*A/The/Ø*) pool is only for _____. Other _____ can't use the pool.
              23.   24. owner   25. person

B: Really? Who makes (*the/a/Ø*) rules?
                        26.

A: (*An/The/Ø*) condo association makes the rules.
       27.

B: (*There are/Are there/Are they*) other rules?
                28.

A: Yes, (*they are/there are/it is*). (*Pets are/The pet is/The pets are*) not allowed.
            29.   30.

    (*There's/It's/They're*) a condo for sale in my building. Do you want to see it?
        31.

B: I don't like (*a condo/condos/the condos*). I prefer (*a/the/Ø*) houses. I don't like to follow
                   32.   33.

    (*a rule/the rules/rules*) of a condo association. I want to make my own decisions.
        34.

WRITING

PART 1 Editing Advice

1. *People* is a plural noun. Use a plural verb form.

    The people in my building ~~is~~ *are* very nice.

2. Don't confuse *there* with *they're*.

    My apartment has two closets. ~~There~~ *They're* not very big.

3. Don't confuse *it's* and *there's*.

    ~~It's~~ *There's* a closet in my bedroom.

4. Don't confuse *have* and *there*.

    ~~Have~~ *There's* a closet in my bedroom.

5. Don't use *the* if the speaker and the listener don't have the same person or thing in mind.

    I have ~~the~~ *a* new roommate.

6. Don't use *the* with a generalization.

    ~~The~~ *H*houses are expensive.

7. Don't use *a* before a plural noun.

    There are ~~a~~ big windows in my living room.

8. Don't use an apostrophe for a plural ending.

    The building has three ~~floor's~~ *floors*.

PART 2 Editing Practice

Some of the shaded words and phrases have mistakes. Find the mistakes and correct them. If the shaded words are correct, write C.

I have a new apartment. It's in ~~the~~ *a* nice neighborhood. There are thirty apartments in my

1.   2.   3.

building.

My apartment is big. They're are four bedrooms and two bathrooms. Has a large closet in

4.   5.

each bedroom.

I love my kitchen. It's a new dishwasher in a kitchen. I hate to wash a dishes. I don't have a

6.   7.   8.   9.

microwave. Some people thinks that's strange, but I don't like the microwaves.

10.   11.

There are five washers and five dryers in the basement. I never have to wait to wash my

12.   13.

clothes.

I like my neighbor's. There very nice people. There's a very interesting women across the

14.   15.   16.   17.

hall from me. We are now friends.

PART 3 Write About It

1. Write a description of your neighborhood. Use *there is/there are* in some of your sentences.
2. Write a description of your apartment, house, or dorm room. Use *there is/there are* in some of your sentences.

PART 4 Edit Your Writing

Reread the Summary of Lesson 3 and the editing advice. Edit your writing from Part 3.

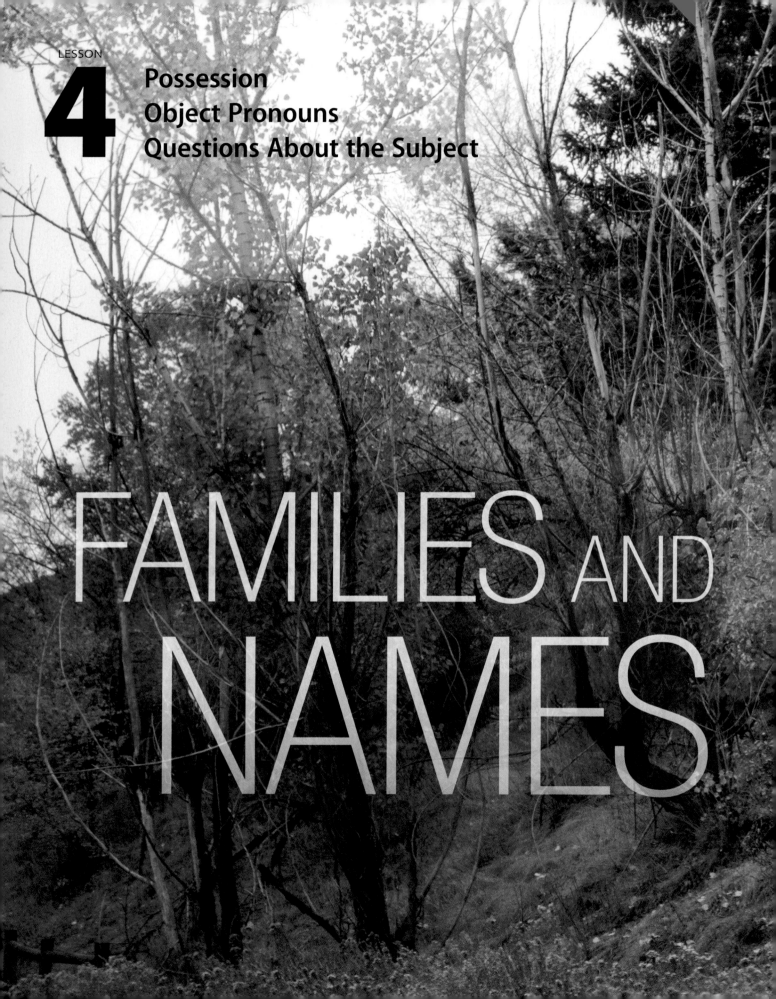

FAMILIES AND NAMES

EXIT 119

No Name ↗

REST AREA

What's in a name? That which we call a rose by any other name would smell as sweet.

—William Shakespeare

Exit sign for No Name, Colorado

Unusual Names

CD 1
TR 16

Read the following article. Pay special attention to the words in bold.

The popularity of names changes. In the United States, some of the most popular **boys'** names today are *Noah*, *Liam*, and *Mason*. Some of the most popular **girls'** names today are *Sophia*, *Emma*, and *Olivia*. The names *Mary* and *John*, once very popular, are not very common anymore.

Your grandparents' names probably seem old and out of fashion, but **your great-grandparents'** names sometimes seem cool now. *Helen*, *Rose*, *Henry*, and *Max*, once not in fashion, are back. The popularity of some names stays the same. For example, *William* is almost always one of the five most popular names for boys.

It's sometimes hard to tell[1] if a name is a **boy's** name or a **girl's** name. *Arizona*, for example, is **the name of a state**. *Dakota* is **the name of an American Indian tribe**. Are these **boys'** names or **girls'** names?

Some celebrities[2] give **their** children unusual names. **David and Victoria Beckham's son's** name is Brooklyn. Singer **David Bowie's son's** name is a rhyme;[3] **his** name is Zowie Bowie. Rock musician Frank Zappa has a daughter with an interesting name. **Her** name is Moon Unit Zappa. Actress **Nicole Richie's** daughter is Sparrow James Midnight Madden. Actor Antonio Sabato Jr. has a son with a very long name. **His** name is Antonio Kamakanaalohamaikalani Harvey Sabato III. The long name is a Hawaiian word meaning "a gift from the heavens."

Do you prefer a common name or an unusual name?

---

1 *to tell*: to know
2 *celebrity*: a famous living person
3 *rhyme*: words that sound alike

Most Popular Names in the United States

Year	Boys' Names	Girls' Names
2014	Noah	Emma
2000	Jacob	Emily
1990	Michael	Jessica
1980	Michael	Jennifer
1970	Michael	Jennifer
1960	David	Mary
1950	James	Linda
1940	James	Mary
1930	Robert	Mary
1920	John	Mary

COMPREHENSION CHECK Based on the reading, tell if the statement is true (**T**) or false (**F**).

1. Names, like other things, go in and out of fashion.

2. A lot of people think their grandparents' names are cool.

3. *Mary* is always a popular name for girls.

4.1 Possessive Nouns—Form

Possessive nouns show ownership or relationship.

	Noun	Rule	Examples
Singular nouns	son daughter	Add apostrophe + *s*.	My **son's** name is William. My **daughter's** name is Emma.
Regular plural nouns	girls boys	Add an apostrophe only.	Popular **girls'** names are Sophia and Ava. Popular **boys'** names are Noah and Jacob.
Irregular plural nouns	children women	Add apostrophe + *s*.	What are your **children's** names? Rose and Dorothy are **women's** names.
Names that end in *-s*	James	Add apostrophe + *s*.	Do you know **James's** wife?
Inanimate objects	state	Use *the* ____ *of* ____. Do not use apostrophe + *s*.	Arizona is the name **of a state**.

Language Note:

Sometimes you will see only an apostrophe when a name ends in *s*.

Do you know **James'** wife?

EXERCISE 1 Listen and fill in the blanks with the words you hear.

_____ name is William Henry White. _____ nickname[4] is
<u>　　　1.　　　</u>　　　　　　　　　　　　　　　　　　　　<u>　　　2.　　　</u>

Bill. _____ name is Elizabeth White. _____ nickname is
　　<u>　　3.　　</u>　　　　　　　　　　　　　　　　　<u>　　　4.　　</u>

Lizzy. _____ name is almost the same as _____ name.
　　　<u>　　5.　　</u>　　　　　　　　　　　　　　　<u>　　6.　　</u>

_____ name is Elsbeth. Some married women use only _____
　　<u>　　7.　　</u>　　　　　　　　　　　　　　　　　　　　　　　<u>　　8.　　</u>

last name, but Lizzy uses both _____ maiden name[5] and
　　　　　　　　　　　　　<u>　　9.　　</u>

_____ name. _____ name is Charles. _____
　<u>　10.　</u>　　　　　　<u>　11.　</u>　　　　　　　　　　　　<u>　12.　</u>

friends call him "Charley." _____ teachers prefer to call him by his real name.
　　　　　　　　　　　<u>　13.　</u>

Some people don't like _____ names, but we're happy with
　　　　　　　　　　　<u>　14.　</u>

_____ names. What about you? Do you like _____ name?
　<u>　15.　</u>　　　　　　　　　　　　　　　　　<u>　16.　</u>

---

[4] *nickname*: an informal name
[5] *maiden name*: a woman's family name before she marries

EXERCISE 2 Fill in the blanks with the possessive form of the words given.

1. My _____ parents' names _____ are Rosa and Paco.
   parents/names

2. My _____ are Lara and Marta.
   sisters/names

3. My _____ is Luis.
   brother/name

4. _____ is 4 years old.
   Luis/son

5. My _____ are José and María.
   grandparents/names

6. In my country, *José* and *Luis* are common _____ .
   men/names

7. In my country, *Rosa* and *Marta* are common _____ .
   women/names

8. My _____ has an unusual name: Esma.
   brother/wife

EXERCISE 3 About You Find a partner. Take turns talking about the names in your family. Use possessive nouns.

EXERCISE 4 Some of the following sentences can show possession with *'s* or *s'*. Rewrite these sentences with the correct ending. If the sentence cannot show possession with *'s* or *s'*, write *NC* for "no change."

1. The teacher knows the names of the students.

   The teacher knows the students' names.

2. The name of the school is Carson College.

   _____

3. The name of this textbook is *Grammar in Context*.

   _____

4. What are the names of your parents?

   _____

5. Do you use the last name of your father?

   _____

6. What is the name of your dog?

   _____

7. The names of my sisters are Julie and Jessica.

_____

8. The name of my hometown is Springfield.

_____

4.2 Possessive Adjectives

Possessive adjectives show ownership or relationship. Compare subject pronouns and possessive adjectives.

Examples	Explanation	
	Subject Pronouns	**Possessive Adjectives**
I like **my** name.	I	my
You are a new student. What's **your** name?	you	your
He likes **his** name.	he	his
She doesn't like **her** name.	she	her
Is this your dog? Is it friendly? What's **its** name?	it	its
We use **our** nicknames.	we	our
These are my friends. **Their** last name is Johnson.	they	their
My sister loves **her** husband. My uncle lives with **his** daughter.	A possessive adjective refers to the noun before it.	
My sister's name is Linda. **Her son's** name is Noah.	We can use a possessive adjective and a possessive noun together.	
Emma's husband's name is William.	We can use two possessive nouns together.	

Language Notes:

1. We do not use an apostrophe with the possessive adjective *its*.
2. We use the same possessive form for singular and plural nouns:
   her brothers (NOT: *hers* brother)

EXERCISE 5 Fill in the blanks with the correct possessive adjective.

1. I don't like _____ my _____ name.

2. He loves _____ mother.

3. She loves _____ father.

4. A dog loves _____ owner.

continued

5. Many American women change _____ last names when they get married.

6. Do you use _____ father's last name?

7. I use _____ middle name.

8. We put _____ names at the top of the page.

4.3 Questions with *Whose*

We use *whose* + noun to ask about possession or ownership.

Questions				Answers
Whose + Noun	*Do/Does*	Subject	Verb	
Whose last name	do	you	use?	I use **my husband's** name.
Whose last name	does	your son	use?	He uses **his father's** name.
Whose + Noun	*Be*	Subject		
Whose book	is	this?		It's **Noah's** book.
Whose papers	are	these?		They're **his** papers.

EXERCISE 6 Write a question with *whose* to complete each conversation.

1. **A:** Do you want to see my family photos?

   B: Those are cute children. Are they your kids?

   A: No, they're not.

   B: _Whose kids are they?_____

   A: They're my sister's kids.

2. **A:** There's a book on the floor.

   B: Let me see if it has a name in it.

   A: _____

   B: It's Rita Patel's book.

3. **A:** My husband and I have different last names.

   B: _____

   A: Our son uses my husband's last name.

4. A: Do you have your new class schedule?

B: Yes, I do.

A: _____

B: I have Mr. Green's class for math.

5. A: What's your cat's name?

B: That's not my cat.

A: _____

B: I don't know. It's always near my front door.

6. A: What do you think of celebrities' children's names?

B: I think they're interesting. I like some of them.

A: _____

B: I like Zowie Bowie's name. It's a rhyme.

4.4 Possessive Pronouns

We use possessive pronouns to avoid repetition of a possessive noun.
Compare possessive adjectives and possessive pronouns.

Examples	Explanation		
You don't know my name, but I know **yours**. (*yours* = your name)	**Possessive Adjectives**		**Possessive Pronouns**
	my		mine
	your		yours
Your name is easy for Americans to pronounce. **Mine** is hard. (*mine* = my name)	his		his
	her		hers
	its		—
His signature is hard to read. **Hers** is easy to read. (*hers* = her signature)	our		ours
	their		theirs
Mary's last name is short. **Jennifer's** isn't. (*Jennifer's* = Jennifer's last name)	After a possessive noun, we can omit the noun.		

EXERCISE 7 Write the correct possessive pronoun for the underlined words.

1. Your name is long. ~~My name~~ *Mine* is short.

2. My sister likes her name. I don't like <u>my name</u>.

3. I like my first name. Do you like <u>your first name</u>?

4. My sister uses her middle name. My brother doesn't use <u>his middle name</u>.

5. My wife and I have different last names. My last name is Roberts. <u>Her last name</u> is Paulson.

6. Your last name is easy to pronounce. <u>Their last name</u> is hard.

7. My brother's children are grown up. <u>Our children</u> are still small.

EXERCISE 8 Choose the correct words to complete the conversation.

A: Do you live with (*your*/*yours*) parents?
                      1.

B: No, I don't. Do you live with (*your*/*yours*)?
                                    2.

A: No. (*Mine*/*Mines*) are back home in Korea. They live with (*my*/*mine*) brother.
          3.   **4.**

B: (*Your*/*Yours*) brother is single, then?
       5.

A: No, he's married. He lives with (*his*/*her*) wife and (*our*/*ours*) parents.
                                        6.   **7.**

In (*our*/*ours*) country, married children often live with (*his*/*their*) parents.
      8.   **9.**

B: Here grown children don't usually want to live with (*their*/*theirs*) parents.
                                                              10.

My mom and dad live in another state.

A: Isn't that hard for you?

B: Not really. I have (*my*/*mine*) life, and they have (*their*/*theirs*).
                          11.   **12.**

NAMING CUSTOMS

 Read the following conversation. Pay special attention to the words in bold.

CD 1
TR 18

A: Can I ask **you** some questions about your name?

B: Of course.

A: Tell **me** about your name. What's your full name?

B: William James Thomas Junior.

A: Do people call **you** "William James"?

B: No. No one calls **me** by my middle name. I never use **it**. I use my middle initial[6] when I sign my name: William J. Thomas Jr.

A: Why do you use *junior* after your name?

B: My father and I have the same name. His name is William J. Thomas Senior. My mother calls **him** "William," but she calls **me** "Billy."

A: Billy?

B: Yes. *Bill* and *Billy* are common nicknames for *William*.

A: What's your wife's name?

B: Ann Marie Simms-Thomas. I call **her** "Annie."

A: Why does she have two last names?

B: Simms is her last name, and Thomas is mine. She uses both of **them**.

A: Do you have any children?

B: Yes. We have a son and a daughter. Our son's name is Jacob, but we call **him** "Jake." Our daughter's name is Madison, but everybody calls **her** "Maddie."

A: What do your children call **you**?

B: They call **us** "Mommy" and "Daddy," of course.

---

6 *initial*: the first letter of your first, middle, or last name

COMPREHENSION CHECK Based on the conversation, tell if the statement is true (**T**) or false (**F**).

1. William has a middle name.

2. William's mother calls William's father "Billy."

3. William's wife doesn't use William's last name.

4.5 The Subject and the Object

Examples			Explanation
S	**V**	**O**	The subject (S) comes before the verb (V). The object (O) comes after the verb. The object is a person or a thing.
Madison	has	a nickname.	
I	love	Maddie.	
S	**V**	**P** **O**	An object can follow a preposition (P).
He always talks **about his children**.			
I have a middle **name**. I never use **it**.			An object can be a noun or a pronoun.
He has two last **names**. He uses both of **them**.			

Compare subject and object pronouns.

Examples	Subject Pronouns	Object Pronouns
I like my name. My wife calls **me** "Bill."	I	me
You have a strange name. I want to ask **you** about your name.	you	you
He has a nickname. We call **him** "Jake."	he	him
She uses a nickname. I call **her** "Annie."	she	her
It's a nice name. I like **it**.	it	it
We have two kids. They call **us** "Mommy" and "Daddy."	we	us
They are wonderful kids. We love **them**.	they	them

Language Notes:

1. After a verb or a preposition, we use an object pronoun.

   My mother calls my sister and **me** her "little babies." (NOT: my sister and *I*)

2. In the subject position, we use a subject pronoun.

   My sister and **I** call our mother "Mama." (NOT: My sister and *me*)

EXERCISE 9 Fill in the blanks with an object pronoun that matches the underlined word(s).

1. <u>I</u> want to know more about your name. Tell _____*me*_____ something about it.

2. I use <u>my middle name</u> when I sign my name, but I don't use _____ any other time.

3. <u>My children</u>'s names are Madison and Jacob. We call _____ "Maddie" and "Jake."

4. <u>You</u> are a new student. I don't know _____ .

5. <u>My English teacher</u> is Ms. Kathleen Novak. We call _____ "Kathy."

6. <u>My teacher</u>'s name is Mr. Frank. Do you know anything about _____ ?

7. <u>We</u> have two nephews. They call _____ "Auntie" and "Unc."

EXERCISE 10 Complete the conversation between a foreign student (A) and an American student (B). Use the correct object pronoun.

A: Americans are informal about names. Our teacher calls _____us_____ by our first names.
                                                                    1.

B: What does your teacher call _____ in your country?
                                              2.

A: In my country, when teachers talk to a woman, they call _____ "Miss" or
                                                                        3.

"Madam." When they talk to a man, they call _____ "Sir."
                                                      4.

B: I like it when the teacher calls _____ by our first names.
                                                  5.

A: I don't. There's another strange thing: in my country, we never use a first name for our teachers.

We always call _____ "Professor" or "Teacher." In the United States, our teacher
                        6.

doesn't like it when we call _____ "Teacher." She says it's impolite. But in my
                                        7.

country, "Teacher" is a term of respect.

B: Only small children in the United States call their teacher "Teacher." If you know your teacher's

name, use _____ .
                    8.

A: I can't call _____ "Sophia." It's hard for _____ to change my
                            9.   10.

customs after a lifetime of following _____ .
                                                11.

EXERCISE 11 Fill in the blanks with *I, I'm, my, mine,* or *me.*

1. _____I'm_____ a foreign student.

2. _____ 20 years old.

3. _____ study at the University of Wisconsin.

4. _____ English isn't perfect.

5. Your parents live in Japan. _____ live in the United States.

6. Sometimes my parents visit _____ at the university.

EXERCISE 12 Fill in the blanks with *you, you're, your,* or *yours.*

1. _____You're_____ a good teacher.

2. _____ explain grammar well.

3. We all understand _____ .

4. Our pronunciation is sometimes hard to understand. _____ is clear.

5. _____ a kind teacher.

6. _____ class is very interesting.

EXERCISE 13 Fill in the blanks with *he, he's, his,* or *him.*

1. I have a good friend. _____His_____ name is Paul.

2. _____ an accountant.

3. _____ works in an office.

4. He works with _____ son, Bill.

5. Bill helps _____ in his business.

6. My wife is a doctor. _____ is a computer programmer.

EXERCISE 14 Fill in the blanks with *she, she's, her,* or *hers.*

1. I have a sister. _____Her_____ name is Diane.

2. _____ an interesting person.

3. I call _____ on the phone once a week.

4. _____ has two children.

5. My children go to Dewey School. _____ go to King School.

6. _____ husband is a teacher.

EXERCISE 15 Fill in the blanks with *it, it's,* or *its.*

1. What do you think of your name? Are you happy with _____it_____?

2. _____ a beautiful name.

3. Look at the list of popular names. Is your name on _____?

4. The name *William* is very popular. _____ on the list almost every year.

5. Look at this website. _____ has a list of popular names in the United States.

6. I have a new book. _____ title is *What to Name Your Baby.*

EXERCISE 16 Fill in the blanks with *we, we're, our, ours,* or *us.*

1. _____We're_____ foreign students.

2. _____ come from different countries.

3. _____ in class now.

4. _____ teacher is American.

5. The teacher asks _____ a lot of questions.

6. Your classroom is on the second floor. _____ is on the third floor.

EXERCISE 17 Fill in the blanks with *they, they're, their, theirs,* or *them.*

1. Diane and Richard are my friends. _____They_____ live near me.

2. _____ Americans.

3. _____ have two children.

4. _____ children go to public school.

5. My house is small. _____ is big.

6. I have dinner with _____ once a week.

WHO NAMES Hurricanes?

Hurricane Earl heads towards the United States.

Read the following article. Pay special attention to the words in bold.

CD 1
TR 19

How do hurricanes get their names? Here are some frequently asked questions (FAQs) about naming hurricanes and tropical storms.[7]

Q: **Who names** hurricanes?

A: The World Meteorological Organization (WMO) names hurricanes and tropical storms.

Q: **When does a storm get** a name?

A: It gets a name when its winds reach 39 miles per hour.

Q: **What kind of names does the WMO use?**

A: It uses both men's and women's names. The first storm of the year begins with an *A*. The next storm begins with *B*, and the next one begins with *C*. If the first storm has a woman's name, the next storm has a man's name.

Q: **Why does the WMO use** names?

A: Names are easy to remember.

Q: Do Atlantic and Pacific storms have the same names?

A: No, they don't.

Q: Does the WMO use the same list of names every year?

A: No, it doesn't. It uses six lists of names. Every 6 years, the WMO uses the same list as before. The 2011 list and the 2017 list are the same. The 2013 list and the 2019 list are the same.

Q: **What happens** if a storm is very serious and deadly,[8] like Hurricane Katrina in 2005 or Hurricane Sandy in 2012?

A: The WMO doesn't use the name again. A committee[9] chooses a new name for that letter of the alphabet.

Q: **What name takes** the place of *Sandy*?

A: *Sara* takes the place of *Sandy*.

Q: **What name takes** the place of *Katrina*?

A: *Kate* does.

---

7 *tropical storm*: heavy rains with high wind
8 *deadly*: so dangerous as to cause death
9 *committee*: a group of people organized for a purpose

2017 Hurricane Names

Caribbean, Gulf of Mexico, and North Atlantic			Eastern North Pacific		
Arlene	Harvey	Ophelia	Adrian	Hilary	Selma
Bret	Irma	Philippe	Beatriz	Irwin	Todd
Cindy	Jose	Rina	Calvin	Jova	Veronica
Don	Katia	Sean	Dora	Kenneth	Wiley
Emily	Lee	Tammy	Eugene	Lidia	Xina
Franklin	Maria	Vince	Fernanda	Pilar	York
Gert	Nate	Whitney	Greg	Ramon	Zelda

COMPREHENSION CHECK Based on the reading, tell if the statement is true (**T**) or false (**F**).

1. The WMO uses the same list of names for hurricanes every year.

2. The list of hurricane names is alphabetical.

3. Hurricanes have names of both men and women.

4.6 Subject Questions and Non-Subject Questions

Examples	Explanation
A: What name follows *Maria*? **B:** *Nate* follows *Maria*.	We can ask a subject question with *what* (+ noun) or *who*. We use the -s form of the verb to ask about the present.
A: Who chooses names for hurricanes? **B:** The committee does.	We can make a short answer with the subject + *do/does*.
A: What happens to a name after a deadly storm? **B:** A committee chooses a new name.	We sometimes begin subject questions about the present with *what happens*.
A: Who **do** you **know** on the committee? **B:** I don't know anyone on the committee. **A:** Why **does** the WMO **use** names? **B:** It uses names because they are easy to remember.	We use *do* or *does* and the base form of the verb to ask a non-subject question about the present.
A: Whose name has ten letters? **B:** Annastazia's does. **A:** Whose last name do you use? **B:** I use my father's last name.	We can ask subject questions and non-subject questions with *whose* + noun.

continued

Language Notes:

1. We use *whom* to ask about the object. In informal English, we often use *who* instead of *whom*.

   INFORMAL: **Who** do you know on the committee?

   FORMAL: **Whom** do you know on the committee?

2. In informal English, we use *who* and put the preposition at the end of the question. In formal English, we use *whom* after the preposition.

   INFORMAL: **Who** do you live **with**?

   FORMAL: **With whom** do you live?

3. When we don't know an answer to a question, we sometimes say "Who knows?" This is a subject question.

   A: When is the next hurricane?

   B: Who knows?

4. The answer to a subject question can use the *–s* form or the base form.

   A: Who **has** a long name?

   B: I **have** a long name.

EXERCISE 18 Complete the conversations with the correct form of the word(s) given or *do* or *does*.

1. **A:** Who _____has_____ an uncommon name in your family?
   a. have

   B: My brother _____. His name is Ezekiel. But only a few people call him that.
   b.

   A: Who _____ him that?
   c. call

   B: Our parents _____.
   d.

   A: What _____ him?
   e. you/call

   B: We call him "Zeke."

2. **A:** Who _____ a nickname?
   a. have

   B: I _____.
   b.

   A: What's your nickname?

   B: Alex. My real name is Alejandro. Everyone except one person calls me "Alex."

   A: Who _____ you "Alejandro"?
   c. call

   B: Only my mother _____.
   d.

3. **A:** Whose name _____ over ten letters?
   a. have

   B: Mine _____.
   b.

   A: How many letters _____?
   c. it/have

   B: It has twelve letters: *Scheherazade.*

A: Wow! That's a long name. How _____ it?

d. you/spell

B: S-C-H-E-H-E-R-A-Z-A-D-E.

A: Where _____ ?

e. it/come from

B: It's the name of a queen in a story. What about your name?

A: My name is unusual, too. But it's short: Pax.

B: That's an interesting name. What _____ ?

f. it/mean

A: It means "peace."

4. A: My name is Sandy.

B: _____ your name?

a. you/like

A: I like it, but it's the name of a bad hurricane in 2012.

B: Don't worry. The name is not on the list anymore.

A: Really? Who _____ the names?

b. replace

B: A committee of the WMO _____ .

c.

A: That's good. What's the new name for 2018?

B: I think it's *Sara*.

A: Someone in my family has that name.

B: Who _____ that name?

d. have

A: My aunt _____ .

e.

4.7 Who, Whom, Whose, Who's

Examples	Explanation
A: Who names hurricanes? **B:** The WMO does.	We use *who* to ask a question about the subject.
A: Who(m) do you live with? **B:** I live with my parents.	We use *who* or *whom* to ask a question about the object. *Whom* is very formal.
A: Whose name begins with *X*? **B:** Mine does. It's Xavier.	We use *whose* to ask about ownership or relationship.
A: Who's that man? **B:** That's my dad.	*Who's* is a contraction of *who is*.

EXERCISE 19 Complete the conversation with *who, whom, whose,* or *who's.*

A: _____*Whose*_____ last name do you use?
 1.

B: I use my father's last name. But I don't live with my father.

A: Why not?

B: My parents are divorced.

A: _____ do you live with, then? Your mother?
 2.

B: No. I live with Nina.

A: _____ that?
 3.

B: That's my older sister. I love her, but she's so lazy. She never washes the dishes.

A: _____ washes the dishes, then?
 4.

B: I do. When I ask "_____ turn is it?" she always says, "I know it's my turn,
 5.

but I'm so busy today."

A: Then don't ask. Just tell her it's her turn. _____ pays the rent?
 6.

B: We both do.

A: I guess you need her, then.

B: I guess I do—for now.

EXERCISE 20 Choose the correct word(s) to complete the conversation.

A: (Whose/Who) name is the same as a hurricane?
 1.

B: (*Mine/My*) is.
 2.

A: What's your name?

B: Irene.

A: (*Who/Whom*) names hurricanes?
 3.

B: The WMO does.

A: Do they ever repeat a name?

B: Yes. They repeat names every six years.

A: Who (*decide/decides*) on the names?
4.

B: A committee does.

A: What (*happens/does happen*) to names like *Irene* and *Katrina*?
5.

B: The WMO doesn't use them anymore because the names give people a bad feeling.

EXERCISE 21 Choose the correct word(s) to complete the conversation.

A: The teacher wants us to talk about names. My name is Lisa Simms-Evans.

B: Do you like (*your*/*you're*) name?
1.

A: No, (*its/it's*) too long. I have both (*parents'/parent's*) last names.
2.   3.

B: Do you have any brothers or sisters?

A: I have one brother. (*He's/His*) name is Leslie. (*He's/His*) not happy with (*his/her*) name, either.
4.   5.   6.

B: Why not?

A: Leslie can be a (*girls/girl's*) name. (*Her/His*) wife calls him "Les." My parents and (*I/me*) call
7.   8.   9.

him "More or Less."

B: That's funny.

A: My (*sisters/sister's*) name is Annette. She doesn't like (*her/his*) name, either. Everyone asks her
10.   11.

if (*she's/she*) Annette Bening.
12.

B: (*Who's/Whose*) Annette Bening?
13.

A: (*He's/She's*) an actress.
14.

B: In your family, who (*have/has*) a good name?
15.

A: My goldfish! (*Its/It's*) name is Goldie.
16.

B: Well, class is over. (*Whose is that coat/Whose coat is that*)? Is it (*your's/yours*)?
17.   18.

A: No. It's not (*my/mine*).
19.

B: What about that book on the floor? Is it (*yours/your*) or (*mines/mine*)?
20.   21.

A: (*Who's/Whose*) name is in the book?
22.

B: It says, "Soo Won Park." Let's take it and give it to (*him/his*).
23.

SUMMARY OF LESSON 4

Possessive Nouns—Forms

	Examples
Singular nouns	My **father's** name is Harry.
Regular plural nouns	My **parents'** names are Rose and Harry.
Irregular plural nouns	*Sophia* and *Liam* are common **children's** names.
Inanimate objects	What's the name **of our textbook**?

Pronouns and Possessive Forms

Subject Pronoun	Object Pronoun	Possessive Adjective	Possessive Pronoun
I	me	my	mine
you	you	your	yours
he	him	his	his
she	her	her	hers
it	it	its	—
we	us	our	ours
they	them	their	theirs
who	who(m)	whose	whose

Examples			
Subject Pronoun	Object Pronoun	Possessive Adjective	Possessive Pronoun
I come from Cuba.	The teacher helps **me**.	**My** name is Rosa.	Your name is common. **Mine** isn't.
They come from Korea.	The teacher helps **them**.	**Their** names are Kim and Lee.	Your name is short. **Theirs** is long.
Who comes from Poland?	**Who(m)** does the teacher help?	**Whose** name do you like?	This is my book. **Whose** is that?

TEST/REVIEW

Choose the correct word(s) to complete the conversation between two students.

A: (Who/*Who's*/Whose) your English teacher?
          1.

B: (My/Mine/Me) teacher is Charles Flynn. Who's (your/your's/yours)?
          2.   3.

A: Marianne Peters. She's (Charle's/Charles/Charles's) wife.
                                              4.

B: Oh, really? (His/He's/He) last name is different from (she/her/hers).
                          5.   6.

A: Yes. She uses (her/hers/his) father's last name, not her (husband's/husbands'/husbands).
                           7.   8.

B: Do they have children?

A: Yes.

B: (Whose/Who's/Who) name do the children use?
          9.

A: (They're/Their/They) use both last names.
          10.

B: How do you know so much about (you're/your/yours) teacher and (his/her/hers) children?
                                        11.   12.

A: We talk about (us/our/ours) names in class. We often ask (her/she/him) about American
                        13.   14.

customs. She explains her customs, and we explain (our/us/ours).
                                                          15.

B: Mr. Flynn doesn't talk about (her/his/he's) family in class.
                                        16.

A: Do you call (her/him/he) "Mister"?
                       17.

B: Of course. (He/He's/His) the teacher. In my country, (it's/its/its') not polite to call a teacher by
                      18.   19.

his or her first name.

A: (Its/It's/It) not polite in my country either. But Marianne is American. (She/She's/Her) prefers
          20.   21.

her first name.

B: It doesn't seem right. We need to show respect for our teachers. I prefer to call (they/them/him)
                                                                                              22.

by (they/they're/their) last names. That's the way we do it in my country.
      23.

A: In (me/my/mine), we just say "Professor." But (we/we're/us) in the United States now, so we
           24.   25.

need to follow American customs.

WRITING

PART 1 Editing Advice

1. Don't confuse *you're* (*you are*) and *your* (possessive form).

   ~~Your~~ You're interested in hurricanes.

   What's ~~you're~~ your name?

2. Don't confuse *he's* (*he is*) and *his* (possessive form).

   ~~He's~~ His name is Paul.

   ~~His~~ He's a good student.

3. Don't confuse *it's* (*it is*) and *its* (possessive form).

   ~~Its~~ It's a tropical storm. ~~It's~~ Its wind is over 50 miles per hour.

4. Don't confuse *his* and *her*.

   My brother loves ~~her~~ his daughter.

   My sister loves ~~his~~ her son.

5. Don't confuse *they're* (*they are*) and *their* (possessive form).

   I have two American friends. ~~They're~~ Their names are Haley and Mike.

   ~~Their~~ They're very nice people.

6. Don't use a possessive pronoun before a noun. Use a possessive adjective.

   How do hurricanes get ~~theirs~~ their names?

7. Don't confuse subject pronouns and object pronouns.

   My father and ~~me~~ I have the same name.

   I have a daughter. I love ~~she~~ her very much.

8. Put the apostrophe in the right place.

   My ~~parent's~~ parents' names are Harry and Marge.

9. Don't use an apostrophe for plural nouns.

   My parents have many ~~friend's~~ friends.

PART 2 Editing Practice

Some of the shaded words and phrases have mistakes. Find the mistakes and correct them. If the shaded words are correct, write C.

 ~~Mine~~ <u>My</u> name is Marta López-Hernández. People often ask me, <u>C</u> "Why do you have two last
 1.   **2.**

name's?" I come from Mexico, and Mexicans use both parent's names. My father's last name is
 3.   **4.**   **5.**

López. My mother's last name is Hernández.
       6.

    When a Mexican woman gets married, she drops hers mother's name and adds his
                                           7.   **8.**

husbands' last name. My sister is married. Her name is Celia López de Castillo. His husband is
 9.   **10.**   **11.**

Luis Castillo-Sánchez. Celia and Luis have two kids, Jorge and Rosa. Theirs friends call them
                                               12.   **13.**

"George" and "Rosie." Me and my sister call Rosa "Rosita" and Jorge "Jorgito."
                       14.

    Some people think ours customs are strange because everyone in the family can have a
                                   15.

different last name. Maybe your confused, but it isn't confusing for us.
                           16.   **17.**

    In the United States, some Mexicans use only one last name. Their afraid that Americans
                                                   18.

don't know what to do with all these names. I prefer the Mexican way. Its our custom, and I'm
                                                           19.

proud of it.
     20.

PART 3 Write About It

1. Do you prefer traditional names or unusual names? Explain your answer.

2. Write about naming customs in your culture.

PART 4 Edit Your Writing

Reread the Summary of Lesson 4 and the editing advice. Edit your writing from Part 3.

PLANET IN DANGER

A disastrous break in an underwater oil pipe in 2010
caused great damage to the Gulf of Mexico.

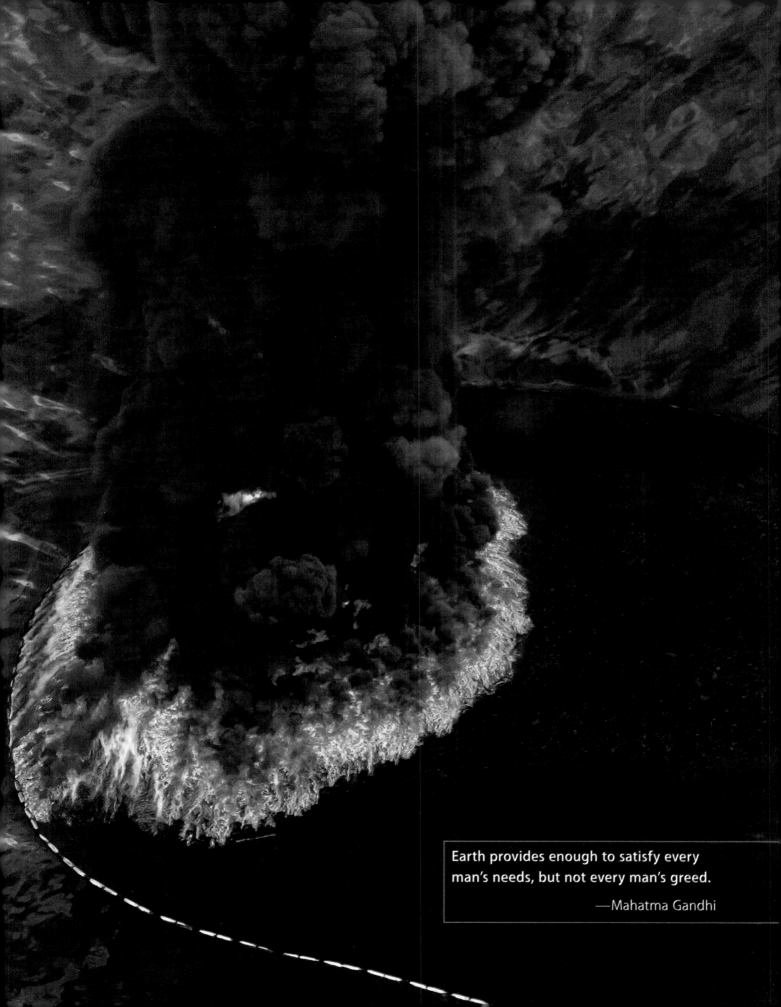

Earth provides enough to satisfy every man's needs, but not every man's greed.

—Mahatma Gandhi

A ring-tailed lemur with a baby in Madagascar

Saving Lemurs

CD 1
TR 20

Read the following conversation. Pay special attention to the words in bold.

A: What **are** you **watching**?

B: I**'m watching** an interesting video about baby lemurs. Do you want to watch it with me?

A: OK. What's it about?

B: Scientists **are raising** about 250 lemurs at Duke University in North Carolina. They**'re breeding**[1] them there.

A: Why **are** they **raising** and **breeding** them at a university? Why **aren't** the lemurs **living** in the wild?[2]

B: Lemurs are the most endangered[3] mammals[4] on the planet. Scientists **are trying** to increase the lemur population. Lemurs **are disappearing** from their native Madagascar. Some species[5] only have a few hundred individuals.

A: Aren't all lemurs from the same species?

B: No. There are about one hundred species. The Duke Lemur Center has twenty-one species. In this video, scientists **are working** at Duke University. Other scientists **are working** with the people of Madagascar. They**'re teaching** the local people how to protect the lemur population. Lemurs are close relatives of humans.

A: Really? Oh look! They're so cute. They**'re looking** at the scientists. Those babies **are playing**. That one**'s climbing** a tree. Oh, and that baby**'s jumping** onto its mother. It looks like the scientists **are enjoying** their job.

---

[1] *to breed*: to help animals produce babies
[2] *the wild*: a natural area where animals live
[3] *endangered*: at risk of disappearing
[4] *mammal*: a warm-blooded animal; the female gives her babies milk
[5] *species*: a group of similar living things

B: Shh! I want to hear this part.

[Video] *"We're weighing the babies. We want to make sure they're gaining weight. If they're gaining weight, they're healthy. Some babies aren't gaining weight. That means they're not healthy. These babies are sleeping. Babies sleep most of the time for the first month."*

A: I think those scientists **are doing** a wonderful thing.

B: I agree. It costs over $7,000 a year to care for a lemur. I**'m thinking** of sending money to help to the Duke Lemur Center.

COMPREHENSION CHECK Based on the reading, tell if the statement is true (**T**) or false (**F**).

1. Lemurs come from Madagascar.

2. Humans and lemurs are closely related.

3. There are 250 species of lemurs.

5.1 The Present Continuous—Forms

Affirmative Statements

Subject	Be	Verb + -ing
I	**am**	
He She It A lemur	**is**	**playing**.
You We They The babies	**are**	

Language Notes:

1. We can make a contraction with a subject pronoun and a form of *be*.

    I am → I'm   You are → You're
    He is → He's   We are → We're
    She is → She's   They are → They're
    It is → It's

2. Most nouns can also form a contraction with *is*. (See page 10 for exceptions.)

    A **man's** talking about lemurs.

3. When the subject is doing two things, we don't repeat the verb *be* after *and*.

    The lemurs **are climbing** and **jumping**.

4. We can put an adverb like *still* or *also* between *be* and the main verb.

    Scientists are working with lemurs at Duke University. They **are also working** with people in Madagascar.

5. The present continuous is sometimes called the present progressive.

continued

Negative Statements

Subject	Be	Not	Verb + *-ing*
I	am		
He She It The lemur	is	not	sleeping.
You We They The babies	are		

Language Notes:

1. The contraction for *is not* = *isn't*. The contraction for *are not* = *aren't*.

   The baby **isn't** gaining weight.

   Those lemurs **aren't** sleeping.

2. There is no contraction for *am not*.

3. We can make a contraction in a negative statement with a subject pronoun and *am, is,* or *are*.

   She's not watching the program.

   They're not sleeping.

EXERCISE 1 Listen to the conversation. Fill in the blanks with the words you hear. Use the correct form of *be* and the words from the box. You can use some verbs more than once.

CD 1
TR 21

cutting	living	losing	studying	watching
dying	looking	not doing	trying	working

A: I 'm watching _____ an interesting program on TV. Do you want to watch
　　　　　　　1.

　　it with me?

B: I _____ much now. Maybe. What is it about?
　　　　　　　　　　　2.

A: It's about parrots. These parrots _____ in the wild in Africa.
　　　　　　　　　　　　　　　　3.

　　A scientist, Steve Boyes, _____ Cape parrots of South Africa.
　　　　　　　　　　　　　　　　4.

　　Boyes and other scientists _____ to protect the land where
　　　　　　　　　　　　　　　5.

　　these parrots live. People _____ down forests. Parrots
　　　　　　　　　　　　　　6.

　　_____ places to make their nests. They
　　　　　　　　7.

　　_____ for food, but they can't find enough. So many of them
　　　　　　　8.

A South African
Cape parrot

_____. Boyes _____
9.   10.

with local people on a project to plant trees. He _____ to
11.

give these parrots a place to make their nests.

5.2 Spelling of the *-ing* Form

Rule	Examples	
We add *-ing* to the base form of most verbs.	eat go study	eat**ing** go**ing** study**ing**
For a one-syllable verb that ends in a consonant + vowel + consonant (CVC), we repeat the final consonant and add *-ing*.	p l a n ↓↓↓ C V C s t o p ↓↓↓ C V C	plan**ning** stop**ping**
We do not repeat a final *w, x,* or *y.*	show mix stay	show**ing** mix**ing** stay**ing**
For a two-syllable verb that ends in CVC, we repeat the final consonant only if the last syllable is stressed.	r e f e r ↓↓↓ C V C b e g i n ↓↓↓ C V C	refer**ring** begin**ning**
For a two-syllable verb that ends in CVC, we don't repeat the final consonant if the last syllable is not stressed.	open offer	open**ing** offer**ing**
If the verb ends in a consonant + *e* or *ue*, we drop the *e* and add *-ing*.	write rescue	writ**ing** rescu**ing**
If the verb ends in *-ie*, we change the *ie* to *y* and add *-ing*.	lie tie	**ly**ing **ty**ing

EXERCISE 2 Write the -ing form of each verb. In two-syllable verbs that end in CVC, the stressed syllable is underlined.

1. play _____playing_____

2. make _____

3. hit _____

4. <u>suf</u>fer _____

5. cut _____

6. ad<u>mit</u> _____

7. try _____

8. <u>hap</u>pen _____

9. stay _____

10. grow _____

11. hurry _____

12. grab _____

13. raise _____

14. fix _____

15. rescue _____

16. do _____

17. breed _____

18. lose _____

19. wait _____

20. serve _____

21. <u>vis</u>it _____

22. oc<u>cur</u> _____

23. die _____

24. disappear _____

EXERCISE 3 Fill in the blanks with the present continuous form of the verbs given. Use contractions when possible.

Some African parrots _____are suffering_____ from diseases.
                                          1. suffer

They _____ their feathers and their beaks.
                   2. lose

They _____ quickly. Today there aren't even 1,000 left. Steve Boyes
              3. disappear

_____ them. He and his team _____
      4. rescue   5. work

to help these birds.

Another species, the African gray parrot, _____ problems, too.
                                        6. have

Some people _____ and _____ them. It is
                7. catch   8. sell

illegal to catch and sell these birds, but people _____ them from their
                                    9. steal

nests. Boyes has a blog about his work with parrots. He _____ to
                                      10. try

educate people about these birds.

5.3 The Present Continuous—Use

Examples	Explanation
We **are watching** a show on TV now. Oh look! That baby lemur **is jumping** onto its mother.	We use the present continuous to describe an action that is in progress at this exact moment.
The babies **are sleeping** now. We **are sitting** in the living room and watching TV.	We use the present continuous with the following verbs to describe a state or condition that we can observe now: *sit, stand, wear, sleep*.
The babies **are gaining** weight. Steve Boyes **is trying** to teach people about parrots.	We use the present continuous to show a longer action that is in progress. It may not be happening at this exact moment.

EXERCISE 4 Write true affirmative or negative statements with the present continuous and the words given.

1. African parrots/lose their homes

   African parrots are losing their homes.

2. the teacher/show us a video about lemurs

   The teacher isn't showing us a video about lemurs.

3. we/learn about animals in this lesson

   _____

4. I/write sentences about animals

   _____

5. Steve Boyes/study lemurs

   _____

6. Boyes/try to rescue parrots

   _____

7. unhealthy baby lemurs/gain weight

   _____

8. many lemurs/live at the Lemur Center

   _____

5.4 Questions with the Present Continuous

Yes/No Questions and Short Answers

Be	Subject	Verb + *-ing*	Short Answer
Am	I		No, you're not.
Is	he she it the lemur	**growing?**	Yes, he is. No, she isn't. Yes, it is. No, it's not.
Are	you we they the babies		Yes, I am. No, we're not. Yes, they are. No, they aren't.

Language Note:

Compare statements and *yes/no* questions.

The lemurs are playing.

Are the lemurs playing?

Wh- Questions

Wh- Word	Be (+ *n't*)	Subject	Verb + *-ing*	
What	**are**	they	**studying?**	
Why	**is**	Boyes	**writing**	a blog?
Why	**aren't**	some babies	**gaining**	weight?

Language Note:

Compare statements and *wh-* questions.

The lemurs are playing.   **The lemurs aren't** sleeping.

Where **are the lemurs** playing?   Why **aren't the lemurs** sleeping?

Subject Questions

Wh- Word as Subject	Be	Verb + *-ing*	
Who	**is**	**studying**	lemurs?
How many lemurs	**are**	**living**	at the Lemur Center?

Language Note:

Compare statements and subject questions.

Someone is studying lemurs.

Who is studying lemurs?

EXERCISE 5 Fill in the blanks to complete each conversation. Use *not* when necessary. Use contractions when possible.

1. **A:** Steve Boyes is studying animals. <u>Is he studying</u> parrots?
   a.

   B: Yes, he <u>is</u> . He _____ parrots in Africa.
   b.c.

   A: Why _____ parrots?
   d.

   B: He's studying parrots because they're dying and he wants to know why.

2. **A:** _____ a lot about animals?
   a.

   B: Yes, I _____ . I'm learning about lemurs and parrots.
   b.

   A: What _____ ?
   c.

   B: I'm learning that these animals are in danger.

3. **A:** Some parrots are losing places to make their nests.

   B: Why _____ places to make their nests?
   a.

   A: Some people are cutting down forests.

   B: I'm asking you a lot of questions. _____ you?
   b.

   A: No. You're not bothering me. You're asking interesting questions.

4. **A:** _____ an article about parrots?
   a.

   B: No, I _____ . I'm reading an article about lemurs.
   b.

   A: Why _____ about lemurs?
   c.

   B: I'm writing an essay about the Duke Lemur Center.

continued

Steve Boyes

5. **A:** What _____ your brother watching on TV?
  a.

  B: He _____ a program about animals.
  b.

  A: Why _____ his homework?
  c.

  B: He isn't doing his homework because he needs to see the program first.

6. **A:** Who _____ care of the lemurs at Duke University?
  a.

  B: Scientists are taking care of them.

  A: How _____ care of them?
  b.

  B: They're trying to make them healthy.

7. **A:** _____ all the lemurs doing well at Duke?
  a.

  B: No, they _____. Some of them aren't gaining weight.
  b.

  A: Why _____ weight?
  c.

  B: Because they're not healthy.

8. **A:** _____ an essay now?
  a.

  B: Yes, I _____. I'm writing an essay for my science class.
  b.

  A: What _____ about?
  c.

  B: I'm writing about endangered species.

EXERCISE 6 About You Find a partner. Ask and answer questions with the words given. Use the present continuous.

1. learn about parrots

   A: *Are you learning about parrots?*

   B: *Yes, I am.*

2. take online classes this semester

3. what other courses/take this semester

4. think about the environment now

5. plan to read more about nature

6. how/your life changing

DISAPPEARING BIRDS

CD 1
TR 22 **Read the following article. Pay special attention to the words in bold.**

Birds are amazing animals. They **live** in all parts of the planet, from hot deserts to the ice of Antarctica. They **fly** nonstop for days. They **find** food easily. They **find** safe places to rest. They **carry** seeds. They **control** bugs. One out of five birds **migrates**.[6] These birds **arrive** at their exact destinations.[7] But, unfortunately, all of this **is changing**.

The bird population **is going** down. This **is happening** to birds in all parts of the planet, from hot places to cold places. Birds **are losing** places to live and make their nests. Their food supply **is going** down. Some penguins of Antarctica **are starving**.[8] Some seabirds, like puffins, **are disappearing**.

Chemicals in the environment **are affecting** bird populations. In Michigan, near an old chemical factory, robins **are dying**. The songs of some birds **are changing**. Some birds **are having** fewer babies. Some birds **are losing** their ability to find their way. Clearly, birds are in trouble. Why **is** this **happening**?

Insects, fish, and other animals **take** in chemicals from the environment. Birds **eat** insects and fish. Some birds **eat** dead animals. This **is giving** birds health problems. If birds **are having** health problems, what **are** these chemicals **doing** to humans? Scientists like Christy Morrissey **are trying** to find out. Morrissey **studies** nature and harmful things in our environment. She **wants** to know how chemicals **affect** these birds.

Birds usually **have** a stable[9] population. When the bird population **goes** down, it **means** something **is happening** to the environment. According to Morrissey, birds **are sending** us messages about our own health and the health of the planet. We **need** to listen to these messages.

---

[6] *to migrate*: to move from one place to another
[7] *destination*: a place where someone is going to
[8] *to starve*: to not have enough food
[9] *stable*: strong and steady

Two puffins on a cliff in Iceland

COMPREHENSION CHECK Based on the reading, tell if the statement is true (**T**) or false (**F**).

1. There are birds in every part of the world.

2. All birds migrate.

3. Birds can help us understand dangers to humans.

5.5 The Present Continuous vs. the Simple Present—Forms

Compare the simple present and the present continuous.

The Simple Present	Examples
AFFIRMATIVE STATEMENT	The gray parrot **lives** in Africa.
NEGATIVE STATEMENT	It **doesn't live** in North America.
YES/NO QUESTION	**Does** it **live** in North Africa?
SHORT ANSWER	No, it **doesn't**.
WH- QUESTION	Where **does** it **live**?
NEGATIVE WH- QUESTION	Why **doesn't** it **live** in North Africa?
SUBJECT QUESTION	What birds **live** in North Africa?

The Present Continuous	Examples
AFFIRMATIVE STATEMENT	Morrissey **is studying** birds.
NEGATIVE STATEMENT	She **isn't studying** lemurs.
YES/NO QUESTION	**Is** she **studying** seabirds?
SHORT ANSWER	Yes, she **is**.
WH- QUESTION	Why **is** she **studying** birds?
NEGATIVE WH- QUESTION	Why **isn't** she **studying** lemurs?
SUBJECT QUESTION	Who **is studying** lemurs?

EXERCISE 7 Listen to the report. Fill in the blanks with the words you hear.

Many animals _____ their places to live. Humans _____ land
　　　　　　　　　　　　1.　　　　　　　　　　　　　　　　　　　　　　2.

from animals. Which animals _____ because of humans? Big cats, such as
　　　　　　　　　　　　　　　　3.

lions, tigers, snow leopards, and cheetahs, are in danger. The population of these animals

_____ quickly. Only 3,000 tigers remain in the wild. What _____
　　　　4.　　　　　　　　　　　　　　　　　　　　　　　　　　　　　　　　　5.

to protect big cats?

　　　Luke Dollar, a National Geographic Emerging Explorer, is a scientist who

_____ on the Big Cats Initiative. This program _____ people
　　　6.　　　　　　　　　　　　　　　　　　　　　　　　　　　　　7.

learn about the problems that big cats _____. People _____
　　　　　　　　　　　　　　　　　　　　　　　8.　　　　　　　　　　　　9.

education about endangered animals. Many people _____ that these animals

                                                    10.

are in danger, and that we _____ much time left to save them.

                                          11.

"_____ to live in a world without lions in the wild?" asks Luke Dollar.

         12.

5.6 The Present Continuous vs. the Simple Present—Use

Examples	Explanation
Gray parrots **live** in Africa. Sometimes I **read** articles about the environment.	We use the simple present with: • general truths or customs • regular activities or repeated actions
We **are reading** about big cats now. The population of big cats **is going** down.	We use the present continuous with: • actions that are in progress now • longer actions that are in progress at this general time

EXERCISE 8 Complete the conversation. Use the present continuous or the simple present form of the verbs given. Use contractions when possible. Include any other words you see.

A: What _____ are you doing _____ here?

         1. you / do

B: I _____ lunch. I always _____

         2. eat   **3.** eat

lunch at this time. But I _____ a video about birds.

              4. also / watch

A: Why _____ it?

         5. you / watch

B: I _____ a class in environmental science.

         6. take

This week we _____ the relationship between

                    7. study

chemicals and bird populations.

A: What _____ ?

         8. you / learn

B: I _____ about chemicals in lakes and oceans.

         9. learn

These chemicals harm fish. A lot of birds _____

                                            10. eat

fish. Look at this video. Do you see that pelican?

It _____ to catch a fish.

      11. dive

A: Cool! Where _____ ?

              12. pelicans / live

B: They _____ close to the water in many parts of

         13. live

the world.

A brown pelican in Ecuador

Scientists study melting ice sheets in Antarctica.

CLIMATE CHANGE

CD 1
TR 24

Read the following article. Pay special attention to the words in bold.

The ice on Antarctica **looks** the same from day to day. But scientists **know** this: the ice **is melting**.[10]

Ice sheets are very big. Changes in the climate cause them to change very slowly. It usually **takes** a long time for ice sheets to melt. So what **is happening** now?

The ocean **is warming**, and big pieces of ice **are breaking** away and **going** into the ocean. This **is causing** the ocean level to rise. Why **is** this **happening**?

Human activity is responsible. Transportation, electricity production, and industry are activities that warm the planet. What **does** this **mean** for us?

Coastal cities, like New York, London, and Tokyo, are in danger of being underwater by the end of the twenty-first century. We **need** to make changes now to prevent[11] this. Some scientists **think** that climate change is unstoppable.[12] We **hope** it's not too late.

---

[10] *to melt*: to change from ice to water
[11] *to prevent*: to stop something from happening
[12] *unstoppable*: impossible to stop

COMPREHENSION CHECK Based on the reading, tell if the statement is true (**T**) or false (**F**).

1. Ice sheets don't change much from day to day.

2. The ocean level is rising.

3. Human activity affects the climate.

5.7 Action and Nonaction Verbs

Examples	Explanation
Scientists **are studying** climate change. Ice **is melting**. Pieces of ice **are breaking** away.	Some verbs are action verbs. These verbs express physical or mental activity. We can use the present continuous with action verbs.
We **need** to make changes now. We **hope** it's not too late. The problem of climate change **seems** difficult. We **care about** the planet.	Some verbs are nonaction verbs. These verbs express a sense or a feeling, not an action. We don't usually use the present continuous with a nonaction verb, even if we are talking about now.
We **are looking at** a photo of an ice sheet. (action) She **is looking for** information about climate change. (action) An ice sheet **looks** the same from day to day. (sense)	*Look* can be both an action and a nonaction verb. *Look at* and *look for* are action verbs. *Look*, as something we sense, is a nonaction verb.
I **am thinking about** the environment. (action) **Are** you **thinking of** studying science? (action) I **think that** climate change is an important issue. (opinion)	*Think* can be both an action and a nonaction verb. *Think of* and *think about* are action verbs. *Think that*, to show an opinion, is a nonaction verb.
Some birds **are having** a hard time finding a place to build a nest. **Do** you **have** time to read the article?	When *have* means to experience something, it is an action verb. When *have* shows possession or relationship, it is a nonaction verb.
We**'re looking at** a video about climate change. (action) We **see** a photo of an ice sheet. (nonaction) **Are** you **listening** to the teacher? (action) **Do** you **hear** the birds outside? (nonaction)	*Look at* and *listen* are action verbs. *See* and *hear* are nonaction verbs.

Language Note:

Groups of common nonaction verbs:

- Senses (usually followed by *like* or an adjective): *smell, taste, look, sound, feel, seem*
- Feelings: *like, love, hate, hope, want, need, prefer, care (about), matter*
- Mental states: *believe, know, hear, see, notice, agree, understand, remember, think (that), realize*
- Other verbs: *mean, cost*

EXERCISE 9 Listen to the report. Fill in the blanks with the verbs you hear. Then work with a partner and circle the nonaction verbs. (Not all simple present verbs are nonaction verbs.)

Some people _____think_____ that climate change is nothing new on Earth. They
　　　　　　　　　1.

often _____ that warming and cooling _____ all the time. This is
　　　　　　2.　　　　　　　　　　　　　　　　　3.

true. But these people _____ one important thing: humans _____
　　　　　　　　　　　　　4.　　　　　　　　　　　　　　　　　　　　　　5.

it now by our activities. Scientists say we _____ to make changes now to stop it.
　　　　　　　　　　　　　　　　　　　6.

Some companies _____ the danger of climate change and our part in it. They
　　　　　　　　　　　7.

_____ to make changes. But some companies _____ to make
　　8.　　　　　　　　　　　　　　　　　　　　　　　　9.

these changes. It _____ money to make changes. Some companies
　　　　　　　　　10.

_____ more about money than the environment.
　　11.

Some activities of modern life _____ our planet. What _____
　　　　　　　　　　　　　　　　12.　　　　　　　　　　　　　　　13.

we _____ about it? Some scientists _____, "Not enough and not
　　　　14.　　　　　　　　　　　　　　　　15.

fast enough."

EXERCISE 10 Complete the conversations with the correct form of the verbs given. Use any other words you see.

1. **A:** What book ____are you reading____?
　　　　　　　　　　　　a. you/read

   B: It's a book about birds. I _____ it. I _____ at the pictures.
　　　　　　　　　　　　　b. not/really/read　　　　　c. just/look

   _____ to see some of the pictures?
　　d. you/want

   A: Sure. Wow. That bird _____ so beautiful. It _____ so
　　　　　　　　　　　　e. look　　　　　　　　　　f. have

   many colors.

   B: These birds are South American parrots. My friend _____ a pet parrot.
　　　　　　　　　　　　　　　　　　　　　　　　g. have

   A: How long _____?
　　　　　　　h. parrots/live

   B: Some parrots _____ over 50 years.
　　　　　　　　　i. live

2. **A:** _____ a science class this semester?
　　　a. you/take

   B: Yes. I _____ a class in environmental science this semester.
　　　　　　b. have

   I _____ about how humans _____ the environment now.
　　c. learn　　　　　　　　　　　　d. harm

   A lot of animals _____ because of us. This is our planet, and we
　　　　　　　　　e. die

   _____ to do something now to take care of it.
　　f. need

128 Lesson 5

A: I _____ human behavior. I _____ that we
g. not/understand   h. think

don't educate young people about these things.

B: I _____. I _____ of getting a degree in
i. agree   j. think

environmental science.

A: What _____ to do with your degree?
k. you/hope

B: I hope to teach high school science.

A: That _____ like a good idea.
l. sound

3. **A:** The water level _____.
a. rise

B: Why _____?
b. it/rise

A: Because the ice on Antarctica _____ fast.
c. melt

B: How _____?
d. scientists/know

A: They _____ ways to measure the speed.
e. have

B: Why _____?
f. it/melt

A: The ocean water _____ warmer.
g. get

B: My brother _____ that climate change is nothing new. He says
h. think

that it _____ all the time.
i. happen

A: Yes, but it _____ faster now because of human activity.
j. happen

4. **A:** Some animals _____ of starvation.
a. die

B: I _____ the word *starvation*. What _____?
b. not/know   c. it/mean

A: It _____ hunger.
d. mean

B: How _____ so much about this?
e. you/know

A: I _____ a great program on TV this week. Every night they
f. watch

_____ about the information we get from birds.
g. talk

B: What kind of information _____ us?
h. birds/give

A: They give us information about harmful chemicals in the environment. If these chemicals

are harming birds, what _____ to us?
i. they/do

SUMMARY OF LESSON 5

Uses of the Present Continuous (With Action Verbs Only)

Use	Examples
For actions that are happening at this moment	She **is watching** a program on TV now. The program **is explaining** climate change.
For longer actions that are in progress at this general time	The planet **is warming**. I **am studying** science this semester.
With a descriptive state with the verbs *sit, stand, wear,* and *sleep*	The baby lemurs **are sleeping**. The scientist **is wearing** a white coat.

Uses of the Simple Present

Use	Examples
For general truths	Lemurs **live** in Madagascar. Some birds **fly** south for the winter.
For regular activities, habits, and customs	I sometimes **watch** nature programs on TV. People often **train** pet parrots to talk.
With places of origin	Steve Boyes **comes** from the United States.
With nonaction verbs	I **know** more about birds now. We **need** to protect the planet.

Action and Nonaction Verbs

Action	Nonaction
The ice **is melting**.	The planet **has** problems.
I **am thinking** about the environment.	I **think** that climate change is a big problem.
We**'re looking** at a book about birds.	Those birds **look** beautiful.
You**'re studying** science.	You **know** a lot about nature.

TEST/REVIEW

Complete the conversation between two students in the library. Use the simple present or the present continuous form of the verbs given. Include any other words you see.

A: Hi, Teresa. What _____*are you doing*_____ here?

1. you/do

B: Hi, Brooke. I _____ for pictures online for my environmental science course.

2. look

A: You have your laptop with you. Why _____ it?

3. you/not/use

B: The computers in the library _____ big monitors. I _____

4. have · 5. want

to see big pictures.

A: _____ to go for a cup of coffee?

6. you/want

B: I _____ time now. I _____ for a classmate.

7. not/have · 8. wait

We _____ on a project together for our class.

9. work

A: What kind of project _____ on?

10. you/work

B: We _____ to write a paper on climate change. Some people

11. need

_____ it _____ now.

12. not/believe · 13. happen

A: What _____ ?

14. you/think

B: I _____ it's a very serious problem.

15. believe

A: I _____ of taking environmental science next semester.

16. think

_____ this class every semester?

17. your teacher/teach

B: I _____ so.

18. think

A: _____ the class?

19. you/like

B: Yes. I _____ it. I especially _____ the teacher.

20. love · 21. like

He _____ tests.

22. not/give

A: Why _____ tests?

23. he/not/give

B: He _____ to give us projects. He _____ we learn more

24. prefer · 25. think

that way.

A: I _____ . He _____ like an interesting teacher.

26. agree · 27. sound

B: He is. Oh, I _____ my friend now. She _____ toward us.

28. see · 29. walk

A: I _____ her. She's in my math class.

30. know

WRITING

PART 1 Editing Advice

1. Don't forget *be* with the present continuous.

   are
   We ᵥlearning about nature.

2. Don't forget *-ing* with the present continuous.

   ing
   She is read ᵥan article about lemurs.

3. Use the correct question form in the present continuous and the simple present.

   is the Earth
   Why ~~the Earth is~~ warming?

   does "starvation" mean
   What ~~means "starvation"~~?

4. Don't use *be* to form the simple present.

   I ~~am~~ know a lot about birds.

5. Don't use the present continuous with a nonaction verb.

   need
   We ~~are needing~~ to take care of our planet.

PART 2 Editing Practice

Some of the shaded words and phrases have mistakes. Find the mistakes and correct them. If the shaded words are correct, write *C*.

       C
I am doing a report on the Sumatran tiger this week. The Sumatran tiger is a
  1.
         has
beautiful animal. It ~~is having~~ black stripes on its orange coat. Unfortunately, this animal
      2.

is disappearing. There are only 400 left.
  3.

    The Sumatran tiger is live in the forests of Sumatra, which is an island of Indonesia.
          4.

Most groups of these tigers have no more than fifty individuals. Why they are disappearing?
             5.   6.

Tigers are needing large areas of forest to live, but people are cutting down forests.
      7.   8.

Why do they destroying forests? Farmers want the land for agriculture. But when
    9.   10.

they cut down the forests, they put the tiger in danger. There is another problem, too.
   11.

Some people killing these animals and selling parts such as skin and bones.
        12.   13.

It is against the law to kill these animals, but some people don't care about the law.
                                    14.

We are need to protect these animals.
   15.

PART 3 Write About It

1. Write about an interesting class you are taking. What are you learning? What do you like about this class?

2. Write about a wild animal that you like. What do you know about this animal? Is this animal having problems in the wild?

PART 4 Edit Your Writing

Reread the Summary of Lesson 5 and the editing advice. Edit your writing from Part 3.

OUR
FUTURE

A man rides a jetpack over Denver, Colorado.

The best thing about the future is that it comes one day at a time.

—Abraham Lincoln

Future Careers

 Read the following article. Pay special attention to the words in bold.

CD 1
TR 26

Are you preparing for your first career or training for a new job? You want a job that **will pay** well. You are probably asking yourself, "How much money **will** this job **pay**?" But there's another very important question. **Will** you **find** a job when you graduate or finish your training? The fastest job growth **will be** in health care, health-care support, construction, and personal care. One-third of new jobs in 2022 **will come** from these four groups.

Health-care occupations **will grow** because the population of the United States is aging.[1] The need for all areas of health care, from home health-care workers to doctors, **will increase**. One profession that **will be** in high demand[2] is nursing. The Bureau of Labor Statistics (BLS) predicts[3] that there **will be** over one-half million openings for nurses in 2022. The number of jobs for personal care helpers **will increase**, too. These workers help people with disabilities[4] take care of their daily needs, like getting dressed or preparing meals.

Jobs in education, accounting, and corporate sales **will** also **grow**. Jobs in STEM professions **will increase**, too. (*STEM* stands for *Science, Technology, Engineering*, and *Mathematics*.) Jobs **will** also **increase** for servers in restaurants, construction workers, and janitors.

Which job opportunities **will decrease**? According to the BLS, we **won't need** as many postal workers in the future since more and more people use e-mail and automatic bill payment. By 2022, the percentage of postal workers **will go** down 28 percent from 2012. Also, we **won't need** as many farm workers in the future.

It is hard to predict the future, but when choosing a career, it is a good idea to look at the Bureau of Labor Statistics reports.

---

[1] *to age:* to get old
[2] *in high demand*: much wanted
[3] *to predict*: to say what will happen in the future
[4] *disability*: a physical or mental condition that limits a person's ability to do certain things

COMPREHENSION CHECK Based on the reading, tell if the statement is true (**T**) or false (**F**).

1. The Bureau of Labor Statistics makes predictions about jobs.

2. Nursing and other health-care professions will grow in the future.

3. The number of jobs for postal workers will decrease in the future.

6.1 The Future with *Will*—Forms

Affirmative and Negative Statements

Examples	Explanation
Nursing jobs **will increase**. There **will be** fewer postal jobs.	For affirmative statements with *will*, we use *will* + the base form of the verb.
I'll become a nurse. **You'll** be proud of me.	We can make contractions with the subject pronouns + *will*: *I'll, you'll, he'll, she'll, it'll, we'll,* and *they'll.*
There **will not** be as many postal jobs. Nurses **won't** have trouble finding a job.	For negative statements with *will*, we use *not* after *will*. The contraction for *will not* is *won't*.

Language Notes:

1. We can put an adverb (*always, never, probably, even, definitely*) between *will* and the main verb.

    Some jobs will **definitely** increase.
    She will **probably** become a doctor.

2. The future of *there is* or *there are* is *there will be.*

    There will be many jobs in STEM professions.

Compare statements, *yes/no* questions, short answers, and *wh-* questions.

Statement	*Yes/No* Question and Short Answer	*Wh-* Question
She **will become** a nurse.	**A: Will** she **become** a hospital nurse? **B:** Yes, she **will**.	When **will** she **become** a nurse?
There **will be** jobs for engineers.	**A: Will** there **be** jobs for scientists? **B:** Yes, there **will**.	What kind of jobs **will** there **be**?
Health-care jobs **will grow**.	**A: Will** farm jobs **grow**? **B:** No, they **won't**.	Why **won't** farm jobs **grow**?
Some jobs **will increase**.	**A: Will** postal jobs **increase**? **B:** No, they **won't**.	Which jobs **will increase**?

🎧 **EXERCISE 1** Listen to the article. Fill in the blanks with the words you hear.

Jobs in the future _____*will be*_____ different from the jobs of today. As people change
1.

jobs or retire, companies _____ to replace workers. New technology also affects
2.

jobs. More people are shopping online, so store workers _____ fewer job
3.

opportunities. Business practices are changing, too. For example, more and more stores are

offering self-service checkout. What _____ this _____ for cashiers?
4.   **5.**

Many people _____ soon _____ without a job. Many factors
6.   **7.**

_____ jobs of the future. The Bureau of Labor Statistics tries to let us know what
8.

the future _____ for workers ten years from now.
9.

EXERCISE 2 Complete the conversation with the verbs from the box. Use *will* and any other words
given. Use contractions when possible. You will use two verbs more than once.

be	find	major	make	remember	show	take

A: I'm planning to study nursing. I'd love to be a doctor, but it _'ll take_____ me too
1.

    long. Nursing is a good profession. I know I _____ a job when I graduate.
2.

    What about you?

B: I'm not sure yet. Both of my parents are teachers, so I _____ in education.
3. probably

    I know I _____ a lot of money as a teacher, but I think it's a wonderful job.
4. not

A: _____ a lot of jobs in the future? That's important to know.
5. there

B: I don't know.

A: There's a great website from the Bureau of Labor Statistics. It shows what the future of a

    profession _____ .
6.

B: Really? How can I find it?

A: Here's my tablet. I _____ you right now. The website says
7.

    that there _____ a need for more teachers. As a teacher,
8.

    you _____ a difference in the lives of young people.
9.

    I _____ my fifth grade teacher. My love of science comes from her.
10. always

6.2 The Future with *Will*—Use

Examples	Explanation
She **will graduate** in four years.	We use *will* for simple facts about the future.
You**'ll be** a great doctor.	We use *will* for predictions.
Do you want to see the BLS website? I**'ll show** it to you on my tablet.	We use *will* when the decision about the future comes at the moment of speaking. An offer to help often has no previous plan.

EXERCISE 3 Find a partner. Take turns making predictions about the future. Use *will* and the words given. Begin each prediction with "I think" or "I don't think."

1. technology/replace teachers

    A: *I don't think technology will replace teachers.*

    B: *I agree.*

2. there/always/be a need for gardeners

3. workers/stay at the same job for a long time

4. we/always/need the Post Office

5. nurses' salaries/increase a lot

6. the United States/bring in doctors from other countries

EXERCISE 4 Find a partner. Complete the conversations between students (S) asking for help from a student counselor (C). Write how the counselor will help. More than one answer is possible.

1. **S:** I'd like to be an accountant, but I don't know anything about the future of accounting.

    C: I'll show you the BLS website. You can find information there.

2. **S:** I don't have enough money for college.

    C: _____

3. **S:** Where's the financial aid office?

    C: _____

4. **S:** I need a letter of recommendation for the nursing program.

    C: _____

5. **S:** I don't understand the information in this booklet.

    C: _____

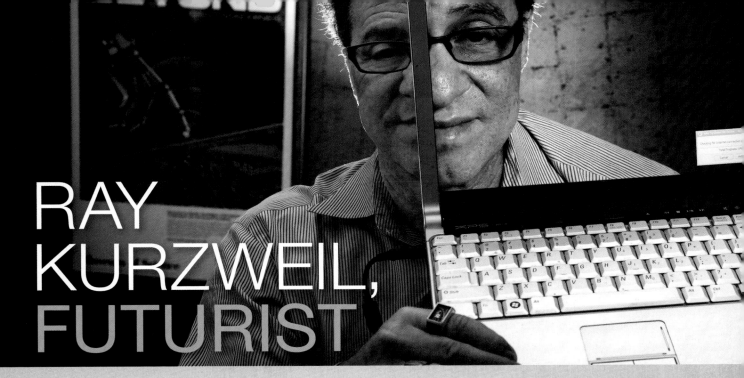

RAY
KURZWEIL,
FUTURIST

 Read the following article. Pay special attention to the words in bold.

CD 1
TR 28

Are computers **going to be** smarter than people someday? Maybe. **Are** they **going to do** even more in the future? Probably. But **are** they **going to tell** stories and **have** a sense of humor?[5] **Will** they **have** feelings? Ray Kurzweil believes this **will happen**.

Who is Ray Kurzweil? He's an author, an inventor, a computer scientist—and a "futurist." He makes predictions about artificial intelligence.[6] He believes that by 2029, computers **are going to do** things better than humans. He predicts that by 2045, computers **will be** one billion times more powerful than all human brains together. Just as we now carry little computers (smartphones) in our hands, someday soon, he says, we**'re going to have** little computers in our brains.

Kurzweil is good at making predictions. For example, here are a few of his predictions from his book *The Age of Intelligent Machines*, published in the late 1980s:

- Documents **will include** more than just words. They **will include** voice, music, and other sounds.
- Computers **will be** as common as pencils and books in schools.
- We **will have** wireless networks to share information.

Today's computers search for answers to our questions, but they don't understand what they are searching. Kurzweil is now working on a project that **will improve** the way computers search. He predicts that one day computers **will** actually **understand** our questions.

Kurzweil also thinks technology **is going to help** us live longer. In fact, he has a very unusual prediction: he thinks that technology **will help** us live forever.[7]

Is this ever **going to happen**? What do you think?

---

[5] *sense of humor:* an ability to understand and say funny things
[6] *artificial intelligence*: computer programs that are able to learn and perform human-like thinking tasks
[7] *forever*: for all future time

COMPREHENSION CHECK Based on the reading, tell if the statement is true (**T**) or false (**F**).

1. Ray Kurzweil's predictions about the future are often correct.

2. All the world's information will be on our smartphones.

3. Kurzweil wants to improve the way computers search.

6.3 The Future with *Be Going To*—Forms

Affirmative and Negative Statements

Examples	Explanation
Computers **are going to be** faster. We **are going to live** longer.	For affirmative statements, we use a form of *be* + *going to* + the base form of the verb.
I'm going to read Kurzweil's book. **Technology's** going to improve.	We can make contractions with pronouns and most subject nouns + a form of *be*.
We**'re not** going to live forever. Computers **aren't** going to have feelings.	For negative statements, we use *not* after *is, am,* or *are*.

Language Notes:

1. We can put an adverb (*always, never, probably, even, actually*) between *be* and *going to*.

    Computers are **probably** going to be smarter than people someday.

2. When the main verb after *be going to* is *go*, we often omit it.

    I**'m going to go** to the library. = I**'m going** to the library.

Pronunciation Note:

In informal speech, we often pronounce *going to* as *"gonna"* (/gənə/) when a verb comes after *to*.

Compare statements, *yes/no* questions, short answers, and *wh-* questions.

Statement	*Yes/No* Question and Short Answer	*Wh-* Question
Computers **are going to be** faster.	**A: Are** they **going to be** smarter? **B:** Yes, they **are**.	How **are** they **going to be** smarter?
She**'s going to read** an article about Kurzweil.	**A: Is** she **going to read** his book? **B:** No, she**'s not**.	Why **isn't** she **going to read** his book?
There **are going to be** more powerful computers in the future.	**A: Are** there **going to be** better smartphones? **B:** Yes, there **are**.	What kind of smartphones **are** there **going to be**?
Some of his predictions **are going to happen**.	**A: Are** all his predictions **going to happen** soon? **B:** No, they **aren't**.	Which predictions **are going to happen**?

EXERCISE 5 Listen to the conversation. Fill in the blanks with the words you hear.

A: There _'s going to be_ _____ a program about artificial intelligence on TV tonight.
1.

B: What time _____ on?
2.

A: At 9 p.m. But I _____ it tonight. I _____ it.
3.   4.

B: Why _____ it tonight?
5.

A: I have a biology test tomorrow. A friend and I _____ to the library to
6.

study. Do you want to watch it with me this weekend? I think I _____ it
7.

on Friday night. _____ free then?
8.

B: Sorry. My brother _____ in town this weekend, so we have a lot of plans.
9.

A: When _____ free?
10.

B: Next weekend.

A: I think I'll watch it this weekend. I _____ an essay about Ray Kurzweil for
11.

my computer class next week.

B: Who's he?

A: A "futurist." He thinks technology _____ people live forever.
12.

B: He sounds a little crazy to me.

6.4 The Future with *Be Going To*—Use

Examples	Explanation
The program **is going to be** on TV at 9 p.m.	We use *be going to* with simple facts about the future.
Kurzweil's prediction: Computers **are going to have** feelings.	We use *be going to* for predictions.
I can't watch the program. **I'm going to meet** a friend at the library.	We use *be going to* when there is a previous plan to do something.

Language Note:

We can also use the present continuous with definite plans for the near future. We usually mention a time.

      I**'m meeting** a friend at 1:00. = I**'m going to meet** a friend at 1:00.

EXERCISE 6 Find a partner. Take turns making predictions about the future. Use *be going to* and the words given.

1. cars/not need drivers

   A: *In the future, cars are not going to need drivers.*

   B: *I agree.*

2. airplanes/fly without pilots

3. the work environment/be different

4. robots/do the jobs of people

5. technology/create new jobs

6. people/live forever

7. students/learn everything on computers

8. scientists/find a cure for most diseases

EXERCISE 7 About You Find a partner. Take turns discussing the statements about the future. Are they true for you?

1. I'm going to take an online course next semester.

2. I'm going to buy a new smartphone soon.

3. I'm going to text my friends today.

4. I'm going to learn more about computers.

5. I'm going to buy an electric car someday.

EXERCISE 8 Find a partner. Ask and answer questions about the future. Use *will* or *be going to* and the words given.

1. people/travel to another planet *(will)*

   A: *Will people travel to another planet?*

   B: *I think so. People will probably travel to Mars.*

2. people/happier in the future *(be going to)*

3. technology/make our lives better *(will)*

4. technology/make our lives worse *(be going to)*

5. computers/be smarter than people *(will)*

6. Ray Kurzweil/live forever *(be going to)*

6.5 Choosing *Will* or *Be Going To*

	Will	*Be Going To*
Predictions	Robots **will** take some jobs away from humans.	Robots **are going to** take some jobs away from humans.
Simple facts	A program about Mars **will** be on TV tonight.	A program about Mars **is going to** be on TV tonight.
Plans	—	I**'m going to** be a nurse.
Decisions about the future that come at the moment of speaking	**A:** Here's a great article on technology. I**'ll** let you borrow it. **B:** Thanks! I**'ll** return it tomorrow.	—

Language Notes:

1. When there is a choice between *will* and *be going to*, *will* sounds more formal.

2. After *think*, *will* is more common than *be going to*.

   Ray Kurzweil thinks he **will** live forever.

EXERCISE 9 Complete the conversation with the verb and any other word(s) given. Use *will* or *be going to*. Sometimes both choices are possible.

A: What _____ are you going to major _____ in?
1. major

B: English. When I go back to my country, I _____ an English
2. start

language school with my brother. English is the most popular language in the world.

A: _____ the most popular language in the world?
3. it/always/be

B: Probably. It's the language of science, business, and entertainment.

A: I think Chinese _____ the number-one language.
4. become

B: I don't think so. I'm reading an interesting article about the future of English.

I _____ you borrow it when I'm finished. I think
5. let

you _____ it.
6. enjoy

A: Thanks, but I _____ time to read it. I'm so busy with school
7. not/have

and my job.

B: If you have a few minutes, I _____ you a little about it. Over 600
8. tell

million people speak English as a second language. Some experts believe that by 2020, only 15

percent of English speakers _____ native speakers.
9. be

A: This sounds like an interesting article. Maybe I _____ it after all.
10. borrow

B: I'm almost finished. I _____ it to you tomorrow. By the way, what
11. give

about you? What _____ in?
12. you/major

A: I _____ a nurse.
13. be

B: You're a very good person. I think you _____ a great nurse.
14. be

Colony⁸ on MARS

CD 1
TR 30 **Read the following article. Pay special attention to the words in bold.**

Will it **be** possible to live on Mars someday? Mars One is an organization that says this **will happen** soon. If its plans **go** well, Mars One **will put** a human colony on Mars by 2025.

Every year, Mars One interviews people who want to go to Mars. When the application to travel was available in 2013, over 200,000 people applied. Mars One **will choose** twenty-four people to start training.

These people **will go** through an eight-year training program. They **will train** in the Arctic region. If a person **doesn't do** well there, Mars One **will choose** another person. When the training **is** finished, four people **will go** on the first mission. When they **arrive** on Mars, they **will work** to create a human colony. They **will learn** to grow their own food. The project **will send** four more people two years later.

There's one big problem: If you **go** to Mars, you **won't come** back. We don't have the technology for a two-way trip. However, many people still want to go there. One person who wants to go is George Hatcher. He is studying planetary science at the University of Central Florida. If Mars One **chooses** him, he **will begin** training. Then, in 2024, the first group of four **will start** their seven-month trip to Mars.

Some people don't believe in the Mars One plan. According to the Massachusetts Institute of Technology, living on Mars probably **won't be** possible by 2025. If the colonists **have** a problem, it **will take** a long time to send them help, and they **will die**.

If George Hatcher **goes** to Mars, he **will have to** leave his family and friends forever. **Will** he **be** happy without them?

---

8 *colony:* a group of people who move to a new place but are still under the government of their home county

An artist's vision of the future Mars One colony

COMPREHENSION CHECK Based on the reading, tell if the statement is true (**T**) or false (**F**).

1. Mars One wants to start a colony on Mars by 2025.

2. A trip to Mars will be a one-way trip for its passengers.

3. Twenty-four people will go on the first trip to Mars.

6.6 The Future with Time Clauses and *If* Clauses

Time or *If* Clause (Simple Present)	Main Clause (Future)	Explanation
If you **go** to Mars,	you **won't come** back.	A clause is a group of words that has a subject and a verb. Some sentences have a time clause or an *if* clause in addition to a main clause. We use the future in the main clause; we use the simple present in the time clause or the *if* clause.
When they **arrive**,	they**'re going to create** a human colony.	
Main Clause (Future)	**Time or *If* Clause (Simple Present)**	
George Hatcher **will go**	if they **choose** him.	
He **isn't going to see** his family again	after he **goes** to Mars.	

Language Note:

If the time clause or the *if* clause comes before the main clause, we use a comma between the two clauses. If the main clause comes first, we don't use a comma.

     If they choose George**,** he will go. (comma)
     George will go if they choose him. (no comma)

EXERCISE 10 Complete the statements about the future. Then find a partner and compare your answers.

1. When the finalists complete the training, _they will travel to Mars_____.

2. If people go to Mars, _____.

3. If Mars colonists have a problem, _____.

4. If Chinese becomes the international language, _____.

5. If people live a long time, _____.

6. If computers become more intelligent than humans, _____.

7. When robots do the work of humans, _____.

8. If the world population continues to grow, _____.

EXERCISE 11 About You Fill in the blanks to make true statements about yourself. Then find a partner and share your statements.

1. When ___ I have more money ___, I'm going to buy a new cell phone.

2. When _____, I'll graduate.

3. If _____, I'm not going to graduate.

4. If _____, I'll probably find a job.

5. If _____, I'll probably live longer.

EXERCISE 12 About You Write a future statement or a question for each of the categories in the chart. Use *will* or *be going to*. Then find a partner and discuss your completed chart.

Category	Future Statement
1. job/career	I'm going to graduate in two years. When I graduate, will I find a job easily?
2. money	
3. learning English	
4. home	
5. family and children	
6. health	
7. fun and recreation	
8. technology	
9. other	

SUMMARY OF LESSON 6

The Future

The Future with *Will*	Examples
Affirmative Statement	He **will become** a nurse.
Negative Statement	He **won't become** a doctor.
Yes/No Question	**Will** he **become** a nurse soon?
Short Answer	Yes, he **will**.
Wh- Question	When **will** he **become** a nurse?
Negative Wh- Question	Why **won't** he **become** a doctor?
Subject Question	Who **will become** a doctor?

The Future with *Be Going To*	Examples
Affirmative Statement	He **is going to study** Chinese.
Negative Statement	He **isn't going to study** Spanish.
Yes/No Question	**Is** he **going to study** Japanese?
Short Answer	No, he **isn't**.
Wh- Question	Where **is** he **going to study** Chinese?
Negative Wh- Question	Why **isn't** he **going to study** Spanish?
Subject Question	Who **is going to study** Spanish?

Uses of *Will* and *Be Going To*	*Will*	*Be Going To*
Predictions	✓	✓
Simple facts	✓	✓
Plans		✓
Decisions about the future that come at the moment of speaking	✓	

The Future with Time and *If* Clauses

Time or *If* Clause (Simple Present)	Main Clause (Future)
After I **finish** the article,	**I'll give** it to you.
If you **study** nursing,	you**'re going to find** a job easily.

Main Clause (Future)	Time or *If* Clause (Simple Present)
I'm going to teach English	when I **go** back to my country.
I'll tell you about the article	if you **have** a few minutes.

Complete the conversation about the future with the word(s) given. Sometimes more than one answer is possible.

A: What ___are you going to do___ tomorrow night?
    1. you/do

B: Not much. I _____ TV after I _____ my
    2. watch   **3.** finish

homework.

A: Do you want to go to a lecture with me? One of my professors _____
    4. talk

about her predictions for the future. The lecture _____ the second in a
    5. be

series of presentations about the future.

B: What time _____?
    6. it/start

A: At 8 p.m. Afterward we _____ a discussion. In the first lecture, she
    7. have

talked about cities of the future. She thinks cities _____ more
    8. have

parks. Also people _____ bicycles more for transportation. There
    9. use

_____ more bike paths. People _____
    10. be   **11.** not/be

so lazy about exercise. We _____ some of our own food.
    12. grow

We _____ all our food from farmers.
    13. not/get

B: How many lectures _____ in this series?
    14. there/be

A: Five. I _____ all of them. I _____ you the link to the
    15. attend   **16.** send

website about the lectures. I know she _____ about politics of the future.
    17. not/talk

B: Why _____ politics?
    18. she/not/discuss

A: That subject makes people angry. So, do you want to go tomorrow?

B: Sure.

A: I _____ to your house around 7:30.
    19. come

B: Thanks. I _____ outside.
    20. wait

A: You don't have to wait outside. I _____ you when I
    21. call

_____ to your house.
    22. get

B: Great.

WRITING

PART 1 Editing Advice

1. For the future with *will*, don't add *be* before the main verb.

    I hope I will ~~be~~ find a good job.

2. Make sure your future sentence has a verb.

    I will _^ happy when I find a job.

be

3. Don't combine *will* and *be going to*.

    Technology ~~will~~ going to improve. OR Technology will improve.

is

4. Don't use the future after a time word or *if*.

    When you ~~will~~ graduate from the nursing program, you will find a job.

5. Use a form of *be* with *going to*.

    He _^ going to write an essay about our future world.

is

6. Use *to* after *going* for the future.

    Are computers going _^ be smarter than humans?

to

7. Use the correct word order for questions.

    Why ~~you aren't~~ going to read the article?

aren't you

PART 2 Editing Practice

Some of the shaded words and phrases have mistakes. Find the mistakes and correct them. If the shaded words are correct, write C. Sometimes more than one answer is correct.

$\overset{C}{\text{We will see}}$ several changes in the future. First, cities $\overset{be}{\underset{\wedge}{\text{will}}}$ much bigger than they
    1.   2.

are today. Right now about 3 billion people live in cities. By the year 2050, that number

will double. It will necessary to make changes for so many people to live together. One
  3.   4.

problem will going to be parking. City planners will need to study the problem. Businesses
        5.   6.

will need to pay drivers for street parking if they want to have customers. I'm glad this will
  7.   8.

happen. Why they aren't going to do this sooner?
         9.

Another change will be with education. Students are going learn STEM skills (science,
         10.   11.

technology, engineering, and mathematics). Some large companies going to become
                                      12.

partners with schools. When students will graduate from high school, they will be have the
                      13.   14.

opportunity to work with the company and learn from a teacher at the company. This is

already happening at one school in New York. Other schools in the United States are going to do
                                                    15.

this in the future.

Many exciting things are going to happen in the future. If I will still be here in 2050, I will
                  16.   17.   18.

see many changes.

PART 3 Write About It

1. Write about a few of your predictions for the future.

2. Write about a few of your plans or goals for the future.

PART 4 Edit Your Writing

Reread the Summary of Lesson 6 and the editing advice. Edit your writing from Part 3.

A seaplane flying over shallow waters

AVIATION

The airplane became the first World Wide Web, bringing people, languages, ideas, and values together.

—Bill Gates

Orville Wright's first flight in 1903 at Kitty Hawk, North Carolina. Wilbur Wright stands and watches.

The Wright Brothers

CD 1
TR 31

Read the following article. Pay special attention to the words in bold.

At one time, people only **dreamed** about flying. The Wright brothers, Wilbur and Orville, **were** dreamers who **changed** the world. They **were** the inventors of the first successful airplane.

From a young age, the brothers **were** fascinated[1] with the idea of flying. When Wilbur **was** 11 and Orville **was** 7, their father **gave** them a flying toy.

When they **were** older, Wilbur and Orville **opened** a bicycle shop in Ohio, where they **designed**, **sold**, and **repaired** bicycles. They **used** their bike shop to design an airplane. The brothers **didn't go** to college, but they **studied** a lot about aviation. They **were** interested in the way birds use their wings. They **studied** three necessary things for flying: lift, control, and power. Wilbur **designed** a small flyer with a gasoline engine. The brothers **flew** it for the first time on December 17, 1903; Orville **was** the pilot. The airplane **stayed** in the air for twelve seconds. It **traveled** a distance of 120 feet. That day they **made**

four short flights in their first "Wright Flyer" (as they **called** it). Only a few U.S. newspapers **reported** this historic moment. A New York newspaper **wrote**, "They are in fact either fliers or liars."

The Wright brothers **continued** to work on their airplane until 1905. For the next two years, they **didn't fly** at all. They **needed** a patent[2] for their invention and to find customers to buy it. They **contacted** the U.S. government, but the government **wasn't** interested. The government **didn't believe** them. The brothers **went** to Europe in 1908. There they **made** more than 200 flights. People **were** amazed. The brothers **became** world celebrities.[3] News of their success **was** now on the front page of newspapers. When they **came** back to America in 1909, they **were** heroes. They **sold** the Wright Flyer to the U.S. Army in 1909.

Airplanes today use the same basic design elements of the Wright Flyer.

---

1 *fascinated*: very interested
2 *patent*: a government license that prevents others from selling the same item
3 *celebrity*: a very famous person

COMPREHENSION CHECK Based on the reading, tell if the statement is true (**T**) or false (**F**).

1. The Wright brothers learned about aviation in college.

2. The U.S. government was immediately interested in the Wright brothers' plane.

3. The Wright brothers were immediately famous after their first flight.

7.1 The Simple Past—Form

Examples	Explanation
They **started** a bicycle business. They **repaired** bicycles.	Regular simple past verbs end in *-ed*. **Base Form** **Simple Past** start start**ed** repair repair**ed**
They **made** four short flights in 1903. They **sold** the Flyer to the U.S. Army.	Irregular simple past verbs do not end in *-ed*. **Base Form** **Simple Past** make made sell sold
Wilbur Wright **was** born in 1867. The Wright brothers **were** inventors.	The verb *be* is irregular. It has two forms in the past: *was* and *were*.

Language Notes:

1. Except for the verb *be*, the simple past form is the same for all subjects.

   They started a business. **I started** a business.

   We flew from Atlanta to Miami. **She flew** from Atlanta to Miami.

2. The verb after *to* does not use the past form.

   The Wright brothers **continued to work** on their plane. (NOT: continued to *worked*)

3. See Appendix H on pages AP10–AP11 for a list of irregular past forms.

 EXERCISE 1 Listen to the article. Fill in the blanks with the verbs in the box. You can use some verbs
CD 1
TR 32 more than once.

came	flew	hoped	rained	waited
cost	got	included	repaired	was
failed	hit	needed	stopped	were

December 17, 2003, _____was_____ the hundredth anniversary of the Wright
                            1.

brothers' first flight. There _____ a six-day celebration at Kitty Hawk, North
                                    2.

Carolina, the location of the first flight. A crowd of 35,000 people _____ to see
                                                                            3.

the flight of a model of the first airplane. The audience _____ some famous
                                                                4.

people, such as Neil Armstrong and Buzz Aldrin. They _____ the first men
                                                            5.

to walk on the moon.

continued

It _____ $1.2 million to make a copy of the original plane. People
6.

_____ to see the Flyer go up in the air. The weather _____ bad
7.   8.

that day. It _____ hard. The crowd _____ with excitement in the
9.   10.

rain. But the Flyer _____ to fly. A wing _____ the ground, and
11.   12.

the plane _____ . Mechanics _____ the engine and wing. The
13.   14.

crowd _____ again for a second try. The plane _____ wind to lift
15.   16.

off, but the winds _____ very calm that day. The Flyer _____ for
17.   18.

twelve seconds in 1903. It never _____ off the ground at all in 2003.
19.

7.2 The Simple Past—Uses

Examples	Uses
Their father **gave** them a toy.	We use the simple past with single, short past actions.
The Wright family **lived** in Ohio.	We use the simple past with longer past actions.
The Wright brothers **made** four short flights on December 17, 1903.	We use the simple past with repeated past actions.

Language Note:

We often use *ago* in sentences about the past. *Ago* means "before now."

The first flight was over 100 years **ago**.

EXERCISE 2 In Exercise 1, underline the regular simple past verbs once and underline the irregular simple past verbs twice. Circle the verb *be*.

EXERCISE 3 Write the base form of each verb. Write *R* for "regular verb." Write *I* for "irregular verb." Write *B* for the verb *be*.

1. _____rain_____ rained _____R_____   9. _____ studied _____

2. _____write_____ wrote _____I_____   10. _____ came _____

3. _____ opened _____   11. _____ gave _____

4. _____ sold _____   12. _____ flew _____

5. _____ started _____   13. _____ were _____

6. _____ happened _____   14. _____ needed _____

7. _____ made _____   15. _____ was _____

8. _____ died _____   16. _____ lived _____

AMAZING AVIATORS[4]

Charles Lindbergh

 CD 1 TR 33 **Read the following article. Pay special attention to the words in bold.**

At the beginning of the twentieth century, flight **was** new. It **was not** for everyone. It **was** only for adventurous people. Two adventurous aviators **were** Charles Lindbergh and Amelia Earhart.

Charles Lindbergh loved to fly. He **was** born in 1902, only a year before the Wright brothers' historic flight. In 1927, a man offered a $25,000 reward for the first person to fly nonstop from New York to Paris. Lindbergh **was** a pilot for the U.S. Mail Service at that time. He wanted to win the prize. He decided to try, and he succeeded. He **was** the first person to fly across the Atlantic Ocean alone. His plane **was** in the air for 33 hours. The distance of the flight **was** 3,600 miles. There **were** thousands of people in New York to welcome him home. He **was** an American hero. He **was** only 25 years old.

Another famous American aviator **was** Amelia Earhart. In 1920, when she **was** 23 years old, she rode in a plane for the first time. As soon as the plane **was** in the air, she **was** sure that she wanted to be a pilot. Earhart believed that men and women **were** equal in intelligence and ability. She took flying lessons and soon bought her own plane. In 1932, when she **was** 34 years old, she **was** the first woman to fly across the Atlantic Ocean alone. Americans **were** in love with Earhart. In 1937, she **was** ready for a bigger challenge.[5] She wanted to fly around the world. She **wasn't** alone; she **was** with a navigator.[6] They disappeared somewhere in the Pacific Ocean. Maybe there **wasn't** enough fuel.[7] Maybe the weather conditions **were** bad. No one really knows what happened to Earhart. It is still a mystery today.

Amelia Earhart

---

[4] *aviator*: a pilot
[5] *challenge*: a difficult job
[6] *navigator*: someone who guides a plane in the right direction
[7] *fuel*: gasoline

COMPREHENSION CHECK Based on the reading, tell if the statement is true (**T**) or false (**F**).

1. Charles Lindbergh was successful in his attempt to cross the Atlantic Ocean.

2. Amelia Earhart was the first person to fly across the Atlantic Ocean.

3. A navigator was with Earhart when she disappeared.

7.3 The Simple Past of *Be*—Forms

Affirmative Statements

Subject	Was/Were	
I He She It Lindbergh	**was**	in New York.
We You They People	**were**	

Negative Statements

Subject	Was/Were + Not	
I He She It Earhart	**was not** **wasn't**	alone.
We You They People	**were not** **weren't**	

Yes/No Questions and Short Answers

Was/Were	Subject		Short Answer
Was	I he she it	on an airplane?	Yes, you **were**. Yes, he **was**. No, she **wasn't**. Yes, it **was**.
Were	we you they		No, we **weren't**. Yes, I **was**. Yes, they **were**.

Wh- Questions

Wh- Word	Was/Were Wasn't/Weren't	Subject	
Why	**was** **wasn't**	I he she it	on an airplane?
	were **weren't**	we you they	

Subject Questions

Wh- Word	Was/Were	
Who	**was**	on the airplane?
How many	**were**	on the airplane?
What	**was**	wrong with Earhart's airplane?

Compare statements, *yes/no* questions, short answers, and *wh-* questions.

Statement	Yes/No Question and Short Answer	Wh- Question
Earhart **was** famous.	**Was** Earhart an inventor? No, she **wasn't**.	Why **was** Earhart famous?
The Wright brothers **were** Americans.	**Were** they from North Carolina? No, they **weren't**.	Where **were** the Wright brothers from?
Newspapers **weren't** interested in the first airplanes.	**Were** newspapers interested in airplanes in 1909? Yes, they **were**.	Why **weren't** they interested in airplanes in 1903?
Lindbergh **was** born in the twentieth century.	**Was** Earhart born in the twentieth century? No, she **wasn't**.	When **was** Earhart born?
Someone **was** with Earhart in 1937.	**Was** Lindbergh with Earhart? No, he **wasn't**.	Who **was** with Earhart?

EXERCISE 4 Complete the conversation between two friends with *was, wasn't, were,* or *weren't*.

A: _____*Were*_____ you interested in the article about Charles Lindbergh and Amelia Earhart?
          1.

B: Yes, I _____ . They _____ very brave people.
          2.   **3.**

A: I agree. At that time women _____ involved in professions like aviation.
          4.

    Many professions _____ only for men. But she believed that women and men
          5.

    _____ able to do the same things.
     6.

B: _____ she married?
     7.

A: Yes, she _____ .
          8.

B: _____ her husband a pilot, too?
     9.

A: No, he _____ .
          10.

B: I _____ sad to read about her disappearance.
      11.

A: I _____ too. But she _____ happy in her profession. In fact,
      12.   **13.**

    she told her husband, "I want to do it because I want to do it."

continued

B: What _____ the problem with her last flight?
14.

A: They _____ in the air for such a long time. Maybe there
15.

_____ enough fuel.
16.

B: Why _____ there enough fuel?
17.

A: I'm not really sure.

7.4 The Simple Past of *Be*—Uses

Examples	Explanation
Lindbergh **was** an aviator.	We use *be* for a classification of the subject.
Lindbergh **was** brave.	We use *be* for a description of the subject.
Lindbergh **was** in Paris.	We use *be* for the location of the subject.
Earhart **was** from Kansas.	We use *be* for the place of origin of the subject.
Earhart **was** born in 1897.	We use *be* with *born*.
There **was** a celebration of the hundredth anniversary of flight in 2003.	We use *was* with *there* for singular nouns.
There **were** thousands of people in New York to welcome Lindbergh.	We use *were* with *there* for plural nouns.
Lindbergh **was** 25 years old in 1927.	We use *be* with ages.

EXERCISE 5 Complete the statements with *was, wasn't, were,* or *weren't*. Then write if each sentence is an example of a classification (C), description (D), location (L), origin (O), *born* (B), age (A), or *there* (T).

1. Lindbergh and Earhart _____*were*_____ famous. _____D_____

2. Lindbergh _____ an inventor. _____

3. The first airplane _____ in the air for 12 minutes. _____

4. Lindbergh and Earhart _____ American heroes. _____

5. Earhart's last flight _____ successful. _____

6. She _____ alone when her plane disappeared. _____

7. Earhart _____ the first woman to fly across the Atlantic Ocean. _____

8. She _____ born in the twentieth century. _____

9. _____ you interested in the story? _____

10. Earhart _____ from Kansas. _____

11. Lindbergh _____ 25 years old when he made his flight across the Atlantic. _____

12. There _____ any reporters to see the flight in 1903. _____

EXERCISE 6 Read each statement. Then use the word(s) given to write a negative statement in the simple past.

1. The Wright brothers were inventors.

   (Earhart and Lindbergh) _Earhart and Lindbergh weren't inventors._____

2. The train was a method of transportation in the early 1900s.

   (the airplane) _____

3. Earhart was from Kansas.

   (Lindbergh) _____

4. The Wright brothers were inventors.

   (Earhart) _____

5. There were a lot of reporters at Kitty Hawk in 2003.

   (in 1903) _____

6. Lindbergh was born in the twentieth century.

   (the Wright brothers) _____

EXERCISE 7 Read each statement. Then use the word(s) given to write a *yes/no* question in the simple past. Write a short answer for each question.

1. The Wright brothers were inventors.

   (Lindbergh) _Was Lindbergh an inventor? No, he wasn't._____

2. The airplane was an important invention.

   (the telephone) _____

3. There were telephones 100 years ago.

   (airplanes) _____

4. Charles Lindbergh was adventurous.

   (the Wright brothers) _____

5. Amelia Earhart was American.

   (Lindbergh) _____

continued

6. Travel by plane is common now.

   (100 years ago) _____

7. I was interested in the story about the aviators.

   (you) _____

EXERCISE 8 Read each statement. Write a *wh-* question in the simple past using the word(s) given. Then find a partner and ask and answer your questions.

1. Charles Lindbergh was famous. (why)

   A: Why was Charles Lindbergh famous? _____

   B: He was one of the first aviators. _____

2. Lindbergh was a hero. (why)

   A: _____

   B: _____

3. Lindbergh was American. (what nationality/Earhart)

   A: _____

   B: _____

4. Earhart was 34 years old when she crossed the ocean. (how old/Lindbergh)

   A: _____

   B: _____

5. Lindbergh was a famous aviator. (who/the Wright brothers)

   A: _____

   B: _____

6. Lindbergh was born in 1902. (when/Earhart)

   A: _____

   B: _____

7. The flight at Kitty Hawk in 2003 wasn't successful. (why)

   A: _____

   B: _____

The Rocket Man

Read the following article. Pay special attention to the words in bold.

When Robert Goddard **was** 17 years old, he **climbed** a cherry tree to cut its dead branches. He **looked** around himself and **imagined** going into space, maybe even to Mars. The year **was** 1899.

As a child, Goddard **loved** to read. He often **visited** the library to borrow books on physical sciences. He **was** a sick child and **didn't graduate** from high school until he **was** 21. He later **became** a physics professor at a university. In his free time, he **built** rockets and **took** them to a field, but they **didn't fly**.

In 1920, Goddard **wrote** an article about rocket travel. When the *New York Times* **saw** his article, a reporter **wrote** that Goddard **had** less knowledge about science than a high school student.

In 1926, Goddard **built** a ten-foot rocket, **put** it into an open car, and **drove** to a field on his aunt's nearby farm. He **lit** the fuse,[8] and the rocket **went** into the sky. It **traveled** at 60 miles per hour to an altitude[9] of 41 feet. Then it **fell** into the field. The flight **lasted** 2.5 seconds. The U.S. government **didn't show** much interest in Goddard's invention. To continue his experiments, Goddard **used** his own money and money from private foundations.[10]

Over the years, his rockets **grew** to 18 feet and **flew** up to 9,000 feet. No one **made** fun of him after he **was** successful. In fact, he **became** known as the father of modern rocketry. He **wrote**, "The dream of yesterday is the hope of today, and the reality of tomorrow."

Goddard **didn't live** to see space flight. He **died** in 1945, but his work **didn't stop**. Scientists **continued** to build bigger and better rockets. In 1969, the American rocket Apollo 11 **took** the first men to the moon. At that time, the *New York Times* **wrote** about its 1920 article: "The *Times* regrets the error."

Robert Goddard with one of his rocket designs in 1928

---

[8] *fuse*: a cord that, when lighted, carries a flame
[9] *altitude*: height
[10] *foundation*: an organization that provides money for projects

COMPREHENSION CHECK Based on the reading, tell if the statement is true (**T**) or false (**F**).

1. Goddard used his aunt's farm to test his rockets.

2. The first rocket was in the air for 60 seconds.

3. The *New York Times* recognized Goddard's success many years later.

7.5 The Simple Past of Regular Verbs

We add *-ed* to the base form of regular verbs to form the simple past.

Examples	Base Form	Simple Past Form
Goddard **climbed** a tree.	climb	climb**ed**
He **looked** around him.	look	look**ed**
The rocket **traveled** for 2.5 seconds.	travel	travel**ed**
Some people **laughed** at his ideas.	laugh	laugh**ed**

EXERCISE 9 Underline the simple past verbs.

1. Goddard <u>climbed</u> a tree to cut its branches.

2. He loved to read.

3. He visited the library to get books about science.

4. He graduated from high school at the age of 21.

5. He studied physical sciences.

6. Goddard wanted to build rockets.

7. He experimented at his aunt's farm.

8. The U.S. government ignored his work at first.

9. Some people laughed at his ideas.

10. He continued his work.

11. He died at the age of 63.

7.6 The Simple Past of Regular Verbs—Spelling

Rule	Base Form	Simple Past
We add -ed to the base form of most regular verbs.	start laugh	started laughed
When the base form ends in e, we add -d only.	die live	died lived
When the base form ends in a consonant + y, we change y to i and add -ed.	carry study	carried studied
When the base form ends in a vowel + y, we add -ed. We don't change the y.	stay enjoy	stayed enjoyed
When the base form of a one-syllable verb ends in a consonant-vowel-consonant (CVC), we repeat the final consonant and add -ed.	s t o p ↓ ↓ ↓ C V C h u g ↓ ↓ ↓ C V C	stopped hugged
When the base form ends in w or x, we don't repeat the final consonant.	show fix	showed fixed
When the base form of a two-syllable verb ends in a consonant-vowel-consonant, we repeat the final consonant and add -ed only if the last syllable is stressed.	r e f e r ↓ ↓ ↓ C V C	referred
When the last syllable of a two-syllable verb is not stressed, we don't repeat the final consonant.	open offer	opened offered

EXERCISE 10 Write the simple past form of each regular verb. In two-syllable verbs that end in consonant-vowel-consonant, the stressed syllable is underlined.

1. play   *played*

2. worry   *worried*

3. hope   _____

4. want   _____

5. like   _____

6. row   _____

7. look   _____

8. shop   _____

9. happen   _____

10. marry   _____

11. pray   _____

12. drag   _____

13. drop   _____

14. vote   _____

15. follow   _____

16. prefer   _____

17. tie   _____

18. mix   _____

19. admit   _____

20. propel   _____

7.7 The Simple Past of Regular Verbs—Pronunciation

Rule	Examples	
We pronounce -ed as /t/ after voiceless sounds /p, k, f, s, ʃ, tʃ/.	jump—jumped cook—cooked cough—coughed	kiss—kissed wash—washed watch—watched
We pronounce -ed as /d/ after voiced sounds /b, g, v, ð, z, ʒ, dʒ, m, n, ŋ, l, r/ and all vowel sounds.	rub—rubbed drag—dragged love—loved bathe—bathed use—used massage—massaged charge—charged	name—named learn—learned bang—banged call—called care—cared free—freed tie—tied
We pronounce -ed as /əd/ after /d/ or /t/ sounds.	wait—waited hate—hated	add—added decide—decided

EXERCISE 11 Find a partner. Take turns pronouncing the base form and the simple past form of each verb in Exercise 10 on page 165.

EXERCISE 12 Complete each statement with the simple past form of a verb from the box.

believe	graduate	live	play	study	want
dream	like	open	receive✓	use	work

1. The Wright brothers _____*received*_____ a flying toy from their father.

2. They _____ with flying toys.

3. They _____ in Ohio.

4. They _____ about flying when they were children.

5. They _____ a lot about flight.

6. They _____ a bicycle shop in Dayton, Ohio.

7. Goddard _____ to go the library a lot when he was young.

8. He _____ to study physical sciences.

9. He _____ from high school at the age of 21.

10. He _____ as a university professor.

11. He _____ in the possibility of going to the moon.

12. He _____ his aunt's farm to test his rockets.

7.8 The Simple Past of Irregular Verbs

Irregular verbs in the simple past do not end in -*ed*.

Examples	Base Form	Simple Past Form
Goddard **built** rockets.	build	built
A newspaper **wrote** an article about him.	write	wrote

There are different ways to form the simple past of irregular verbs.

No Change in Form

beat	cost	fit	hurt	put	set	split
bet	cut	hit	let	quit	shut	spread

Change in Form

feel—felt	mean—meant[1]	dig—dug	sting—stung
keep—kept	sleep—slept	hang—hung	strike—struck
leave—left	sweep—swept	spin—spun	swing—swung
lose—lost	weep—wept	stick—stuck	win—won
awake—awoke	speak—spoke	begin—began	sing—sang
break—broke	steal—stole	drink—drank	sink—sank
choose—chose	wake—woke	ring—rang	spring—sprang
freeze—froze		shrink—shrank	swim—swam
bring—brought	fight—fought	blow—blew	grow—grew
buy—bought	teach—taught	draw—drew	know—knew
catch—caught	think—thought	fly—flew	throw—threw
arise—arose	rise—rose	bleed—bled	meet—met
drive—drove	shine—shone	feed—fed	read—read[2]
ride—rode	write—wrote	lead—led	speed—sped
sell—sold	tell—told	find—found	wind—wound
mistake—mistook	take—took	lay—laid	say—said[3]
shake—shook		pay—paid	
swear—swore	wear—wore	bite—bit	light—lit
tear—tore		hide—hid	slide—slid
become—became	forgive—forgave	fall—fell	run—ran
come—came	give—gave	hold—held	sit—sat
eat—ate	lie—lay	see—saw	
forget—forgot	shoot—shot	stand—stood	
get—got		understand—understood	
build—built	send—sent	be—was/were	have—had
lend—lent	spend—spent	do—did	hear—heard
		go—went	make—made

Language Notes:

[1] *meant*: rhymes with *sent*   [2] *read*: is pronounced like *red*   [3] *said*: rhymes with *bed*

EXERCISE 13 Complete each statement with the simple past form of the verb given.

1. The Wright brothers' father _____*gave*_____ them a flying toy.
   _{give}

2. The brothers _____ a dream of flying.
   _{have}

3. They _____ interested in flying after seeing the toy.
   _{become}

4. They _____ many books about flight.
   _{read}

5. They_____ bicycles in Ohio.
   _{sell}

6. They _____ the first gas-powered airplane.
   _{build}

7. They_____ for the first time in 1903.
   _{fly}

8. Only a few people _____ the first flight.
   _{see}

9. Between 1903 and 1909, they _____ some changes to the airplane.
   _{make}

10. In 1909, they _____ their plane to the U.S. Army.
    _{sell}

11. The Wright brothers _____ celebrities when they returned to America in 1909.
    _{be}

12. The airplane was an important invention because it _____ people from different
    _{bring}

    places closer together.

13. Thousands of people _____ to North Carolina for the hundredth anniversary of flight.
    _{go}

EXERCISE 14 Complete each statement with the simple past form of a verb in the box.

be	drive	fly	see	think
become ✓	fall	put	take	write

1. Goddard _____*became*_____ interested in rockets when he was a child.

2. He _____ a professor of physics.

3. People _____ that space travel was impossible.

4. Goddard _____ his first rocket in a car and _____ to his aunt's farm.

5. The rocket _____ for a couple of seconds, and then it _____ to the ground.

6. Goddard never _____ the first moon landing.

7. The *New York Times* _____ about their mistake 49 years later.

8. Apollo 11 _____ the first men to the moon in 1969.

7.9 Negative Statements with the Simple Past

Regular Verbs

Subject	Verb	
You	**looked** **didn't look**	at the sky.
We	**traveled** **didn't travel**	to North Carolina.
She	**returned** **didn't return**	to New York.

Irregular Verbs

Subject	Verb	
She	**had** **didn't have**	an accident.
He	**went** **didn't go**	to Paris.
It	**flew** **didn't fly**	for a long time.

Language Notes:

1. We use *didn't (did not)* + the base form for regular and irregular verbs.

2. Remember: The simple past forms of the verb *be* are *was, were, wasn't,* and *weren't.*

EXERCISE 15 Complete each statement with the negative form of the underlined verb.

1. Goddard <u>believed</u> in space flight. Other people _____*didn't believe*_____ in space flight at that time.

2. The Wright brothers <u>dreamed</u> about flying. They _____ about rockets.

3. They <u>sold</u> bicycles. They _____ cars.

4. Their 1903 airplane <u>had</u> a pilot. Their first airplane _____ a pilot.

5. The Wright brothers <u>wanted</u> to show their airplane to the U.S. government. The government _____ to see it at first.

6. The Wright brothers <u>built</u> the first airplane. They _____ the first rocket.

7. Goddard <u>thought</u> his ideas were important. Other people _____ his ideas were important at first.

8. In 1920, a newspaper <u>wrote</u> that he was foolish. The newspaper _____ about the possibility of rocket travel.

9. In 1926, his rocket <u>flew</u>. Before that time, his rockets _____ .

10. The first rocket <u>stayed</u> in the air for 2.5 seconds. It _____ in the air for a long time.

11. Goddard <u>saw</u> his rockets fly. He _____ rockets go to the moon.

12. A rocket <u>went</u> to the moon in 1969. A rocket _____ to the moon during Goddard's lifetime.

13. Earhart <u>was</u> with someone when she disappeared. She _____ alone.

Evelyn "Mama Bird" Johnson
at the Moore-Murrell Airport
in Tennessee

"Mama Bird" Johnson

 CD 2
TR 2
Read the conversation between two friends. Pay special attention to the words in bold.

A: I just read an article about a very special female pilot, Evelyn Bryan Johnson.

B: Why **was** she so special?

A: Evelyn was born in 1909, just six years after the Wright brothers made their first flight.

B: When **did** she **begin** flying?

A: In 1944. She wanted a hobby[11] because she was lonely.

B: **Did** she **like** flying right away?

A: Yes, she **did**.

B: What kind of planes **did** she **fly**?

A: She started with small private planes. Then she learned to fly seaplanes, multi-engine planes, and helicopters. She had more flying hours than any other female pilot in history.

B: How many flying hours **did** she **have**?

A: About 57,000 hours. That's over six years! And she traveled over five million miles. That's about twelve round-trip flights to the moon! She became known as "Mama Bird" Johnson.

B: Who **gave** her that name?

A: One of her students **did**. She trained over 5,000 pilots. She did a lot of other things, too.

B: What else **did** she **do**?

---

11 *hobby*: an activity done for pleasure

A: She worked as a flight examiner,[12] she raced planes, and she ran a tourist flight service.

B: **Did** she ever **work** outside of aviation?

A: Yes, she **did**. But when she took her first flying lesson, she knew this was the career for her.

B: When **did** she **stop** flying?

A: She stopped flying in her mid-90s when her eyesight[13] became bad.

B: **Did** she finally **retire** in her 90s?

A: Not exactly. She continued to give lessons and flight exams. She worked as the manager of an airport almost till the end of her life.

B: When **did** she **die**?

A: In 2012.

B: How old **was** she when she died?

A: She was 102.

B: Why **didn't** she **receive** any awards?

A: Who **said** she didn't receive any awards? She won over thirty awards. She's in the National Aviation Hall of Fame, along with the Wright brothers, Robert Goddard, and Neil Armstrong, who was the first man on the moon.

---

[12] *flight examiner*: someone who tests the skills of trainee pilots
[13] *eyesight*: the ability to see

COMPREHENSION CHECK Based on the reading, tell if each statement is true (**T**) or false (**F**).

1. Evelyn Johnson learned to fly many kinds of airplanes.

2. She had more flying hours than all other pilots.

3. Besides being a pilot, she was also a flight instructor.

7.10 Questions with the Simple Past

Yes/No Questions and Short Answers

Did	Subject	Base Form		Short Answer
Did	I you he she it we they	**fly**	fast?	Yes, you **did**. No, I **didn't**. Yes, he **did**. No, she **didn't**. Yes, it **did**. No, we **didn't**. Yes, they **did**.

continued

Wh- Questions

Wh- Word	*Did/Didn't*	Subject	Base Form
Where When Why How	**did**	I you he she	
Why	**didn't**	it we they	**fly**?

Subject Questions

Wh- Word	Simple Past Verb	
Who	**called**	her "Mama Bird"?
Which pilots	**took**	lessons from her?
What	**happened**	to Earhart?

Compare statements, *yes/no* questions, short answers, and *wh-* questions.

Statement	Yes/No Question and Short Answer	*Wh-* Question
Johnson **flew** large planes.	**Did** she **fly** seaplanes? Yes, she **did**.	What kind of planes **did** she **fly**?
She **managed** an airport.	**Did** she **manage** a big airport? No, she **didn't**.	Which airport **did** she **manage**? Why **didn't** she **manage** a big airport?
Many pilots **took** lessons from her.	**Did** her husband **take** lessons from her? No, he **didn't**.	How many pilots **took** lessons from her?

Language Note:

Compare questions with *be* to other simple past questions.

> **Was** she a good pilot?   When **was** she born?
>
> **Did** she **win** awards?   When **did** she **die**?

EXERCISE 16 Read each statement. Then complete the *yes/no* questions and short answers in the simple past. Use pronouns in your answers.

1. **A:** Evelyn Johnson graduated from high school.

   B: _____ Did she graduate _____ from college?

                      a.

   A: Yes, _____ she did _____.

             b.

2. **A:** Johnson worked as a pilot for many years.

   B: _____ as a flight instructor, too?

              a.

   A: Yes, _____.

             b.

3. **A:** She trained many pilots.

B: _____ any commercial jet pilots?
　　　　　　　　a.

A: Yes, _____ .
　　　　　　b.

4. **A:** She taught many pilots to fly.

　　B: _____ many women to fly?
　　　　　　　　　a.

　　A: No, _____ . Only 5 percent of her students were women.
　　　　　　b.

5. **A:** Johnson had some accidents.

　　B: _____ any serious accidents?
　　　　　　　　　a.

　　A: Yes, _____ .
　　　　　　　b.

6. **A:** She won many awards.

　　B: _____ any awards for bravery?
　　　　　　　　　a.

　　A: Yes, _____ .
　　　　　　　b.

7. **A:** She knew many pilots.

　　B: _____ the Wright brothers?
　　　　　　　　　a.

　　A: No, _____ .
　　　　　　b.

EXERCISE 17 Read each statement. Use the word(s) given to write a *yes/no* question and short answer in the simple past.

1. The Wright brothers had a dream.

   (Goddard) _Did Goddard have a dream?_

   (yes) _Yes, he did._

2. Wilbur Wright died in 1912.

   (in an airplane crash) _____

   (no) _____

3. The Wright brothers built an airplane.

   (Goddard)_____

   (no) _____

4. Earhart loved to fly.

   (Lindbergh) _____

   (yes) _____

continued

5. Lindbergh crossed the ocean.

(Earhart) _____

(yes) _____

6. Lindbergh worked for the U.S. Mail Service.

(Earhart) _____

(no) _____

7. Lindbergh was famous.

(Earhart) _____

(yes) _____

8. Lindbergh was born in the twentieth century.

(Earhart) _____

(no) _____

9. People didn't believe the Wright brothers at first.

(Goddard) _____

(no) _____

EXERCISE 18 Complete each question using the simple past.

1. **A:** Evelyn Johnson trained many pilots.

   B: How many pilots _____*did Johnson train*_____?

   A: She trained over 5,000 pilots.

2. **A:** Not many of her students were female.

   B: How many of her students _____?

   A: Only about 5 percent.

3. **A:** She rescued a helicopter pilot after his helicopter crashed.

   B: How _____ him?

   A: She got under the blades of the helicopter, turned off the motor, and sprayed it with a fire extinguisher.

4. **A:** Someone gave her the nickname "Mama Bird."

   B: Who _____ her the nickname "Mama Bird"?

   A: One of her students gave her the nickname.

5. **A:** Johnson became the manager of an airport.

   B: When _____ the manager of an airport?
   a.

   A: When she was 45 years old.

   B: How long _____ the manager of an airport?
   b.

   A: She was the manager for over 50 years.

6. **A:** She loved to fly.

   B: Why _____ to fly?

   A: She said, "It's a different world from anything else. When you get up there and you fly around, everything is so beautiful."

7. **A:** Sometimes she had airplane accidents. Something serious happened two times.

   B: What _____ these two times?
   a.

   A: Her engine failed, and she landed her plane in fields.

   B: _____ seriously injured?
   b.

   A: No, she wasn't.

8. **A:** She was born in 1909, 6 years after the first flight of the Wright brothers.

   B: Where _____ ?
   a.

   A: She was born in Kentucky.

   B: _____ the Wright brothers?
   b.

   A: No, she didn't. She never met the Wright brothers.

9. **A:** She retired from flying in her mid-90s.

   B: Why _____ from flying?
   a.

   A: Her eyesight got worse. Also, she had an accident and lost her leg.

   B: What kind of accident _____ ?
   b.

   A: She had a car accident.

10. **A:** She died at the age of 102.

    B: When _____ ?

    A: She died in 2012.

EXERCISE 19 Complete each question using the simple past.

1. **A:** What kind of engine ___*did the first airplane have*___?

   B: The first airplane had a gasoline engine.

2. **A:** Where _____ their plane?

   B: The Wright brothers built their plane in their bicycle shop.

3. **A:** Why _____ the first flight in 1903?

   B: Newspapers didn't report it because they didn't believe it.

4. **A:** Where _____?

   B: Lindbergh worked at the U.S. Mail Service.

5. **A:** Why _____ the ocean?

   B: He crossed the ocean to win prize money.

6. **A:** How much money _____?

   B: He won $25,000.

7. **A:** How old _____ when he crossed the ocean?

   B: Lindbergh was 25 years old when he crossed the ocean.

8. **A:** Where _____?

   B: Earhart was born in Kansas.

9. **A:** Where _____?

   B: Her plane disappeared in the Pacific Ocean.

10. **A:** What _____ to her plane?

    B: Nobody knows what happened to her plane.

11. **A:** Who _____ with Earhart?

    B: A navigator flew with Earhart.

12. **A:** Why _____ in the Wright brothers' airplane?

    B: The government wasn't interested because they didn't believe the Wright brothers.

13. **A:** When _____ on the moon?

    B: The first man walked on the moon in 1969.

14. **A:** Why _____ the first moon landing?

   B: Goddard didn't see the first moon landing because he died in 1945.

EXERCISE 20 About You Write questions in the simple past using the words given. Then find a partner and ask and answer your questions.

1. when/you/fly in a plane for the first time

   When did you fly in a plane for the first time?

2. who/be/with you

   _____

3. what/be/your first impression of flying

   _____

4. what/be/your longest trip

   _____

5. you/like the articles about aviation in this lesson

   _____

6. which article/you/like the best

   _____

7. you/know about Robert Goddard before you read the story

   _____

8. you/know anything about Amelia Earhart before you read the story

   _____

9. you/see the first moon landing

   _____

SUMMARY OF LESSON 7

The Simple Past of *Be*

	Was	*Were*
AFFIRMATIVE STATEMENT	He **was** in Paris.	They **were** in Paris.
NEGATIVE STATEMENT	He **wasn't** in London.	They **weren't** in London.
YES/NO QUESTION	**Was** he in Rome?	**Were** they in Rome?
SHORT ANSWER	No, he **wasn't**.	Yes, they **were**.
WH- QUESTION	When **was** he in Paris?	When **were** they in Paris?
NEGATIVE *WH-*QUESTION	Why **wasn't** he in Rome?	Why **weren't** they in Rome?
SUBJECT QUESTION	Who **was** in London?	How many people **were** in Paris?

The Simple Past of Other Verbs

	Regular Verb	Irregular Verb
AFFIRMATIVE STATEMENT	They **worked** in a bike shop.	You **flew** to Florida.
NEGATIVE STATEMENT	They **didn't work** in a factory.	You **didn't fly** to New York.
YES/NO QUESTION	**Did** they **work** in Ohio?	**Did** you **fly** to Miami?
SHORT ANSWER	Yes, they **did**.	No, I **didn't**.
WH- QUESTION	Where **did** they **work**?	Where **did** you **fly**?
NEGATIVE *WH-* QUESTION	Why **didn't** they **work** in a factory?	Why **didn't** you **fly** to Miami?
SUBJECT QUESTION	Who **worked** in a factory?	How many people **flew** to Miami?

TEST/REVIEW

Choose the correct word(s) to complete the conversation between two students.

A: You (*didn't come*/*wasn't come*/*didn't came*) to class last week.
  _1._

  I (*was*/*were*/*did*) worried about you.
  _2._

B: I (*didn't*/*wasn't*/*weren't*) in town.
  _3._

A: Where (*you go*/*was you go*/*did you go*)?
  _4._

B: I (*went*/*did go*/*was go*) to Washington, DC.
  _5._

A: (*Did you go*/*You did go*/*Did you went*) alone?
  _6._

B: No, I (*didn't*/*wasn't*/*not*). One of my brothers went with me.
  _7._

A: Which brother (*went*/*did go*/*did went*) with you?
  _8._

B: My brother Jackson.

A: (*You did drive*/*Did you drove*/*Did you drive*) there?
  _9._

B: No, we (*weren't*/*didn't*/*don't*). We (*flied*/*flew*/*fly*).
  _10._ _11._

A: Washington isn't so far from here. Why (*you didn't drive*/*didn't you drive*/*didn't you drove*)?
  _12._

B: We (*finded*/*found*/*were find*) cheap airline tickets. Anyway, we
  _13._

  (*didn't want*/*didn't wanted*/*weren't want*) to have a car in Washington. Parking is expensive,
  _14._

  and the streets are confusing. The subway system is very good. We (*take*/*took*/*taked*) the
  _15._

  subway everywhere.

A: Where (*you stayed*/*did you stayed*/*did you stay*)?
  _16._

B: We (*stayed*/*staied*/*stayyed*) in a hotel.
  _17._

A: What (*did you do*/*did you did*/*you did*) in Washington?
  _18._

B: We (*visit*/*visitted*/*visited*) the government buildings, of course. But I (*did*/*was*/*were*) more
  _19._ _20._

  interested in the museums. I especially (*was loved*/*loved*/*did love*) the Air and Space Museum.
  _21._

  We (*see*/*seen*/*saw*) the Wright brothers' first airplane—the real one!
  _22._

A: There (*was*/*had*/*were*) a lot of progress in flight in the twentieth century.
  _23._

B: Yes. The first flight was in 1903. Only 66 years later, astronauts (*were*/*was*/*did*) on the moon.
  _24._

WRITING

PART 1 Editing Advice

1. Use the base form, not the past form, after *to*.

          take
   I wanted to ~~took~~ flying lessons.

2. Use the base form after *did* or *didn't*.

          finish
   Orville Wright didn't ~~finished~~ high school.

        find
   Did they ~~found~~ Earhart's plane?

3. Use correct question formation.

       did Goddard invent
   When ~~Goddard invented~~ the rocket?

4. Use *be* with *born*. Don't add *-ed* to *born*. Don't use *be* with *died*.

         was born
   Wilbur Wright ~~borned~~ in 1867. He ~~was~~ died in 1912.

5. Use the correct past form.

       built   *was*
   Goddard ~~builded~~ rockets. He ~~were~~ interested in engineering.

6. Use *be* with age.

        was
   Evelyn Johnson ~~had~~ 102 years old when she died.

7. Don't confuse *was* and *were*.

       were
   Where ~~was~~ you yesterday?

8. Don't use *did* in a subject question.

       happened
   What ~~did happen~~ to Amelia Earhart?

PART 2 Editing Practice

Some of the shaded words and phrases have mistakes. Find the mistakes and correct them. If the shaded words are correct, write *C*.

        had   *C*

A: Last week, we ~~have~~ an interesting homework assignment. We had to write about a famous person.
               1.   2.

B: Who you wrote about?
          3.

A: I writed about Yuri Gagarin.
      4.

B: Who's that?

A: He was the first person in space.
       5.

B: Was he an American?
      6.

A: No, he didn't. He was Russian.
         7.   **8.**

B: When he went into space?
           9.

A: In 1961.

B: Did he went alone?
     10.

A: Yes. But he wasn't the first living thing in space. There was dogs, chimpanzees, and even turtles
            11.   **12.**
in space before him.

B: Is Gagarin still alive?

A: No. He was died in 1968.
        13.

B: When did he born?
       14.

A: He borned in 1934. He had only 34 years old when he died in 1968. He never seen the moon
     15.   **16.**   **17.**   **18.**
landing. That was happened in 1969.
          19.

B: How did Gagarin died? What was happened?
     20.   **21.**   **22.**

A: He were in a plane crash.
     23.

B: That's so sad.

A: Yes, it is.

PART 3 Write About It

1. Use the information from Part 2 to write a paragraph about Yuri Gagarin.

2. Choose another famous person from aviation or space exploration. Write a paragraph about what this person did.

PART 4 Edit Your Writing

Reread the Summary of Lesson 7 and the editing advice. Edit your writing from Part 3.

The Downtown Container Park shopping
center in Las Vegas, Nevada

SHOPPING

If you are not content today, there is nothing you can buy tomorrow to change that.

—Joshua Becker

Shopping in the Digital Age

CD 2
TR 3

Read the following article. Pay special attention to the words in bold.

Do you like **to shop** online? Or do you prefer **to go** into a store, look at a product, and talk to a salesperson? Maybe you like **to do** a combination of both these things. Smart shoppers know how **to use** different methods **to get** the best price. In order **to make** money, businesses need **to understand** the habits of today's shoppers.

One common shopper strategy[1] is "showrooming." This means that customers go into a store, look at the product, talk to a salesperson, and then use their smartphones or other mobile devices **to find** a better price. "Reverse showrooming" is another strategy: customers first go online **to do** research and then go into a store **to get** the product the same day. One thing is for certain: shoppers are now using many strategies to get the best price.

The number of online shoppers is rising, but not as fast as retailers[2] first thought. People still like **to go** into stores. Teens especially prefer **to shop** at the mall. Shopping for them is not about finding the best price; it's a social experience.

In order **to keep** customers coming into stores, managers need **to train** salespeople well. In-store shoppers want salespeople **to give** them a lot of attention, **be** polite, and **know** a lot about the product.

What products do shoppers like **to buy** online? The number one online purchase[3] is electronics. It's easy **to research** these products and **compare** prices online.

Online shopping doesn't work for every product. People prefer **to shop** for food in a store. If you're buying a new car, you can research prices online, but you still need **to drive** the car. If you're buying a mattress, online reviews[4] can't tell you if it's comfortable for you. You still need **to go** into the store and **lie** on it.

---

1 *strategy*: a plan to achieve a goal
2 *retailer*: a company that sells products to the public
3 *purchase*: something you buy
4 *review*: an article about customer opinions

COMPREHENSION CHECK Based on the reading, tell if the statement is true (**T**) or false (**F**).

1. Online shopping is growing faster than expected.

2. Showrooming includes both online research and in-store research.

3. For teens, shopping is often a social experience.

8.1 Infinitives—Overview

An infinitive is *to* + the base form of a verb.

Examples	Explanation
Do you like **to shop** online?	We use an infinitive after certain verbs such as *like*.
It's important **to compare** prices.	We use an infinitive after certain expressions beginning with *it*.
Are you surprised **to know** about shopping apps?	We use an infinitive after certain adjectives such as *surprised*.
Stores need to understand shoppers' habits **to stay** in business.	We use an infinitive to show purpose.

Language Notes:

1. When we connect two infinitives with *and*, we usually omit *to* after *and*.

   You need **to go** into the mattress store and **lie** on the bed.

2. An infinitive never shows tense. Only the first verb shows tense.

   He needs **to buy** a new car. (NOT: He needs to *buys*)

   He tried **to sell** his old car. (NOT: He tried to *sold*)

CD 2
TR 4

EXERCISE 1 Listen to the report. Fill in the blanks with the words you hear.

Businesses use several strategies _____*to get*_____ customers. Do you ever go to a
                                      1.

supermarket and see someone giving away free samples of food? Shoppers sometimes like

_____ a new product before buying it. Stores want you _____ the
        2.   **3.**

product, so they give you a sample and a coupon.

Many stores have special offers each week. They know that once you're in the store for the

sale item, it's convenient for you _____ other items there, too.
                                          4.

Another way to get a customer's attention is with good service. A salesperson may ask you,

"Do you want me _____ this to your car for you?" There's no extra charge for
                        5.

this service. It isn't necessary _____ this person for the service.
                                        6.

Do you ever bring your own bags to a supermarket? It isn't necessary _____
                                                                             7.

it. But some supermarkets give you a small amount of money for each bag.

continued

There is so much competition between businesses. They need _____ all
                                                                8.
kinds of strategies _____ our attention and encourage us _____
                            9.   10.
at their store.

8.2 Verbs + Infinitives

Examples	Explanation
I need **to buy** a new TV. I want **to get** a good price.	An infinitive can follow certain verbs.

We can use an infinitive after these verbs:

begin	forget	love	promise
continue	hope	need	start
decide	know how	plan	try
expect	like	prefer	want

Pronunciation Notes:

1. In informal speech, we pronounce *want to* /wɑnə/. In very informal writing, such as text messaging, we often write *wanna*.

2. We often pronounce *to* like /tə/ after a consonant sound, /də/ after a vowel sound, or /ə/ after a /d/ sound.

    I plan to buy a new smartphone. (/tə/)

    Try to get the best price. (/də/)

    I need to compare prices. (/ə/)

EXERCISE 2 Fill in the blanks with the infinitive form of the verbs from the box.

be	compare	read	spend
buy ✓	get	shop	wait

1. I want _____ to buy _____ a new TV.

2. I decided _____ about $500.

3. I need _____ prices online before going to the stores.

4. I want _____ the best price.

5. I like _____ reviews of products before I decide.

6. I know how _____ a smart shopper.

7. I don't like _____ on Saturdays because the stores are crowded.

8. I prefer to shop in a store. I don't like _____ 8 to 10 days to get a product.

EXERCISE 3 About You Find a partner. Ask and answer questions using the words given. Use infinitives.

1. like/shop

    A: *Do you like to shop?*

    B: *Yes, I do.* OR *No, I don't.*

2. try/compare prices

3. plan/buy something new soon

4. prefer/shop alone

5. like/shop online

6. know how/use shopping apps

EXERCISE 4 About You Find a partner. Ask and answer the questions.

1. When do you like to shop?

    A: *When do you like to shop?*

    B: *I like to shop on the weekend.*

2. What big item do you plan to buy soon?

3. Do you prefer to pay with a credit card, a debit card, or cash?

4. Where do you like to shop?

5. What do you need to know before making a big purchase?

8.3 *It* + *Be* + Adjective + (Noun) + Infinitive

Examples				Explanation
It	*Be* (+ *Not*)	Adjective (+ Noun)	Infinitive	We often use an infinitive after an expression with *it*.
It	is	convenient	**to use** a shopping app.	
It	isn't	a good idea	**to buy** a bed online.	
It's easy **for me to use** a shopping app. It's hard **for my grandfather** to shop online.				We can add *for* + a person (noun or object pronoun) before the infinitive.

An infinitive can follow these adjectives:

convenient	difficult	expensive	hard	impossible	possible
dangerous	easy	fun	important	necessary	practical

EXERCISE 5 About You Complete each statement about your shopping experiences. Use *for* + a person, if you like. Then discuss your answers with a partner.

1. It's necessary _____ for me to get a new smartphone _____.

2. It's important _____.

continued

3. It's not convenient _____.

4. It's convenient _____.

5. It's impossible _____.

6. It's difficult _____.

7. It's not expensive _____.

8. It isn't a good idea _____.

8.4 *Be* + Adjective + Infinitive

Examples				Explanation
Subject	*Be*	**Adjective**	**Infinitive**	We often use an infinitive after certain adjectives.
I	am	ready	**to talk** to a salesperson.	
She	is	happy	**to help** you.	

We can use an infinitive after these adjectives:

afraid	happy	pleased	proud	sad
glad	lucky	prepared	ready	

EXERCISE 6 Fill in the blanks with the infinitive form of the verbs from the box.

buy ✓	do	help	make	use
bother	have	go	spend	

A: I need _____to buy_____ a new car. I'm not ready _____ a decision. I don't
              1.   2.

know what I need _____ first. I'm afraid _____ so much money
                        3.   4.

and maybe get a bad car.

B: I can help you.

A: I don't want _____ you. I know you're very busy.
              5.

B: I'm happy _____ you. There are websites that give information about new and
              6.

used cars. Let's look at my tablet. This site is free. Here's another good site, but it's not free.

A: Oh.

B: Don't worry. You can use this service for free at the library.

A: Great. It's convenient for me _____ to the library.
              7.

How can I compare cars on one of these sites?

B: Don't worry. It's easy _____ these sites. If you have a problem, ask the librarian
          8.

for help.

A: Thanks for all your advice. I'm lucky _____ you as a friend.
                                          9.

8.5 Verb + Object + Infinitive

Examples				Explanation
Subject	Verb	Object	Infinitive	After *like, want, need, ask, expect,*
We	expect	the clerk	**to know** about the product.	and *encourage,* we can use a noun
I	asked	her	**to give** me information.	or an object pronoun (*me, you, him,*
You	want	the employees	**to be** polite.	*her, it, us, them*) + an infinitive.
She	needs	them	**to answer** her questions.	

EXERCISE 7 Choose the correct word(s) to complete each conversation.

Conversation 1 (between a salesman and a shopper)

A: Do you want (me/I) (to help/help) you find something?
                    1.   2.

B: Yes. We could use your help. Our daughter asked (*we buy/us to buy*) her a new cell phone.
                                                        3.

We don't know which plan to choose.

A: How much does she talk on the phone?

B: She never stops talking on the phone. I want (*her to use/that she use*) it just for important calls,
                                                4.

but she chats and texts with her friends all the time.

A: Here's a plan I want (*you to consider/that you consider*). It has unlimited calls and texts.
                          5.

B: You don't understand. We want (*her/she*) to use the phone less, not more.
                                   6.

Conversation 2 (between two friends)

A: I'm going to buy a tablet on Saturday. I need (*that you/you to*) come with me.
                                                  1.

B: Why? How do you want (*that I/me to*) help you?
                            2.

A: You just bought a new tablet, so you can give me advice.

Conversation 3 (between a husband and wife at the supermarket)

A: Oh, look. There's free food over there. Do you want (*me to get/I get*) you a little hotdog?
                                                          1.

B: No. They just encourage (*us/we*) to spend our money on things we don't need.
                               2.

continued

Conversation 4 (between a supermarket clerk and a customer)

A: Excuse me, miss. You have a lot of bags. Do you want (*me/I*) (*to help/helping*) you take them
    1.   2.

to your car?

B: Thanks. Do I need (*pay/to pay*) for this service?
                        3.

A: No, of course not. We're happy (*to help/help*) our customers.
                                    4.

EXERCISE 8 Complete the conversation between two brothers. Fill in the blanks with the first verb given, an object pronoun, and then the second verb given.

A: Mom and Dad say I spend too much money. They _____ *expect me to save* _____
                                                            1. expect/save

my money for the future. I _____ me alone.
                                2. want/leave

B: You do? I thought you _____ you a car.
                                3. wanted/buy

A: Well, I do. You know how much I hate to take the bus. I _____
                                                                4. want/talk

to them for me. Tell them I need a car.

B: I'm not going to do that. They're trying to _____ more responsible.
                                                    5. encourage/be

A: I *am* responsible.

B: No, you're not. Remember when you told Mom and Dad you wanted a new tablet? You

_____ one for you. There was nothing wrong with
        6. expected/buy

your old one. And remember when you lost your cell phone? You told Dad because

you _____ you a new one.
        7. wanted/buy

A: Well, I'm still in school, and I don't have much money.

B: Mom and Dad _____ and start to take responsibility
                        8. expect/graduate

for yourself. You buy too much stuff.

A: No, I don't. By the way, did I tell you I broke the screen on my cell phone?

8.6 Infinitives to Show Purpose

Examples	Explanation
I use coupons **in order to save** money. I use the Internet **to compare** prices.	We can use infinitives to show purpose. *To*, for purpose, is the short form of *in order to*.
In order to use this website, you need to pay. **To find** a better price, he used a shopping app.	The infinitive phrase can come at the beginning of a sentence. If so, we use a comma after the infinitive phrase.

EXERCISE 9 Complete the conversation between two friends. Fill in the blanks with the infinitive form of the verbs from the box.

change	compare	learn	look for	make	print	take ✓

A: Do you want to see my new camera?

B: Sure. Does it take good pictures?

A: Absolutely. I use this camera _____to take_____ most of my pictures.
                                           1.

B: I just use my smartphone.

A: This camera takes better pictures than a smartphone.

B: Was it expensive?

A: Not really. I went online _____ prices. Then I went to several stores in this city
                                        2.

_____ the best price.
        3.

B: Do you ever make prints of your pictures?

A: Sometimes. I buy high-quality paper _____ photos for my album. Sometimes
                                                    4.

I make little books of my vacations.

B: Is it hard to use the camera?

A: At first I had to read the manual carefully _____ how to take good pictures.
                                                          5.

But now it's easy. I'll take a picture of you. Smile.

B: Let me see it. My eyes are closed in the picture. Take another picture of me.

A: OK. This one's better.

B: I don't like the background. It's too dark.

A: I can use a photo-editing program _____ the color.
                                                6.

B: Can you use the program _____ me more handsome?
                                      7.

EXERCISE 10 About You Fill in the blanks to make true statements. Then find a partner and discuss your answers.

1. To take good pictures, _you need good lighting_____.

2. To take a good selfie, _____.

3. In order to be a better shopper, _____.

ARE FREE TRIALS[5] REALLY FREE?

 Read the following article. Pay special attention to the words in bold.

You're surfing the Internet[6] and see an offer for a free trial for a product or service. It **might** be an offer for free magazines. Or it **may** be a subscription[7] to a music app. You **may** already have a free music app, but you **have to** listen to a lot of ads. With a paid service, you **don't have to** listen to ads. You **can** even download music and listen to it offline.

Should you accept the offer? If it's free, what **can** you lose? Try it. You **might** like it. Right? Well, it **might not** be such a good deal after all. Why not?

First, you **have to** give the company your e-mail address. Companies often sell your e-mail address to other companies. You **may** start to receive a lot of unwanted ads.

Second, it's easy to start a free trial, but it's hard to cancel[8] the service when the trial period is up.[9] You call the phone number on the website (if you **can** find it!), and someone tells you, "You **can't** cancel by phone. You **have to** cancel online."

Why **must** they make it so hard to cancel? Think about it—why **should** they make it easy? Your free trial is now a charge to your credit card. You **might not** notice the charge until you get your next bill. Before you sign up for a free trial, you **should** read the cancellation policy.[10] It **might** be in very small writing. You **should** mark your calendar to cancel before the trial period ends.

If you decide to keep the service or product, use your credit card, not your debit card. If there's a problem, the credit card company **can** usually help you.

Here's the best advice: if you don't need the service or product, don't take it just because it's free. Free trials **can** sometimes cost you a lot of money.

---

5 *free trial*: a short period to test a product or service at no cost
6 *to surf the Internet*: to search casually for information online
7 *subscription*: an agreement to use a product or service for a certain period of time
8 *to cancel*: to stop something
9 *to be up*: to be finished
10 *cancellation policy*: the rules about canceling something

COMPREHENSION CHECK Based on the reading, tell if the statement is true (**T**) or false (**F**).

1. A paid subscription gives you service without ads.

2. It is sometimes hard for you to cancel a free trial.

3. Online companies can make money when they have your e-mail address.

8.7 Modals and Phrasal Modals—Overview

The modal verbs are *can, could, should, would, may, might,* and *must.*

Examples	Explanation
You **can start** a free trial easily. You **should read** the cancellation policy.	The base form of the verb follows a modal.
The free trial **might not** be a good idea. You **cannot** cancel this subscription online.	To form the negative, we put *not* after the modal. We write the negative of *can* as one word: *cannot.*
I **can't** find the phone number on the website. You **shouldn't** use a debit card for an online purchase.	We can form a contraction for *cannot* (*can't*), *should not* (*shouldn't*), *must not* (*mustn't*), and *would not* (*wouldn't*). There is no contraction for *may not* and *might not.*

Language Note:

Notice these patterns with a modal:

AFFIRMATIVE STATEMENT:	We **can cancel** online.
NEGATIVE STATEMENT:	We **can't cancel** by phone.
YES/NO QUESTION:	**Can** we **cancel** by e-mail?
SHORT ANSWER:	No, you **can't.**
WH- QUESTION:	How **can** we **cancel?**
NEGATIVE WH- QUESTION:	Why **can't** we **cancel** by phone?
SUBJECT QUESTION:	Who **can cancel** this?

Phrasal modals are like modals in meaning.

Phrasal Modal	Examples
have to be able to be allowed to	You **have to** cancel by Friday. I **am** not **able to** understand the cancellation policy. The company **is allowed to** sell your e-mail address.

EXERCISE 11 Listen to the report. Fill in the blanks with the words you hear.

CD 2
TR 6

Manufacturers often send coupons to shoppers to encourage them to buy a new product.

If you receive a coupon for a new kind of toothpaste, you _____ want to try it.
1.

continued

Coupons have an expiration date.[11] You _____ pay attention to this date

2.

because you _____ use the coupon after this date.

3.

   Stores have weekly specials, but there's usually a limit. You _____ buy more

4.

than the limit. If you see a sign that says, "3 for $5," you _____ buy three items

5.

to get the special price. You _____ buy just one or two.

6.

   What _____ you do if a store has a special but you _____ find

7.   8.

the item on the shelf? If the item is sold out,[12] you _____ go to the customer

9.

service desk and ask for a "rain check." A rain check allows you to buy this item at the sale

price even after the sale is over. A rain check has an expiration date. You _____

10.

use the rain check by this date.

   If you see a sign that says "rebate," this means that you _____ get money

11.

back from the manufacturer. You _____ mail the proof of purchase[13] and

12.

the receipt to the manufacturer. Also, you _____ fill out a small form.

13.

It _____ take 6 to 8 weeks to get your money. You _____

14.   15.

keep a copy of the receipt.

8.8 Can, Be Able To, Be Allowed To

Examples	Explanation
Can you find the phone number of this website? I**'m** not **able to** find the phone number.	We use *can* or *be able to* for ability.
The offer says "free trial." What **can** I lose? Free trials **can** sometimes cost money.	We use *can* for possibility.
Can I download music for free? **Are** we **allowed to** sample the food? The sign says "Limit two." You **can't** buy more than two of this sale item.	We use *can* or *be allowed to* for permission. The negative shows prohibition.

---

[11] *expiration date*: the last day a coupon can be used
[12] *to be sold out*: to have no more left
[13] *proof of purchase*: the document(s) to show you bought a product

Language Note:

Be permitted to has the same meaning as *be allowed to*.

> **Are** we **permitted to** sample the food?

Pronunciation Notes:

1. In affirmative statements, we usually pronounce *can* as /kən/.

> I **can** go tomorrow. (/kən/)

2. In negative statements, we usually pronounce *can't* as /kænt/. The stress is stronger than in affirmative statements.

> I **can't** go today. (/kænt/)

3. Sometimes it is hard to hear the *t* in *can't*. The vowel sound and the word stress help us hear the difference between *can* and *can't*.

4. In a short answer, we pronounce *can* as /kæn/ and *can't* as /kænt/.

> Can you help me? Yes, I **can**. (/kæn/)
>
> Can I pay by check? No, you **can't**. (/kænt/)

EXERCISE 12 About You These statements are true for most U.S. supermarkets. Check (√) the ones that are true about a supermarket in your country. Then find a partner and discuss your answers.

1. _____ You can use coupons.

2. _____ You can sometimes buy two items for the price of one.

3. _____ You can buy stamps.

4. _____ You can get a rain check.

5. _____ You're allowed to pay with a check.

6. _____ You're allowed to return an item if you're not happy with it.

7. _____ You can get free bags.

8. _____ Small children can sit in a shopping cart.

9. _____ If you have a small number of items, you can go to a special checkout lane.

10. _____ You can ask someone to help you take your bags to your car.

11. _____ You're sometimes able to get free samples.

EXERCISE 13 Complete the conversation between two friends. Fill in the blanks with the phrases from the box.

'm not able to finish	can give	can say
're not allowed to apply	can help ✓	can't wait

A: I need some help with this website.

B: I _____can help_____ you. What's the problem?
        1.

A: I _____ the registration for this free trial. It's for a magazine.
        2.

It's a sports magazine, and I love sports.

B: I have a subscription to this magazine. I _____ you my magazine in about a week.
        3.

A: I _____ a week. The sports news will be old.
        4.

B: OK. Let me see what we need to do. Oh, I see the problem. You _____
        5.

for this offer. It says that it's only for people over the age of 18. You're 17, right?

A: I _____ that I'm 18.
        6.

B: I don't think that's a good idea.

8.9 Should

We use *should* for advice.

Examples	Explanation
You **should** compare prices before you buy.	*should* = It's a good idea.
You **shouldn't** buy things you don't need.	*shouldn't* = It's not a good idea.

EXERCISE 14 About You If someone from another country is going to live in the United States, what advice would you give him or her about shopping? Work with a partner to write sentences of advice. Use modals.

1. You should shop for summer clothes in July and August. Summer clothes are cheapest at that time.

2. _____

_____

3. _____

_____

EXERCISE 15 Complete the conversation between a husband and wife at the supermarket. Fill in the blanks with the phrases from the box.

shouldn't buy	should use	shouldn't eat	should look at	should take
should be	should we buy ✓	should come	should we pay	should bring

A: _____Should we buy_____ ice cream? It's on sale.
        1.

B: It's a hot day. And we have to stop at the post office before we go home.

We _____ it today. It'll melt.
                2.

A: How about candy for the kids? They always ask us for candy.

B: That's not a good idea. They _____ so much candy. Where's our
                                    3.

shopping list? We _____ our list and not buy things we don't
                        4.

need. We _____ careful about how we spend our money.
            5.

A: You're right. OK. Milk is on our list.

B: You _____ the expiration date. This milk carton has tomorrow's
            6.

date. You _____ milk from the back row. It's usually fresher.
            7.

A: Really?

B: You almost never come shopping with me. You _____ with me
                                                    8.

more often. You can learn to be a better shopper.

A: You're right. Look. That sign says, "Bring your own bags. Get 10¢ for each bag." Next time,

we _____ our own bags. You see? I'm learning.
        9.

B: Great. _____ with a credit card or use cash?
            10.

A: I've got enough cash. Let's use cash.

8.10 *Must* and *Have To*

We use *must* and *have to* for necessity.

Examples	Explanation
You **must** cancel your free trial by Friday. To get a rebate, you **must** send the proof of purchase.	*Must* has a very official, formal tone.
When you sign up for a free trial, you **have to** use your credit card or debit card.	*Have to* is less formal than *must*.

continued

Language Note:

Another way to express necessity is with *have got to*. We usually make a contraction with a pronoun and *have* or *has*.

> I**'ve got to** cancel this trial by January 10.
>
> She**'s got to** pay by credit card.

EXERCISE 16 Fill in the blanks with the phrases from the box.

has to go	must show	have to return ✓
must send	have to buy	have to use

1. Eggs are on sale for $2.19 a dozen, "Limit two." I have three cartons of eggs. I ___have to return___ one of the cartons.

2. I have a coupon for cereal. The expiration date is tomorrow. I _____ it by tomorrow, or I won't get the discount.

3. The coupon for cereal says "Buy 2, get 50¢ off." Do I _____ two in order to get the discount?

4. She has a rebate application. She _____ the proof-of-purchase symbol and the receipt to the manufacturer.

5. He wants to pay by check. The cashier asks for his driver's license. He _____ his driver's license.

6. She has twenty-six items in her shopping cart. She can't go to a lane that says "10 items or fewer." She _____ to another lane.

8.11 *Not Have To* and *Must Not*

Examples	Explanation
To get a rebate, you **must** mail in a receipt. To get a rebate, you **have to** mail in a receipt.	In affirmative statements, *have to* and *must* are very similar in meaning. *Must* is more formal.
Stores **must not** sell an item after the expiration date.	In negative statements, *must not* shows that something is prohibited.
I usually shop on my tablet. **I don't have to** go into a store.	*Don't have to* shows that something is not necessary; there is a choice.

Language Note:

Must not is very formal. Informally, we use *can't*.

> Stores **can't** sell an item after the expiration date.

EXERCISE 17 Fill in the blanks with the correct verbs from the box. You can use some verbs more than once.

buy	carry	go	pay	take	use

1. If you sample a product, you don't have to _____buy_____ it. But if you decide to buy it, you will usually get a coupon.

2. If you have just a few items, you don't have to _____ a shopping cart. You can use a basket.

3. You don't have to _____ your own bags to the supermarket. But if you do, some stores will give you a small amount of money for the bags.

4. I don't have to _____ to the library to get information on a product. I can get most information on my mobile device.

5. When you're leaving a supermarket, you don't have to _____ your bags to your car. A sales assistant can do it for you.

6. I don't have to _____ with cash. I can use my credit card.

7. I don't have to _____ into a store to buy electronics. But I have to shop in a store for certain items, like a mattress.

8.12 *May, Might,* and *Will*

Examples	Explanation
A free trial **may** cost a lot of money. I have a coupon for a new toothpaste, so I **might** try it.	*May* and *might* have the same meaning. They show possibility for the future.
If you're a careful shopper, you **will** save money.	*Will* shows certainty about the future.

Language Note:

Compare *maybe* (adverb) with *may* or *might* (modal verbs):

Maybe my friend **will** buy a new tablet.

My friend **may** buy a new tablet.

My friend **might** buy a new tablet.

EXERCISE 18 Fill in the blanks with the phrases from the box. More than one answer may be possible.

might get	might want	may receive
might not be	may be	may try

1. If she sends the rebate form today, she ___may receive___ a check in about six weeks.

2. Meg needs to go shopping. She's not sure what her kids want. They _____ to try a new kind of cereal.

3. She's not sure if she should buy the small or the large size of cereal. The large size _____ cheaper.

4. The store sold out of all the coffee that was on sale. The clerk said, "We _____ more tomorrow."

5. The milk has an expiration date of June 27. Today is June 27. She's not going to buy the milk because it _____ good.

6. She's not sure what kind of toothpaste she should buy. She might buy the one she usually buys, or she _____ a new kind.

EXERCISE 19 Complete each statement. Write what *may* or *might* happen. Use *will* if you think the result is certain. Find a partner and compare your answers.

1. If you shop online, _you might find a better price_____.

2. If you go into a store and talk to a salesperson, _____

   _____.

3. If you buy shoes online, _____

   _____.

4. If you try a free sample in a supermarket, _____

   _____.

5. If you bring your own bags to a supermarket, _____

   _____.

6. If you don't cancel a free trial on time, _____

   _____.

SHOPPING TIPS[14]

Read the following article. Pay special attention to the words in bold.

Here are some shopping tips to help you make smart choices and save money:

1. If you have a favorite store, **search** online for store coupons. **Google** the name of the store and the word *coupon*. You can print the coupon or have it on your smartphone.

2. We often see sales such as "Buy one, get one free." **Ask** yourself, "Do I really need this item?" **Don't buy** something just because it's on sale.

3. **Ask** about the return policy. Can you return the item? If so, what is the time limit for a return?

4. If you receive a gift card, **use** it as soon as you can. Some gift cards have an expiration date.

5. **Shop** for groceries with a list. You'll save money if you use your list. **Don't shop** when you're hungry. Hungry shoppers often buy a lot of junk food.[15]

6. If possible, **don't take** small children to a store where they can see candy or toys. Kids often say, "**Buy** me this; **buy** me that."

7. If you shop online, **ask** about the refund[16] policy. If you return the item, who pays for shipping?[17]

8. If you shop online, **pay** with a credit card. **Read** your bill as soon as you receive it. **Look** for charges you don't recognize.

9. **Look** for discounts. Teachers get discounts at some stores. College students and senior citizens often get discounts.

Careful shopping can help you save a lot of money.

COMPREHENSION CHECK Based on the reading, tell if the statement is true (**T**) or false (**F**).

1. You can find the coupons for some stores online.

2. Some stores give discounts to students.

3. Not all companies offer free shipping on returns.

---

[14] *tip*: a piece of advice
[15] *junk food:* food that tastes good but is bad for you
[16] *refund*: money returned to the customer
[17] *shipping*: the cost to send something

8.13 Imperatives

Examples	Explanation
Use a gift card right away. **Don't shop** for food when you're hungry.	The imperative is the base form of the verb. For a negative, we put *don't* before the verb. The full form, *do not*, is not common in conversation.
Google *coupon* and the name of a store. **Ask** about the refund policy. Mommy, **buy** me a toy! **Do** your best.	We use the imperative for: • instructions • suggestions • demands • encouragement
Have a nice day. **Take** care.	We use the imperative in certain social expressions.

Language Notes:

1. We can put *always* or *never* before an imperative.

   Always take a list with you. **Never** shop for groceries when you're hungry.

2. The subject of an imperative is *you*, but we don't include *you* in the sentence.

EXERCISE 20 Fill in the blanks with the correct words from the box.

ask	don't buy	don't lose	take
compare ✓	don't forget	find	train

1. Before you buy an electronic device, _____*compare*_____ prices online.

2. If you go to a store, _____ a salesperson who knows about the product.

3. _____ a lot of questions.

4. _____ a mattress online. You need to go into the store and try it.

5. _____ your receipt. If you need to return an item, you may need your receipt.

6. Always _____ your own bags to a supermarket. It's good for the environment.

7. If you take a free trial offer, _____ to cancel before the ending date.

8. If you are a store manager, _____ your salespeople well.

EXERCISE 21 About You Write sentences advising someone about shopping in a country you know about. Use imperatives. Compare your sentences with a partner.

1. _Take your own bags to the supermarket. Bags aren't free in supermarkets._

2. _____

3. _____

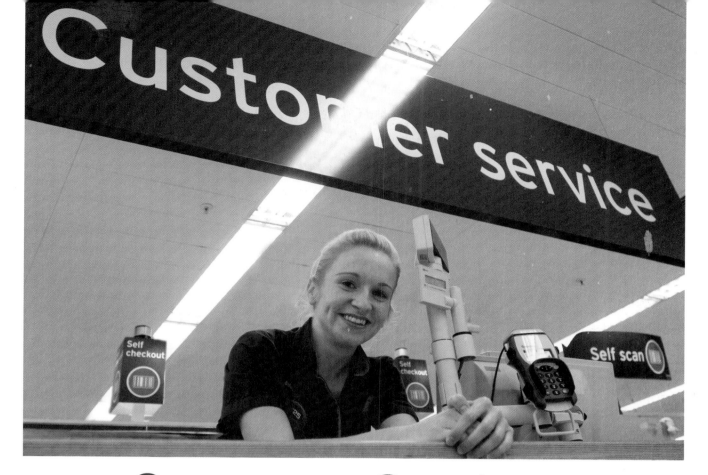

At the Customer Service Counter

 Read the following conversation between a customer service representative (A) and a customer (B) in a supermarket. Pay special attention to the words in bold.

A: **Can** I help you?

B: Yes. I**'d like** to cash a check.

A: You need to fill out an application. You can use that computer over there.

B: Do I have to do it on the computer? Do you have a paper application?

A: Yes, we do. Here's one. Please fill it out.

B: I don't have a pen. **Could** I use your pen?

A: There are pens over there.

A few minutes later:

A: **May** I see your driver's license?

B: Here it is.

A: Let me check your application. Oh, you wrote in the gray box. That's for us to complete, not for the customer. Why don't you fill out another form? Here's a new one.

B: Thanks.

A few minutes later:

B: Here's my application. **Could** you cash my check now?

A: I'm sorry, sir. We have to wait 7 to 10 days. **Can** I help you with anything else?

B: Yes. I**'d like** to buy some stamps.

COMPREHENSION CHECK Based on the conversation, tell if the statement is true (**T**) or false (**F**).

1. The customer filled out the check-cashing application on a computer.

2. The customer filled out the application correctly.

3. The customer cashed a check the same day.

8.14 Modals and Other Expressions for Politeness

Examples	Explanation
Would **Can** **Could** } you cash my check, please?	We use *would, can,* and *could* in a question to make a request. These sentences are more polite than "Cash my check."
May **Could** **Can** } I use your pen, please?	We use *may, could,* and *can* in a question to ask for permission. These sentences are more polite than "Give me your pen."
I **would like** to cash a check. **Would** you **like** to use my pen?	*Would like* has the same meaning as *want. Would like* is more polite than *want.*
I**'d** like to cash a check. He**'d** like to buy stamps.	The contraction with *would* after a pronoun is *'d.*
Why don't you fill out another form?	We use *Why don't you . . . ?* to offer a suggestion.
Why don't we walk to the supermarket. **Let's** walk to the supermarket. **Let's not** take the car.	We use *Why don't we . . . ?* or *Let's (not)* to make a suggestion that includes the speaker.
May **Can** } I help you?	Salespeople often use these questions to offer help to a customer.

EXERCISE 22 Complete the conversation between a salesperson (A) and a customer (B) in an electronics store. Choose the correct words. If both answers are correct, circle both choices.

A: (May I/Would I) help you?
    1.

B: Yes. (*I'd want/I'd like*) to buy a new computer. (*May you/Could you*) show me some
            2.   3.

    under $600?

A: (*Would you like/Do you like*) to see the laptops or the desktops?
            4.

B: (*Can you/Would you*) show me the laptops, please?
            5.

A: (*Could we/Why don't we*) go to the next aisle? Our laptops are over there. How do you
            6.

    plan to use your computer?

B: I like to play games and watch movies.

A: This computer is great for games.

B: (*Could you/May you*) tell me the price?
7.

A: We have a great deal on this one. It's $599.99. If you buy it this week, you can get a $100 rebate

from the manufacturer.

B: (*Can I/Would I*) take it home and try it out?
8.

A: That's not a problem. If you're not happy with it, you can return it within fourteen days and get

a full refund.

B: OK. I'll take it.

A: That'll be $635.99 with tax. (*Do you want/Would you like*) to buy a service contract?
9.

B: What's that?

A: If you have any problems with the computer for the next two years, we will replace it for free.

The contract costs $129.99.

B: Hmmm. I don't know.

A: (*Why don't you think about it?/Let's think about it.*) You have ten days to buy it. We have
10.

information in this brochure about the service contract.

B: Thanks.

A: Have a nice day.

B: You too.

SUMMARY OF LESSON 8

Infinitives

After verbs	Do you like **to shop**?
After expressions with *it*	It's important **to save** the receipt.
After adjectives	The sales clerk is happy **to help** you.
After object nouns or pronouns	I want you **to show** me your laptops.
To express purpose	We use coupons **to save** money.

Modals

can can't	The clerk **can** give you information. You **can** shop online. You **can** borrow my tablet. **Can** I cash a check here? You **can't** park here. It's a bus stop. I **can't** help you now. I'm busy.	Ability Possibility Permission Permission request Prohibition Inability
should shouldn't	You **should** compare prices. You **shouldn't** shop when you're tired.	A good idea Not a good idea
may may not	**May** I borrow your pen? I **may** buy a new car. You **may not** understand the instructions.	Permission request Possibility Possibility
might might not	A "free" trial **might** cost a lot of money. You **might not** remember to cancel.	Possibility Possibility
must must not	You **must** cancel your trial by Friday. Stores **must not** sell food after the expiration date.	Necessity Prohibition
would would like	**Would** you help me shop for a tablet? I **would like** to buy the newest model.	Request Want
could	**Could** you help me shop for a tablet?	Request

Phrasal Modals

have to not have to	She **has to** buy a new computer. She **doesn't have to** buy the most expensive model.	Necessity Lack of necessity
be allowed to	You**'re allowed to** take a shopping cart to your car.	Permission
be able to	**Are** you **able to** understand the warranty?	Ability

Imperatives

Save your money.	**Don't buy** another tablet.

Suggestions

let's (not)	**Let's** compare prices online.	**Let's not** waste our money.
why don't we/you	**Why don't we** compare prices?	**Why don't you** use a shopping app?

TEST / REVIEW

Choose the correct word(s) to complete the essay. If both answers are correct, circle both choices.

I want (*get/to get*) the best price when I shop. I know you do, too. So I (*would/'d*) like you
1.   2.

(*follow/to follow*) my advice.
3.

First, (*is/it's*) important (*compare/to compare*) prices. If you see something you like at a
4.   5.

store, (*you get/get*) the information about the product. If you have a camera on your phone,
6.

(*is/it's*) a good idea (*take/to take*) a picture of the tag (*for having/to have*) all the information
7.   8.   9.

about it. You (*don't have to/shouldn't*) go from store to store. You can (*to go/go*) online and look
10.   11.

for this item from another seller. You (*may/might*) find a better price.
12.

If you like the store where you first saw the item, you can go back and talk to a salesperson

about your research. Tell him that you want (*that he match/him to match*) the price.
13.

You (*should/must*) read sales ads carefully. You (*must/might*) find that the item is not
14.   15.

available at all stores. Some people like (*call/to call*) first (*to/for*) be sure that the item is at
16.   17.

the store. Nowadays, (*it's/is*) difficult (*to get/for get*) a real person on the telephone. Often we
18.   19.

(*have to wait/should wait*) a long time before a person picks up our call. Yesterday I made a
20.

call. It was frustrating (*to wait/waited*) on the phone for long time, but it was faster than going
21.

to the store.

When you decide on an item, you (*have to/should*) ask about price policy. If the item goes
22.

on sale in the next few weeks at this company or another company, (*can you/you can*) bring in
23.

your receipt and get the lower price?

Be careful of "Buy one, get one free" offers. These offers sound good. The store

(*wants that we/wants us to*) buy something we (*might not/must not*) even need.
24.   25.

I hope you follow my advice. I (*would/might*) like you (*to learn/learn*) from
26.   27.

my experience.

WRITING

PART 1 Editing Advice

1. Don't use *to* after a modal.

   I should ~~to~~ buy a new computer.

2. Don't forget *to* for an infinitive.

   Do you like ^shop? *(to)*

   It's important ^save your receipt. *(to)*

3. Use the base form in an infinitive.

   I tried to ~~found~~ a good price. *(find)*

4. Don't forget *it* in certain expressions.

   ~~Is~~ important to be a careful shopper. *(It's)*

5. Use *to,* not *for,* to show purpose.

   I went online ~~for~~ compare prices. *(to)*

6. Use the object pronoun and an infinitive after *want, expect, need, ask,* etc.

   I want ~~that he~~ explain the product to me. *(him to)*

PART 2 Editing Practice

Read the following e-mail. Some of the shaded words and phrases have mistakes. Find the mistakes and correct them. If the shaded words are correct, write *C*.

Dear Mom,

Recently I bought a new tablet, and I wanted to ~~got~~ the best price. Now you want I help
1. *(C)*   **2.** *(get)*   **3.**

you buy a new TV.

I want you be a good shopper. First, do the research. Is important to compare prices at
4.   **5.**   **6.**

different stores. Buy the Sunday newspaper for look at ads.
7.

You can to look for prices online, too. Remember that if you buy something online, you
8.
sometimes have to pay for shipping, too. Go to the stores and try use the product. It
9.   10.
might look good online, but you need to see it and try it out. It's not always easy make a
11.   12.   13.
decision. But if you follow this advice, you can be a smart shopper. Let me know if you need
14.
help with something else. I'm always happy help you. When you can help me with my school
15.   16.
paper? I want you help me check the grammar.
17.

Love,
Toni

PART 3 Write About It

1. Write about a purchase you made recently (such as a smartphone, camera, refrigerator, or microwave). Describe how the shopping experience was for you. How did you decide what to buy? Was it easy to make a decision? Did you get a good price?

2. Write about your experience shopping for food. Do you take a list? Do you use coupons? Do you always go to the same store? Do you take your own bags to the supermarket? Does it take you a long time to shop?

PART 4 Edit Your Writing

Reread the Summary of Lesson 8 and the editing advice. Edit your writing from Part 3.

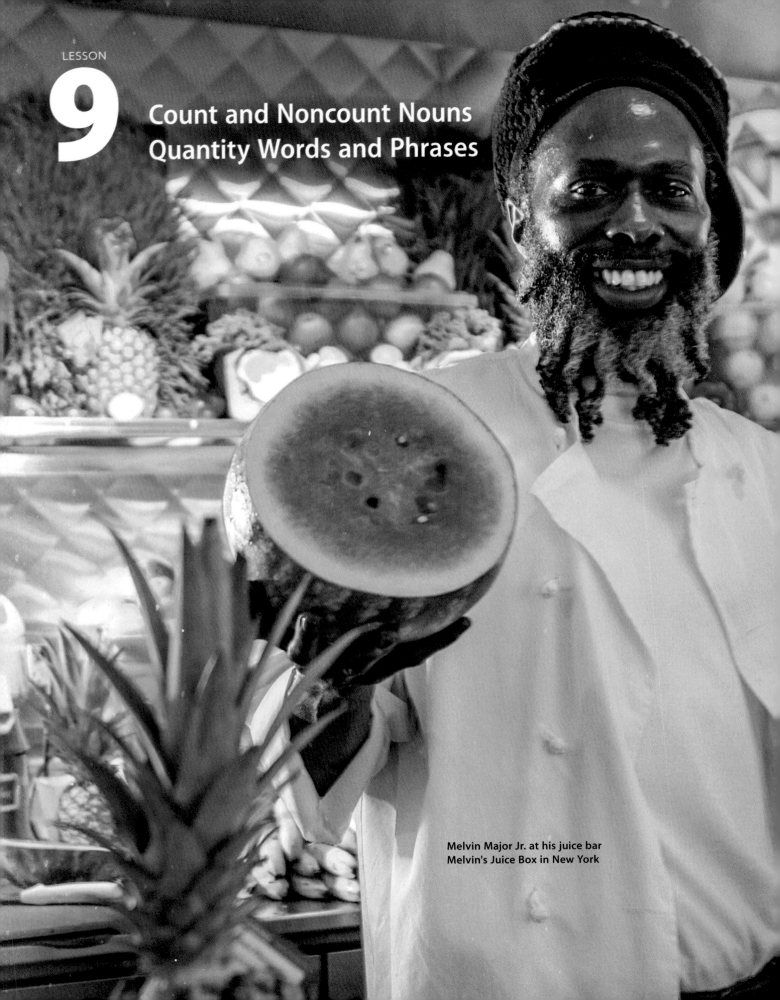

Melvin Major Jr. at his juice bar
Melvin's Juice Box in New York

Don't eat anything your great-grandmother wouldn't recognize as food.

—Michael Pollan

Healthy Living

Prices visible on signs:

1.59 | +3.99 | +3.99 | | Celery Root +1.99 | Sweet Fennel +1.99 | Bunch Beets +1.99 | Daikon Radish +1.59 | Easter Egg Radish +1.29 | Sunchokes +3.99 | Burdock Gobo +4.99

Organic Food

CD 2
TR 9

Read the following article. Pay special attention to the words in bold.

Do you ever buy organic **food**? At one time, you could only find organic **fruits**, **vegetables**, **grains**, dairy **products**, and **meat** in a special **store**. Now more and more **supermarkets** are selling organic **products**. What, exactly, does "organic" mean? How is it different from nonorganic **food**? And why is it so expensive?

Organic **meat**, **eggs**, and dairy **products** come from **animals** raised without growth **hormones**.[1] It takes longer for these **animals** to grow. **Farmers** grow organic **fruits** and **vegetables** without **pesticides**.[2] Farming without **chemicals** requires more **work**, so the **product** is more expensive.

Organic **products** are better not only for your **health** but also for the **health** of the **planet**. Organic farming does less than nonorganic farming to harm the **soil**, the **water**, and the **air**. It is also better for the **workers** on the **farm**. They don't have to breathe harmful **pesticides**.

If a **family** wants to buy organic **food** but can't afford it, what can they do? Some nonorganic **items** have fewer **pesticides** than others. These are **onions**, **avocados**, **corn**, **pineapples**, **cabbage**, **cantaloupe**, **watermelon**, and sweet **potatoes**. If possible, avoid nonorganic **apples**, **strawberries**, **celery**, **peaches**, **spinach**, **blueberries**, and **lettuce**. It is important to wash all fresh **produce** to remove **dirt** and **chemicals**.

Is all organic **food** healthy for you? Not always. Many organic **products** may have a lot of **sugar**, **salt**, **fat**, or **calories**. It's important to check the **ingredients**, even on organic **products**.

Whether you buy organic **food** or not, the healthiest **products** are fresh **products**.

---

[1] *growth hormone*: a chemical that helps animals grow faster
[2] *pesticide*: a chemical used to kill insects

COMPREHENSION CHECK Based on the reading, tell if the statement is true (**T**) or false (**F**).

1. In the United States, you can only find organic food in special stores.

2. Farming with chemicals is easier than farming without chemicals.

3. Workers on nonorganic farms breathe in pesticides.

9.1 Count and Noncount Nouns—An Overview

There are two groups of nouns: count and noncount nouns.

Examples	Explanation
I eat an **apple** every day. She eats two **eggs** for breakfast.	We use a count noun in the singular form or plural form. We can put *a*, *an*, or a number before a count noun.
Do you buy organic **meat**? I like to eat **corn** in the summer.	We use a noncount noun in the singular form only. We don't put *a*, *an*, or a number before a noncount noun.

CD 2
TR 10

EXERCISE 1 Listen to the report. Fill in the blanks with the words you hear.

Packaged _____ at the supermarket have a lot of
            1.

nutrition facts. This _____ can help you make healthy
               2.

_____ . But it can also be confusing. Let's look at some
    3.

of the categories on a package of _____ .
                     4.

- SERVING SIZE. If the package says "serving size: ½ cup" and you use

   a whole cup, double the _____ .
                5.

- CALORIES. This section also shows the number of calories

   from _____ .
        6.

- FAT. Not all _____ are the same. The fat in
              7.

   _____ , olive _____ , and
       8.   **9.**

   _____ is healthy. It helps control cholesterol.
       10.

   Many _____ , potato _____ ,
            11.   **12.**

   and other _____ contain unhealthy fats.
           13.

continued

- SODIUM. Limit your intake of _____. It can raise your blood pressure.[3]

  14.

- CARBOHYDRATES. Carbs[4] give us energy. But there are good carbs and bad carbs. Healthy carbs come from

  _____, _____, _____, and whole _____. Brown

  15.   16.   17.   18.

  _____ is healthier than white rice. Avoid _____ and _____ made

  19.   20.   21.

  from white _____. _____ is a bad carb. It provides empty calories and can lead

  22.   23.

  to type 2 diabetes. _____ also has sugar, but is has _____ and

  24.   25.

  _____, too.

  26.

- PROTEIN. _____, _____, _____, and _____ are

  27.   28.   29.   30.

  healthy sources of protein. Limit red _____.

  31.

9.2 Groups of Noncount Nouns

There are several types of noncount nouns.

Group A: Nouns that have no distinct, separate parts (we look at the whole)				
air	cholesterol	honey	oil	soup
blood	coffee	juice	paper	tea
bread	dirt	meat	rain	water
butter	fat	milk	soil	yogurt
cheese				

Group B: Nouns that have parts too small or insignificant to count							
grass	hair	popcorn	rice	salt	sand	snow	sugar

Group C: Nouns that are classes or categories of things (the members of the group are not the same)	
candy (candy bars, chocolates, mints)	jewelry (necklaces, bracelets, rings)
clothing (sweaters, pants, dresses)	mail (letters, packages, postcards)
fruit (apples, peaches, pears)	money or cash (nickels, dimes, dollars)
furniture (chairs, tables, beds)	poultry (chickens, ducks, turkeys)
homework (essays, exercises, readings)	produce (oranges, apples, corn)

Group D: Nouns that are abstractions				
advice	friendship	intelligence	music	truth
art	fun	knowledge	noise	unemployment
beauty	happiness	life	nutrition	work
education	health	love	patience	
experience	information	luck	pollution	

---

[3] *blood pressure*: measurement of the force in which blood moves through the body

[4] *carb*: an informal word for "carbohydrate"

Group E: Some fruits and vegetables that are usually noncount nouns				
asparagus	cabbage	celery	grapefruit	lettuce
broccoli	cauliflower	corn	kale	spinach

Language Notes:

1. Some nouns work as both count and noncount nouns.

   We ate **chicken** for dinner. (*chicken* = food)

   He has one hundred **chickens** on his farm. (*chickens* = live animals)

2. *Food, fruit, juice,* and *fat* can be count or noncount nouns. As count nouns, they refer to categories or kinds.

   Eggs and cheese are **foods** that contain cholesterol. (*foods* = kinds of food)

   Lemons and oranges are **fruits** that contain vitamin C. (*fruits* = kinds of fruit)

3. When we refer to part of a food, it's a noncount noun. When we refer to the whole, it's a count noun.

   We baked two **pies**. We ate some **pie** for dessert.

   I bought two large **watermelons**. We ate some **watermelon** after dinner.

EXERCISE 2 Complete the chart with the words from the box.

information ✓	chemical	choice ✓	advice	bean	salt	sugar	rice	egg
ingredient	homework	snack	bread	pasta	fruit	meat	dirt	fat
vegetable	cookie	health	peach	work	soil	seed	nut	oil

Noncount Nouns	Count Nouns
information	choice

EXERCISE 3 Fill in the blanks with the noncount nouns from the box.

advice	coffee	milk ✓	salt
candy	information	olive oil	sugar

1. Babies need to drink a lot of _____ milk _____, but adults don't.

2. Children like to eat _____, but it's not good for them. It has a lot of sugar.

3. A lot of people drink _____ in the morning.

4. _____ is a good source of fat.

5. Potato chips contain a lot of _____.

6. Soda and candy contain a lot of _____.

7. You can get _____ about nutrition from a food package.

8. Ask your doctor for _____ about a healthy diet.

EXERCISE 4 A nutritionist (A) is talking to a patient (B) about the patient's eating habits. Fill in the blanks with the singular form of the words given for noncount nouns and the plural form for count nouns.

A: You should eat ____ vegetables ____ every day.
               1. vegetable

B: I eat veggies. I especially love _____.
                          2. potato

A: That's not the best vegetable for you.

B: Why not?

A: They can raise the sugar level in the blood. It's almost like eating _____.
                                                              3. sugar

B: Really? I didn't know that.

A: French _____ are especially bad for you. They contain unhealthy fats, which
           4. fry

    affect your _____. It's better to eat _____, _____,
               5. cholesterol   **6.** carrot   **7.** broccoli

    _____, and _____. Do you eat enough _____?
          8. spinach   **9.** pea   **10.** fruit

B: Yes. I especially love _____, _____, and _____.
                            11. banana   **12.** strawberry   **13.** cherry

A: That's great.

B: I drink a lot of _____ and eat a lot of _____. These are good
                14. milk   **15.** yogurt

    sources of calcium, right?

A: Yes. But it's not clear how much dairy we need. Other sources of calcium are white

_____, _____, and _____.
　　　16. bean　　　　　　　　17. almond　　　　　　　　18. orange

B: I take a lot of _____ and _____. That's good, right?
　　　　　　　　　　　19. vitamin　　　　　　　　20. mineral

A: Yes. But the best source is from _____, not from _____.
　　　　　　　　　　　　　　　21. food　　　　　　　　　　　22. pill

9.3 Units of Measure with Noncount Nouns

We don't use *a/an* or a number before a noncount noun. We use a unit of measure that we can count—for example, two *glasses* of milk. We measure by:

Container	Portion	Measurement	Shape or whole piece	Other
a bottle of water a carton of milk a bag of flour a can of soda (pop) a cup of coffee a glass of juice a bowl of soup a tube of 　toothpaste	a slice/piece of 　bread a piece of meat a slice/piece of cake a slice of pizza a piece of candy	a spoonful of sugar a teaspoon of salt a cup of oil a pound of meat a gallon of milk a pint of ice cream a scoop of ice cream	a loaf of bread an ear of corn a piece of fruit a head of lettuce a bar of soap a stalk of celery a candy bar	a piece of mail a piece of furniture a piece of advice a piece of 　information a work of art a homework 　assignment a piece of paper

Language Note:

We can use *a helping of* or *a serving of* for almost any food.

　　How many *helpings of* fruit did you have today?

EXERCISE 5 Fill in the blanks with a logical unit of measure for the noncount nouns. More than one answer is possible.

1. She drank two _____*cups of*_____ coffee.

2. She ate a _____ meat.

3. She bought two _____ meat.

4. She bought a _____ bread.

5. She ate two _____ bread.

6. She bought a _____ rice.

7. She ate a _____ rice.

8. She put one _____ sugar in her coffee.

9. She ate a _____ soup.

10. She ate two _____ corn.

The IMPORTANCE of WATER

CD 2
TR 11

Read the following article. Pay special attention to the words in bold.

How **much** water should you drink? Four glasses a day? Eight glasses a day? There's **no** easy answer to that question. You sometimes hear, "Drink eight 8-ounce glasses of water every day." We probably need the equivalent[5] of eight glasses of fluid[6] a day. We get **some** water from the food we eat. Watermelon, for example, is 90 percent water. If you drink milk, juice, soda, tea, or coffee, you're also getting water from these sources. Be careful with soda and **some** juices. They can contain **a lot of** sugar, which isn't good for you. The best source of water is water!

Water makes up about 60 percent of your body weight. **Many** factors determine your need for water: your health, your physical activity, and even where you live.

Do you live in a hot or humid climate? Then you probably lose water through sweat. Do you live in a cold climate? Then your house is probably heated in the winter. Heated air dries your skin, so you need **some** water to replace what you lose.

Physically active people (such as people who run marathons) lose **a lot of** water through sweat. They also lose sodium. **Some** athletes use sports drinks because they contain not only water but also sodium. The problem with commercial sports drinks is that they contain **a lot of** sugar. There are **a few** good alternatives[7] to sports drinks: coconut water, raisins, bananas, and watermelon juice. If you look online, you can find **some** good recipes for natural sports drinks. These recipes usually contain **some** honey, **a little** salt, and natural fruit juices like orange juice.

A lot of people use bottled water. However, there isn't **much** proof[8] that bottled water is better than tap water. One thing is for sure: water is important for our health.

---

5 *equivalent*: same amount as
6 *fluid*: liquid
7 *alternative*: another choice
8 *proof*: evidence that something is true

1. Everyone needs eight glasses of water a day.

2. If you live in a hot, humid climate, you lose water through sweat.

3. People who run marathons need to replace not only water but sodium, too.

9.4 *Many*, *Much*, and *A Lot Of* with Large Quantities

We use *many* with count nouns. We use *much* with noncount nouns. We use *a lot of* with both count and noncount nouns.

	Count	Noncount
AFFIRMATIVE STATEMENT	**Many** people use bottled water. **A lot of** people use bottled water.	I drink **a lot of** water.
NEGATIVE STATEMENT	Broccoli doesn't have **many** calories. Broccoli doesn't have **a lot of** calories.	He doesn't drink **much** coffee. He doesn't drink **a lot of** coffee.
QUESTION	Did you buy **many** oranges? Did you buy **a lot of** oranges? **How many** oranges did you buy?	Does he drink **much** water? Does he drink **a lot of** water? **How much** water does he drink?

Language Notes:

1. We don't usually use *much* in affirmative statements. We use *a lot of* in affirmative statements.
2. We can omit the noun after quantity words.

    I don't drink much coffee. Do you drink *much*?
3. When the noun is omitted, we use *a lot*, not *a lot of*.

    I drink **a lot of** water, but she doesn't drink **a lot**.

EXERCISE 6 Fill in the blanks with *much, many, a lot of,* or *a lot*. In some cases, more than one answer is possible.

1. Athletes need to drink _____*a lot of*_____ water.

2. _____ people carry a water bottle with them.

3. Children usually drink _____ milk, but adults don't drink _____.

4. There are _____ sports drinks in the supermarket.

5. I drink _____ coffee in the morning, but I don't drink _____ in the afternoon.

6. Is there _____ water in spinach?

7. How _____ glasses of water did you drink today?

8. How _____ fruit did you eat today?

9. I have _____ recipes for healthy meals.

10. It isn't good to eat _____ candy.

9.5 *A Few* and *A Little* with Small Quantities

We use *a few* with count nouns. We use *a little* with noncount nouns.

Count	Noncount
I ate **a few** raisins.	He put **a little** sugar in the tea.
She keeps **a few** bottles of water in her car.	Do you want **a little** milk in your coffee?

EXERCISE 7 Fill in the blanks with *a few* or *a little*.

1. It's important to eat _____*a little*_____ fruit every day.

2. It's important to eat _____ pieces of fruit every day.

3. I use _____ milk in my coffee.

4. Do you want _____ sugar in your coffee?

5. We put _____ carrots in the soup.

6. We put _____ celery in the soup.

7. We put _____ salt in the soup.

8. After I exercise, I drink _____ glasses of water.

9. Eat _____ raisins after you exercise.

9.6 *A/An, Some, No,* and *Any*

	Singular Count	Plural Count	Noncount
AFFIRMATIVE STATEMENT	I ate **a** peach. I ate **an** apple.	I ate **some** peaches. I ate **some** apples.	I drank **some** water.
QUESTION	Do you want **a** banana?	Do you want **any** raisins? Do you want **some** grapes?	Did you put **any** salt in the soup? Did you put **some** oil in the soup?
NEGATIVE STATEMENT	I didn't buy **a** watermelon.	There aren't **any** potatoes in the soup. There are **no** potatoes in the soup.	There isn't **any** salt in the soup. There is **no** salt in the soup.

Language Notes:

1. We can use *any* or *some* for questions with plural count nouns and noncount nouns.

2. We use *any* after a negative verb. We use *no* after an affirmative verb.

    I didn't eat **any** raisins. OR I ate **no** raisins. (NOT: I *didn't* eat *no* raisins.)

EXERCISE 8 Fill in the blanks with *a, an, some, no,* or *any.* In some cases, more than one answer is possible.

1. I ate _____*an*_____ apple.

2. Did you buy _____ bananas?

3. I didn't buy _____ potatoes.

4. Did you eat _____ fruit today?

5. I didn't put _____ beans in the soup.

6. There are _____ apples in the refrigerator. I bought them yesterday.

7. There are _____ grapes in the refrigerator. We need to buy some.

8. Do you want _____ orange?

9. Do you want _____ cherries?

10. I ate _____ rice.

11. I didn't eat _____ strawberries.

12. There's _____ milk in my coffee. I drink it black.

EXERCISE 9 Fill in the blanks with *a lot of, much, many, some, a little, any,* or *no.* In some cases, more than one answer is possible.

1. Eggs have ____*a lot of*____ cholesterol.

2. You shouldn't eat so much red meat because it has _____ fat.

3. Only animal products contain cholesterol. There is _____ cholesterol in fruit.

4. Diet sodas use a sugar substitute. They don't have _____ sugar.

5. There is _____ sugar in a cracker, but not much.

6. Plain popcorn is healthy, but popcorn with butter has _____ fat.

7. Coffee has caffeine. Tea has _____ caffeine, too, but not as much as coffee.

8. She doesn't drink _____ tea. She usually drinks coffee.

9. I usually put _____ butter on a slice of bread.

10. I put _____ milk in my coffee. Do you want _____ milk for your coffee?

11. My sister is a vegetarian. She doesn't eat _____ meat.

12. Does the cake have _____ sugar?

13. How _____ apples did you use for the apple pie?

EXERCISE 10 About You Find a partner. Ask and answer questions about what you eat and drink. Ask questions with *much*. Use quantity words in your answers.

1. eat/candy

   A: *Do you eat much candy?*

   B: *No. I don't eat any candy.*

2. drink/orange juice

3. eat/rice

4. drink/milk

5. eat/fish

6. eat/chicken

7. eat/bread

8. drink/water

9. eat/cheese

10. drink/apple juice

11. drink/tea

12. eat/cheese

13. drink/soda

EXERCISE 11 Complete the conversation between a husband (A) and wife (B). Choose the correct word(s). If both answers are correct, circle both choices.

A: Where were you today? I called you (*much*/*many*) times, but I just got your voice mail. I left
1.

(*much*/*a lot of*) messages. I started to get worried about you.
2.

B: Sorry. I forgot to take my cell phone. I went to the supermarket today. I bought (*a few*/*a little*) things.
3.

A: What did you buy?

B: There was a sale on coffee, so I bought (*a lot of*/*much*) coffee. I didn't buy (*any*/*no*) strawberries
4.   5.

because the price was too high. I bought (*some*/*any*) grapes instead. And I bought (*a*/*any*)
6.   7.

watermelon, too.

A: How (*much*/*many*) money did you spend?
8.

B: I spent (*much*/*a lot of*) money because of the coffee. I bought five one-pound bags.
9.

A: It took you a long time.

B: Yes. There were (*a lot of*/*many*) people in the store. And there was (*a lot of*/*much*) traffic, so it
10.   11.

took me (*a lot of*/*much*) time to drive home.
12.

A: There's not (*much/many*) time to cook dinner.
　　　　　　　　　　　　13.

B: Maybe you can cook today and let me rest.

A: I don't have (*any/no*) time. I have (*a lot of/a lot*) work to do. I have to finish a report.
　　　　　　　　　14.　　　　　　　　　　　　　15.

B: Maybe we should just order a pizza tonight.

EXERCISE 12 Complete the conversation between a server (A) and two customers (B) and (C) in a restaurant. Fill in the blanks with an appropriate quantity word. In some cases, more than one answer is possible.

A: We have _____*some*_____ specials today. Would you like to hear about them?
　　　　　　　　1.

B: No, thank you. For now, we'd both like _____ coffee, please.
　　　　　　　　　　　　　　　　　　　　　　　　　2.

A: Do you want _____ cream for your coffee?
　　　　　　　　　　　　　3.

B: Yes. I'd like _____ cream.
　　　　　　　　　　　4.

C: I don't need _____ cream. I like my coffee black.
　　　　　　　　　　　5.

A: Are you ready to order now?

C: We need _____ more time to decide.
　　　　　　　　6.

continued

A few minutes later:

A: Can I take your order now?

B: Yes. I'd like the scrambled eggs and a _____ toast. I'd also like

                               7.

_____ orange juice.

        8.

A: Do you want _____ butter or jam with your toast?

                      9.

B: No, thanks.

A: And you, sir?

C: I'd like _____ pancakes.

             10.

A: Do you want _____ syrup with your pancakes?

                11.

C: Yes, please.

Later:

A: Would you like _____ dessert?

               12.

C: What do you have?

A: We have a fresh cherry pie. We have a special today: a _____ pie with a

                                13.

_____ of ice cream for only $1.99.

       14.

B: We're trying to lose weight. Do you have _____ other choices?

                           15.

A: We have _____ fresh fruit.

        16.

C: That sounds good. Please bring us one _____ of fruit and two spoons.

                      17.

We can share. And we'd like _____ more coffee, please.

                18.

After the customers finish eating:

A: Would you like anything else?

B: Just the check. I don't have _____ cash with me. Can I pay with a credit card?

                      19.

A: Of course.

EAT Less, LIVE Longer

Read the following article. Pay special attention to the words in bold.

About 68 percent of Americans are overweight. The typical American consumes[9] **too many** calories and **too much** fat and doesn't get enough exercise. Many American children are overweight, too. About one-quarter of 2- to 5-year-olds and one-third of school-age children are overweight or obese[10] in the United States. Children spend **too many** hours watching TV and not enough time getting exercise. They see **too many** commercials for food products every day. Ninety-eight percent of food commercials during children's TV shows are for foods that have a lot of fat, sugar, or sodium.

Eating fewer calories can help us live longer. Doctors studied people on the Japanese island of Okinawa. Okinawans eat 40 percent less than the typical American. The Okinawan diet is low in calories and salt. Okinawans also eat **a lot of** fruit, vegetables, and fish and drink **a lot of** green tea and water. Many Okinawans in their 80s have excellent health. Okinawa has **a lot of** people over the age of 100—two and a half times the average in the United States. However, as younger Okinawans start to eat like Westerners, they will probably have much shorter lives than their grandparents.

How can we live longer and healthier lives? The answer is simple: eat less and exercise more.

---

9   *to consume*: to eat or drink
10 *obese*: very overweight

An 89-year-old Okinawan gathers seaweed.

COMPREHENSION CHECK Based on the reading, tell if the statement is true (**T**) or false (**F**).

1. The majority of Americans are overweight.

2. Children see a lot of commercials for food on TV.

3. Okinawans usually live longer than Americans.

9.7 *A Lot Of* and *Too Much/Too Many*

Examples	Explanation
There are **a lot of** healthy older people in Okinawa. I don't eat **a lot** in the morning.	We use *a lot (of)* to show a large quantity. It is a neutral term.
I ate **too many** cookies. Now I don't feel well. If you drink **too much** coffee, you won't sleep tonight.	*Too much* and *too many* show that a quantity is excessive and causes a problem. We use *too many* with count nouns. We use *too much* with noncount nouns.
If you eat **too much**, you will gain weight.	We use *too much* after a verb.

EXERCISE 13 Complete the conversation between a mother (A) and her 12-year-old son (B). Choose the correct word(s).

A: I'm worried about you. You spend too (*much*/*many*) hours watching TV. And you eat too
  _1._

  (*much*/*many*) junk food and don't get enough exercise. You're gaining weight.
  _2._

B: Mom, I know I watch (*a lot of*/*a lot*) TV, but I learn (*a lot of*/*a lot*) from TV.
  _3._   _4._

A: No, you don't. Sometimes you have (*a lot of*/*too much*) homework, but you turn on the TV
  _5._

  as soon as you get home from school. I'm going to make a rule: no TV until you finish

  your homework.

B: Oh, Mom. You have too (*much*/*many*) rules.
  _6._

A: There are (*a lot of*/*too many*) things to do besides watching TV. Why don't you go outside
  _7._

  and play? When I was your age, we played outside.

B: "When I was your age." Not again. You always say that.

A: Well, it's true. We had (*too much*/*a lot of*) fun outside playing with friends. I didn't have
  _8._

  (*a lot of*/*too much*) toys when I was your age. Also, we helped our parents (*a lot*/*too much*)
  _9._   _10._

  after school. We cleaned the house and washed the dishes.

B: My friend Josh cleans the basement and takes out the garbage. His mom pays him

(*too much/a lot of*) money for doing those things.
　　　　　11.

A: You're not Josh, and I'm not Josh's mother. I'm not going to pay you for things you should do.

B: OK. Just tell me what to do, and I'll do it.

A: There are (*a lot of/too much*) leaves in the yard. Why don't you put them in garbage bags?
　　　　　　　　　12.

And you can walk the dog, too. He's getting fat. He eats (*too much/too many*) and sleeps
　　　　　　　　　　　　　　　　　　　　　　　　13.

all day. Both of you need more exercise.

EXERCISE 14 About You Fill in the blanks to make true statements about yourself. Then find a partner and discuss your answers.

1. I sometimes eat too much _____.

2. I sometimes drink too much _____.

3. I sometimes watch too many _____.

9.8 *Too* and *Too Much/Too Many*

Examples	Explanation
The potatoes are **too** salty. I can't eat them. Please walk faster. You walk **too** slowly.	We use *too* with adjectives and adverbs.
I don't eat ice cream because it has **too much** fat and **too many** calories.	We use *too much* before noncount nouns. We use *too many* before count nouns.

Language Note:

We often use *too, too much,* and *too many* to complain about something.

　　This tea has **too much** sugar. I can't drink it.

EXERCISE 15 A group of students is complaining about the school cafeteria. They are giving reasons why they don't want to eat there. Fill in the blanks with *too, too much,* or *too many.*

1. The food is _____ *too* _____ greasy.

2. There are _____ students there.

3. The lines move _____ slowly.

4. The food is _____ expensive.

5. There's _____ noise.

6. They put _____ salt in the food.

EXERCISE 16 Fill in the blanks with *too, too much,* or *too many* if a problem is presented. Use *a lot (of)* if a problem is not presented.

1. Strawberries are _____*too*_____ expensive this week. Let's not buy them.

2. Some kids spend _____ time watching TV. They don't get enough exercise.

3. Oranges have _____ vitamin C.

4. I don't eat potato chips. They have _____ calories and

   _____ fat.

5. Babies drink _____ milk.

6. If you drink _____ coffee, you won't sleep.

7. If you exercise, you need to drink _____ water.

8. I exercised _____, and now I feel much better.

9. _____ older Okinawans are very healthy.

EXERCISE 17 Complete the conversation between a doctor (A) and a patient (B). Fill in the blanks with an appropriate quantity word or unit of measure. In some cases, more than one answer is possible.

A: I'm looking at your lab results, and I see that your cholesterol level is very high. Also your blood

   pressure is _____*too*_____ high. Do you use _____

   _{1.}   _{2.}

   salt on your food?

B: Yes, Doctor. I love salt. I eat _____ potato chips and popcorn.

   _{3.}

A: That's not good. What else do you usually eat?

B: For breakfast I usually have _____ coffee and a doughnut. I don't

   _{4.}

   have _____ time for lunch, so I eat _____

   _{5.}   _{6.}

   cookies and drink _____ soda while I'm working. I'm so busy that I

   _{7.}

   have _____ time to cook at all. So for dinner, I usually stop at a

   _{8.}

   fast-food place and get a burger and fries.

A: That's a terrible diet! How _____ exercise do you get?

   _{9.}

B: I never exercise. I don't have _____ time at all. I own my own

   _{10.}

   business, and I have _____ work. Sometimes I work 80 hours

   _{11.}

   a week.

A: I'm going to give you an important _____ advice. You're going to

12.

have to change your lifestyle.

B: I'm _____ old to change my habits.

13.

A: That's not true. I'm going to give you a booklet about staying healthy. It has

_____ information that will teach you about diet and exercise.

14.

Please read it and come back in three months.

EXERCISE 18 About You Write three sentences of advice about being healthy. Use quantity words and units of measure. Then find a partner and compare your sentences.

1. _____

_____

2. _____

_____

3. _____

_____

Quantity Words and Phrases with Count and Noncount Nouns

Quantity Words and Phrases	Singular Count EXAMPLE: *grape*	Plural Count EXAMPLE: *grapes*	Noncount EXAMPLE: *milk*
the	✓	✓	✓
a/an	✓		
one	✓		
two, three, etc.		✓	
some (with affirmative statements and questions)		✓	✓
any (with negative statements and questions)		✓	✓
no	✓	✓	✓
a lot of		✓	✓
much (with negative statements and questions)			✓
many		✓	
a little			✓
a few		✓	
several		✓	

TEST / REVIEW

Choose the correct word(s) to complete the essay.

I had (*some*/*any*/*a little*) problems when I first came to the United States. First, I didn't

1.

have (*much*/*a*/*some*) money. (*A few*/*A little*/*A few of*) friends of mine lent me (*some*/*a*/*any*)

2. 3. 4.

money, but I didn't feel good about borrowing it.

Second, I couldn't find (*a*/*an*/*no*) apartment. I went to see (*some*/*a little*/*an*) apartments,

5. 6.

but I couldn't afford (*not any*/*any*/*none*) of them. For (*a little*/*a few of*/*a few*) months, I had to

7. 8.

live with my uncle's family, but the situation wasn't good.

Third, I started to study English, but I soon found (*a*/*any*/*some*) job and had

9.

(*no*/*any*/*not any*) time to study. I work (*a lot of*/*too much*/*a lot*) and earn enough for my

10. 11.

apartment and other expenses, but I don't have (*no*/*any*/*some*) free time.

12.

Fourth, I'm gaining weight. I started eating (*much*/*many*/*a lot of*) junk food. I know I

13.

should eat a healthier diet, but I don't have time to cook. In the morning, I just have

(*a cup of coffee*/*a cup coffee*/*cup of coffee*) and run out the door. I know I should get

14.

(*some*/*much*/*a few*) exercise every day, but I just don't have the time. I have

15.

(*too much*/*too many*/*a lot*) things to do.

16.

Little by little my life is starting to improve. I'm saving (*a few*/*a little*/*a*) money and

17.

starting to eat better.

WRITING

PART 1 Editing Advice

1. Don't put *a* or *an* before a noncount noun.

   some
   My doctor gave me ~~an~~ advice about nutrition.

2. Don't use the plural form with noncount nouns.

   glasses of water
   He drank three ~~waters~~ today.

3. Don't use a double negative.

   any
   He doesn't have ~~no~~ time for breakfast. OR He has no time for breakfast.

4. Don't use *much* with an affirmative statement.

   a lot of
   We prepared ~~much~~ soup.

5. Don't use *a* or *an* before a plural noun.

   He ate ~~a~~ potato chips with his sandwich.

6. Use the plural form with plural count nouns.

   s
   He ate a lot of grape.

7. Omit *of* after *a lot* when the noun is omitted.

   I drank a lot of water yesterday, but I didn't drink a lot ~~of~~ today.

8. Use *of* with a unit of measure.

   of
   I ate two pieces bread.

9. Don't use *of* after *many, much, a few*, or *a little* if a noun follows directly.

   He put a little ~~of~~ milk in his coffee.

10. Only use *too/too much/too many* if there is a problem.

    very   *a lot of*
    My grandfather is ~~too~~ healthy. He gets ~~too much~~ exercise.

11. Don't use *too much* before an adjective or an adverb. Use *too*.

    I can't exercise today. I'm too ~~much~~ tired.

    You're walking too ~~much~~ slowly.

PART 2 Editing Practice

Some of the shaded words and phrases have mistakes. Find the mistakes and correct them. If the shaded words are correct, write *C*.

My parents gave me a̶ good advice: stay healthy. They told me to get good nutrition and to
1.   *C* **2.**

exercise every day. My parents follow their own advice, and, as a result, they're too healthy.
3.

I try to follow their advices, but sometimes I can't. I'm very busy, and sometimes I don't have
4.

no time for exercise. When I was in high school, I had a lot of free time, but now I don't have
5.

a lot of. So for breakfast, I just have a cup coffee with a little of sugar and two pieces of toast.
6.   **7.**   **8.**   **9.**

I have a lot of friend at college, and we often go out to eat after class. They always want
10.

to go to a fast food places. I know the food is too much greasy. When I suggest healthier
11.   **12.**

restaurants, they say they're too expensive. When I get home from work at night, I just heat up
13.

a frozen dinner. I know this is not healthy, but what can I do?

PART 3 Write About It

1. Describe your eating habits in a typical day.

2. Describe food and eating habits in your native country or culture. What is a typical breakfast, lunch, and dinner? What times do people eat? Do people generally eat a healthy diet?

PART 4 Edit Your Writing

Reread the Summary of Lesson 9 and the editing advice. Edit your writing from Part 3.

10 Adjectives and Adverbs
Noun Modifiers
Too/Very/Enough

Dr. Pardis Sabeti, a computational biologist, uses genetic research to fight diseases such as Ebola.

Arrays
Unit B

GREAT WOMEN

Women must try to do things as men have tried. When they fail, their failure must be but a challenge to others.

—Amelia Earhart

Helen Keller

Read the following article. Pay special attention to the words in bold.

Do you know of anyone with a disability[1] who did **remarkable** things? Helen Keller was a truly **amazing** woman.

Helen Keller was a **healthy** baby. But when she was 19 months old, she had a **sudden** fever.[2] The fever disappeared, but she became **blind** and **deaf**. Because she couldn't hear, it was **difficult** for her to learn to speak. As she grew, she was **angry** and **frustrated**[3] because she couldn't understand or communicate. She became **wild**, throwing things and kicking and biting.

When Helen was seven years old, a teacher, Anne Sullivan, came to live with Helen's family. First, Anne taught Helen how to talk with her fingers. Helen was **excited** when she realized that things had names. Then Anne taught Helen to read using the braille system. Helen learned these skills **quickly**. However, learning to speak was harder. Anne continued to teach Helen **patiently**. Finally, when Helen was ten years old, she could speak **clearly** enough for people to understand her.

Helen was very **intelligent**. She went to a school for blind students, where she did very **well**. Then she went to college, where she graduated with honors[4] when she was 24 years old. Helen traveled all over the United States, Europe, and Asia with Anne to raise money to build schools for **blind** people. Her **main** message was that **disabled** people are like everybody else. They want to live life **fully** and **naturally**. Helen wanted all people to be treated **equally**.

Anne Sullivan "talking" to Helen Keller using her fingers

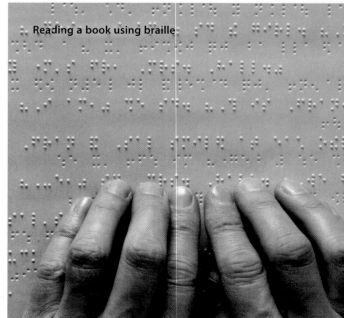

Reading a book using braille

---

[1] *disability*: a physical or mental limitation
[2] *fever*: a body temperature that is higher than normal
[3] *frustrated*: angry at being unable to do something
[4] *with honors*: having high academic grades

COMPREHENSION CHECK Based on the reading, tell if the statement is true (**T**) or false (**F**).

1. Helen Keller learned to speak when she was seven years old.

2. Anne Sullivan was Helen's teacher.

3. Helen raised money to build schools for blind people.

10.1 Adjectives; Adverbs of Manner

Examples	Explanation
Helen was a **healthy** baby. She seemed **intelligent**. She became **blind**. Anne was a **wonderful** teacher.	Adjectives describe nouns. We can use adjectives before nouns or after the verbs *be, become, look, seem, sound, taste, feel,* and *smell.*
Anne taught Helen **patiently**. Helen learned **quickly**. People want to live life **fully**.	Adverbs of manner tell how we do things. We form most adverbs of manner by putting *-ly* at the end of an adjective.

EXERCISE 1 Listen to the report. Fill in the blanks with the words you hear.

CD 2
TR 14

A _____ site in Washington, DC, is the Vietnam Veterans[5] War Memorial.
     1.

Four million people visit it _____ . It is _____ and
                              2.   3.

_____ with the names of _____ soldiers from the war carved
     4.   5.

into _____ stone. Who created this _____ memorial? Was it a
        6.   7.

_____ artist? No. It was Maya Lin, a 21-year-old student at Yale University.
     8.

In 1980, there was a _____ contest to create a memorial. Lin went to
                          9.

Washington to study the space _____ . She wanted visitors to a war
                                   10.

memorial to look at death _____ . A committee looked at almost 1,500
                              11.

applications and thought Lin's design was _____ . She won. Was she
                                               12.

_____ to win? Yes, of course. But some war veterans protested
     13.

_____ against her _____ design. They wanted a more
     14.   15.

_____ design: statues of soldiers with an _____ flag.
     16.   17.

But Lin's design became a reality. In 1982, the memorial was finished. Lin continues

to create _____ works of art.
              18.

Maya Lin

---

[5] *veteran:* someone who was in the military

EXERCISE 2 Label the words you wrote in Exercise 1 as adjectives (adj) or adverbs (adv).

1. _____adj_____   6. _____   11. _____   16. _____

2. _____   7. _____   12. _____   17. _____

3. _____   8. _____   13. _____   18. _____

4. _____   9. _____   14. _____

5. _____   10. _____   15. _____

10.2 Adjectives

Examples	Explanation	
Anne was a **good** friend to Helen. I have many **good** friends.	Adjectives are always singular.	
Helen Keller felt **frustrated** when she couldn't communicate. Maya Lin was **excited** to win the contest.	Some -ed words are adjectives: *married, divorced, educated, excited, frustrated, disabled, worried, finished, tired, crowded*.	
Helen had an **interesting** life. She was an **amazing** woman.	Some -ing words are adjectives: *interesting, boring, amazing, exciting*.	
The War Memorial is a **very** popular site.	We can put *very* before an adjective.	
Helen was a **normal**, **healthy** baby. The War Memorial has a **simple**, **beautiful** design.	We can put two adjectives before a noun. We sometimes separate the two adjectives with a comma.	
Some people have an easy childhood. Helen had a hard **one**. What about the other designs? Were there other good **ones**?	After an adjective, we can substitute a singular noun with *one* or a plural noun with *ones* to avoid repeating the noun.	

EXERCISE 3 Fill in the blanks with the adjectives from the box.

blind	excited	frustrated	intelligent	traditional	wild
dead	equal	healthy ✓	patient	unusual	young

1. Helen Keller was a _____healthy_____ baby.

2. Before Helen learned to communicate, she felt _____.

3. She became _____, sometimes throwing things.

4. Helen's teacher, Anne Sullivan, was a _____ person.

5. When Helen learned to communicate, she became _____.

6. Helen was _____ and did well in school.

7. _____ people learn to read with the braille method.

8. Helen wanted _____ treatment for blind people.

9. Maya Lin was very _____ when she won the contest. She was only 21.

10. Her design was _____ because it didn't show soldiers and flags.

11. Some people didn't like her design. They wanted a more _____ design.

12. The War Memorial has the names of _____ soldiers.

EXERCISE 4 About You Complete each statement with your opinion. Then find a partner and compare your answers.

1. In my opinion, _____ is a great person.

2. I think _____ is a popular place.

3. I think _____ is a patient person.

4. In my opinion, _____ is a beautiful monument.

5. I think _____ is an unusual woman.

EXERCISE 5 Fill in the blanks with the adjectives from the box. Add *one* or *ones*.

great	long	new	patient	serious ✓	simple

1. **A:** I prefer funny stories.

   B: I don't. I prefer _____*serious ones*_____. I especially liked the story of Maya Lin.

2. **A:** I'm reading a book about Helen Keller. It has over 400 pages.

   B: Wow! It's a _____ .

3. **A:** Do you have any good ideas for your next essay?

   B: I have a _____ . I'm going to write about a remarkable woman.

4. **A:** I don't like strict teachers.

   B: I don't either. I prefer _____ .

5. **A:** Many traditional war memorials have soldiers and flags.

   B: I prefer _____ , like the Vietnam Memorial in Washington, DC.

6. **A:** Maya Lin designed many memorials.

   B: I know. When is she going to design a _____ ?

Lilly Ledbetter

🎧 CD 2 TR 15

Read the following article. Pay special attention to the words in bold.

For every dollar a man makes in the United States, a woman makes 78 cents. Even a woman with a **college** education makes 7 percent less than a college-educated man in a similar position.

Lilly Ledbetter started to work as a manager at a **tire** company in 1979. At that time, her boss told her a **company** rule: Employees must not discuss **salary** information with each other. Nineteen years later, a coworker told her that three men in similar positions made as much as 40 percent more than Ledbetter.

How could this happen? She was a good worker. In fact, one year she won the top **performance** award.[6] She often worked 12-**hour** shifts[7] as a **night** supervisor to earn **overtime** pay. She had a lot of expenses: **house** and **car** payments and **college** tuition for her kids. As a result of her lower salary all these years, her **retirement** benefits would be less. Ledbetter was angry.

She decided to fight back. She sued[8] the company. The company moved her to a job lifting 80-**pound** tires. (She was 60 years old at the time.) Her case went all the way to the Supreme Court in 2006, but she lost. The Court said it was too late to sue. The limit is 180 days.

Ledbetter didn't give up.[9] She explained to members of Congress how unequal pay affects all women. In 2009, Congress and President Barack Obama finally passed a law called the "Lilly Ledbetter Fair Pay Act." This law says that employees can report discrimination[10] if they discover unfairness not just 180 days after the first **pay**check, but 180 days after *any* **pay**check.

Ledbetter didn't benefit from her fight. She received nothing from the company. But she said, "I'm just thrilled[11] that this has finally passed and sends a message to the Supreme Court: You got it wrong."

---

6 *performance award*: an award for excellent work
7 *shift*: a period of paid work time
8 *to sue*: to go to court to get money from someone who caused you damage or suffering
9 *to give up*: to stop doing something
10 *discrimination*: unfair treatment because of race, gender, or religion
11 *thrilled*: very excited and happy

Lilly Ledbetter in front of the tire company she worked for

COMPREHENSION CHECK Based on the reading, tell if the statement is true (**T**) or false (**F**).

1. When Lilly Ledbetter started her job, she had to lift heavy tires.

2. The company didn't let employees discuss their salaries.

3. Ledbetter won her Supreme Court case.

10.3 Noun Modifiers

Examples	Explanation
Workers couldn't discuss **salary** information. Ledbetter had to make **car** payments.	We can use a noun to describe another noun. The first noun acts as an adjective.
Ledbetter's **law**suit went to the Supreme Court. How much did she get in each **pay**check?	Sometimes we write the two nouns as one word. The noun modifier and the noun become a compound noun.
Ledbetter didn't have a **college** education. Some students go to a **city** college.	The first noun is more specific than the second noun. A *college education* is a specific kind of education. A *city college* is a specific kind of college.
She put money in her **checking** account.	Sometimes the first noun ends in *-ing*.
Maya Lin finished her **master's** degree.	Sometimes the first noun ends in *'s*.
A company that makes tires is a **tire** company. A tire that is 80 pounds is an 80-**pound** tire. A woman who is 60 years old is a 60-**year**-old woman.	When two nouns come together, the first noun is always singular. When we use a number before the noun, we usually attach it to the noun with a hyphen.

Language Note:

There are many noun + noun combinations. Here are some common ones:

art museum	driver's license	haircut	summer vacation
bachelor's degree	drugstore	master's degree	text message
baking dish	earring	math course	TV show
cell phone	eyebrow	reading glasses	washing machine
daylight	fingernail	running shoes	wedding ring
dishwasher	flashlight	skiing accident	winter coat
doorknob	garbage can	shopping cart	

EXERCISE 6 Complete each statement with a noun + noun combination.

1. A memorial about war is a _____war memorial_____.

2. A student in college is a _____.

3. Language that communicates with signs is _____.

4. Sight with eyes is _____. (*one word*)

5. A wall made from stone is a _____.

6. A store that sells books is a _____. (*one word*)

continued

7. A woman who is 60 years old is a _____ .

8. A box for mail is a _____ . (*one word*)

9. A shift of twelve hours is a _____ .

10. A student with honors is an _____ .

EXERCISE 7 Fill in the blanks by putting the words given in the correct order. Make any necessary changes to the nouns. Choose the correct article (*a* or *an*) where you see a choice.

Last night I saw a _____TV program_____ about the Paralympic Games. In the
                  1. program/TV

Paralympic Games, athletes with physical disabilities compete. One of the athletes in the

program was Christina Ripp Schwab. Christina is in a _____ .
                                        2. chair/wheels (*one word*)

But that didn't stop her from becoming a _____ .
                                  3. player/basketball

She became interested in basketball when she was just a

_____ . She played on her _____ at
      4. child/10 years old   5. team/college

the University of Illinois. In 2005, she got her _____
                                      6. degree/bachelor's

in _____ . In 2008, she won a _____ at the
        7. community/health   8. medal/gold

Paralympic Games in China.

Christina Ripp Schwab plays for the U.S. at the 2008 Beijing Paralympic Games.

Another great athlete from the Paralympic Games is Gina McWilliams.

As a child, she loved sports, but when she was 26 years old, she was in a/an

_____ and lost part of her right leg. She tried many sports before
        9. accident/car

deciding on floor volleyball. At the 2008 Paralympic Games, she and her team won the

_____ . Now Gina works as a/an _____
        10. silver/medal   **11.** athletic/director

for disabled adults and children.

10.4 Adverbs

Examples	Explanation
Lilly Ledbetter acted **responsibly**. The company treated women **unfairly**. Helen Keller learned sign language **quickly**.	An adverb of manner tells how we do something. It usually follows the verb phrase. We form most adverbs of manner by putting *-ly* at the end of an adjective.
She was **probably** happy with the new law. **Eventually**, Ledbetter's case went to the Supreme Court. **Unfortunately**, she didn't win her case.	Other common *–ly* adverbs are *eventually, annually, frequently, certainly, suddenly, recently, directly, completely, generally, repeatedly, naturally, finally, probably, (un)fortunately, extremely, constantly*.
She worked **hard**. (adverb) She had a **hard** job. (adjective) She wakes up **early**. (adverb) She has an **early** shift. (adjective)	Some adverbs and adjectives have the same form: *hard, fast, late, early*.
She did **well** in school. (adverb) She went to a **good** school. (adjective)	The adverb *well* is completely different in form from the adjective *good*.
The company treated her **very** badly.	We can use *very* before an adverb.

Language Notes:

1. The adverbs *hard* and *hardly* have different meanings.

    She works 12 hours a night. She works *hard*.

    I *hardly* ever work overtime. (*hardly ever* = almost never; rarely)

2. The adverbs *late* and *lately* have different meanings.

    She came home after midnight. She came home *late*.

    She doesn't have much interest in her job *lately*. (*lately* = recently)

3. *Real* is an adjective. *Really* is an adverb. In conversation, many people use *real* in place of *really*.

    Her job was *real* hard. (conversational English)

    Her job was *really* hard. (formal English)

EXERCISE 8 Choose the correct words to complete each conversation.

1. **A:** Anne Sullivan was a (*great*/*greatly*) teacher.

   B: I agree. She taught Helen Keller (*patient*/*patiently*).

2. **A:** Did Helen learn (*quick*/*quickly*)?

   B: Yes, she did. But she never learned to speak (*clear*/*clearly*).

3. **A:** Did Helen do (*good*/*well*) in college?

   B: Yes. She was an (*excellent*/*excellently*) student.

4. **A:** Maya Lin's War Memorial is very (*beautiful*/*beautifully*).

   B: I agree. It deals with death (*honest*/*honestly*).

5. **A:** Did Lilly Ledbetter benefit (*direct*/*directly*) from her fight for equality for women?

   B: No, she didn't, (*unfortunate*/*unfortunately*). She learned about her pay inequality (*late*/*lately*).

6. **A:** Lilly Ledbetter worked (*hard*/*hardly*).

   B: I know. She felt (*happy*/*happily*) when the Fair Pay Act (*final*/*finally*) passed in Congress.

   But equal pay for women isn't changing (*fast*/*fastly*).

7. **A:** I work the night shift and sleep in the day. I (*hard*/*hardly*) ever have time to see my family.

   B: That's (*certain*/*certainly*) a difficult way to live.

10.5 Spelling of -*ly* Adverbs

Adjective Ending	Adjective	Rule	Adverb
Most endings	glad honest	Add -*ly*.	glad**ly** honest**ly**
y	easy lucky	Change *y* to *i* and add -*ly*.	eas**ily** luck**ily**
consonant + *le*	simple comfortable	Drop the *e* and add -*y*.	simpl**y** comfortabl**y**
ll	full	Add -*y*.	full**y**
e	nice free	Add -*ly*.*	nice**ly** free**ly**

Language Note:

* One common exception is: *true—truly*.

EXERCISE 9 Write the adverb form of each adjective.

1. bad _____badly_____
2. good _____
3. lazy _____
4. true _____
5. brave _____
6. full _____
7. probable _____

8. polite _____
9. fast _____
10. constant _____
11. terrible _____
12. beautiful _____
13. responsible _____
14. early _____

EXERCISE 10 Fill in the blanks with the adverb form of the adjectives given.

1. Congress _____finally_____ passed a new law.
          final
2. Companies should treat everyone _____.
                                          equal
3. Lilly Ledbetter works _____ for women's rights.
                              hard
4. At first, Helen Keller didn't learn to talk _____.
                                                      easy
5. She wanted to live life _____.
                                full
6. Maya Lin studied the space in Washington _____.
                                                  careful
7. She designed the wall _____.
                              simple
8. Four million people visit the Vietnam War Memorial _____.
                                                            annual
9. At first, some people protested _____ against Maya Lin's memorial.
                                          strong
10. When you visit the wall, you will _____ feel sad.
                                            probable
11. The wall is _____ beautiful.
                      real

EXERCISE 11 Fill in the blanks with the adjectives given, or change the adjectives to adverbs if necessary.

I know two people who are opposites. One is my coworker Paula. She complains

____constantly____ about everything. She's never _____. She says that
  1. constant   2. happy

everyone is _____. When she drives, she behaves _____ to other
                3. impolite   4. rude

drivers. She says nobody drives _____. She finds something wrong with
                                      5. good

everyone. I met her for lunch last week. I arrived about 5 minutes _____, and
                                                                          6. late

she was _____ with me.
              7. angry

continued

My friend Karla is _____ different from Paula. She works
8. complete

_____ but never complains. She has a _____ attitude about life.
9. hard   **10.** positive

She's an _____ person and travels _____. She's always learning
11. active   **12.** frequent

new things. She's studying French and can speak it _____ now. She learns
13. fluent

_____ and is _____ about everything. She goes to museums
14. quick   **15.** curious

_____ and knows a lot about art. She is a _____ friend.
16. frequent   **17.** good

EXERCISE 12 Choose the correct words to complete this report.

When Helen Keller was a (~~small child~~/child small), she behaved (wild/wildly) because she
1.   **2.**

couldn't communicate (good/well) with her family. When she was seven years old, her parents
3.

found a (good/well) teacher, Anne Sullivan, to work with her.
4.

Anne was from a (poorly/poor) immigrant family. She had a (hard/hardly) life.
5.   **6.**

When she was a child, she had a disease that made her almost blind. When she was an

eight-(year/years)-old girl, her mother died. A few years later, her father left the family.
7.

When she was 14 years old, she could not see (clear/clearly) and she could not read. But
8.

she got the opportunity to go to a school for blind students. At the age of 14, she started

(school elementary/elementary school). She was (intelligent/intelligently) and graduated from
9.   **10.**

high school as the best student.

After graduation, she heard about a job to teach a blind girl, Helen Keller. Anne went to

live with Helen's family. Anne taught Helen that things had names. Within a month, Helen

learned (signs/sign) language. After that, Helen learned (quick/quickly) and wanted to study
11.   **12.**

in school. Anne attended (classes college/college classes) with Helen, spelling out the lectures
13.

and reading to her after class. She continued to help Helen for the rest of her life. Her

(sight eyes/eyesight) became worse, and she became (complete/completely) blind. She died
14.   **15.**

in 1936. Helen lived until 1968.

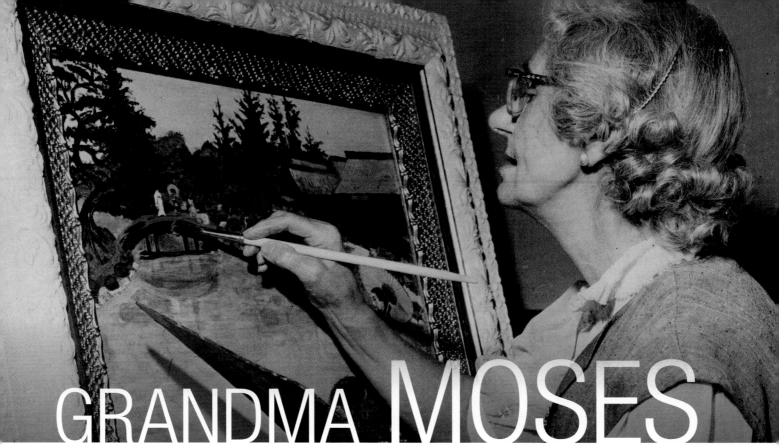

GRANDMA MOSES

 Read the following article. Pay special attention to the words in bold.

CD 2
TR 16

Anna Mary Robertson was born in 1860. She had a **very** hard life. She didn't have much formal education. At the age of 12, she started to work as a housekeeper in farmers' homes. One of her employers noticed that Anna Mary was interested in art and gave her some art materials.

When she was 27 years old, Anna Mary met Thomas Moses, who worked on the same farm. They got married and started to raise a family. They continued to work on other people's farms. Anna Mary was interested in art, but she was **too** busy working and raising their five children to paint. She and her husband eventually saved **enough** money to buy their own farm. Their children grew up and Thomas died. Anna Mary continued to take care of the farm.

When Anna Mary Moses was in her seventies, she became **too** weak to do farm work. She liked to do embroidery,[12] but as she grew older, she couldn't continue because of arthritis, which caused her pain in her joints. It was **too** hard for her to work with a needle. Her sister suggested that she try painting.

It was easy **enough** for Anna Mary to hold a paintbrush. She painted pictures of farm life. Louis Caldor, a New York City art collector, saw her paintings in a store window and bought them. He took them to galleries and museums in New York City. At first, the owners of the galleries weren't interested. They said that at 78 years old, Anna Moses was **too** old and her career would be **too** short. But Caldor didn't stop trying to show her paintings. Soon galleries and museums started to become interested. Because she started painting late in life, newspapers started calling her "Grandma Moses."

When she was 92, Grandma Moses wrote her autobiography.[13] At the age of 100, she illustrated[14] a book. She was still painting until her death at age 101. Grandma Moses created 1,600 paintings.

---

[12] *embroidery*: the art of sewing a design on cloth
[13] *autobiography*: a person's written story about his or her life
[14] *to illustrate*: to make drawings

COMPREHENSION CHECK Based on the reading, tell if the statement is true (**T**) or false (**F**).

1. Anna Mary started to paint when she was in school.

2. She continued to do embroidery even when she was very old.

3. Her paintings show life on a farm.

10.6 *Very* and *Too*

Examples	Explanation
Grandma Moses was **very** old when she wrote her autobiography. She painted **very** well.	*Very* shows a large degree. We can put *very* before adjectives and adverbs.
Grandma Moses became **too** weak to do farm work. Lilly Ledbetter brought her case to the Supreme Court, but it was **too** late.	*Too* shows that there is a problem. We can put *too* before adjectives and adverbs. We sometimes use an infinitive phrase after the *too* phrase.

Language Note:

For emphasis, we can put *much* before *too*.

> Lilly Ledbetter brought her case to court *much too* late.

EXERCISE 13 Fill in the blanks with *very* or *too*.

1. Helen Keller was _____ very _____ intelligent.

2. She became _____ wild, and her parents needed help with her.

3. Anne Sullivan worked _____ patiently with Helen.

4. At first, some people thought Maya Lin's design was _____ unusual. They wanted a more traditional design.

5. Most people love her memorial. They think it's _____ beautiful.

6. She was _____ happy when the committee chose her design.

7. Lilly Ledbetter worked _____ hard for her company.

8. Ledbetter learned about pay inequality for women _____ late to do anything about it.

9. Christina Ripp Schwab is _____ talented. She won a gold medal at the Paralympics.

10.7 Enough

Examples	Explanation
Grandma Moses was **talented enough** to get the attention of an art collector. She painted **skillfully enough** to get her paintings in art museums.	*Enough* means "as much as needed." We use *enough* after adjectives and adverbs.
When she was younger, she didn't have **enough time** to paint.	We use *enough* before nouns.

EXERCISE 14 Fill in the blanks with the words given and *enough*.

1. Helen Keller was _____<u>intelligent enough</u>_____ to graduate from college.
   intelligent

2. Anne Sullivan was _____ to work with Helen.
   patient

3. She had _____ to teach Helen many things.
   time

4. Maya Lin's project was _____ to win the competition.
   good

5. Lilly Ledbetter didn't have _____ about
   information
   the salaries of other workers.

6. She wasn't _____ to lift heavy tires.
   strong

7. Did she make _____ to send her children to college?
   money

8. Grandma Moses painted _____ to get the attention of
   well
   a New York art collector.

SUMMARY OF LESSON 10

Adjectives and Adverbs

Adjective	Adverb
Anne Sullivan was **patient**.	She taught Helen **patiently**.
The Vietnam War Memorial is **beautiful**.	Maya Lin designed it **beautifully**.
Helen Keller was a **good** student.	She did **well** in school.
Lilly Ledbetter had a **late** shift.	She worked **late**.
Gina McWilliams had an **unfortunate** accident.	**Unfortunately**, she lost part of her leg.

Adjective Modifiers and Noun Modifiers

Adjective Modifier	Noun Modifier
a **hard** job	a **factory** job
a **new** company	a **tire** company
good sight	**eye**sight
expensive tuition	**college** tuition
a **young** child	a 7-**year**-old child

Very, Too, and *Enough*

very + adjective	Lilly Ledbetter was **very brave**.
very + adverb	She worked **very hard**.
too + adjective	You're never **too old** to learn something new.
too + adverb	Some workers work **too slowly**.
adjective + *enough*	Ledbetter was **brave enough** to fight for her rights.
adverb + *enough*	Helen Keller spoke **clearly enough**. People understood her.
enough + noun	Ledbetter didn't make **enough money**.

TEST/REVIEW

Choose the correct word(s) to complete the essay.

We just read a story about Grandma Moses. We learned that you are never

(~~too old~~/too much old) to learn something new. Grandma Moses was a 72-(*year/years*)-old
1. **2.**

grandmother when she started to paint. She couldn't do embroidery because of

(*health problems/problems health*), but she could hold a (*brushpaint/paintbrush*). She made
3. **4.**

many beautiful (*paintings oil/oil paintings*). She continued painting until she died at the age
5.

of 101. I think her story is (*too/very*) interesting.
6.

I always thought I was (*too old/very old*) to learn a (*foreign language/language foreign*),
7. **8.**

but now that I'm in the United States, I need to learn it. Most of the students in my

(*English class/class English*) are (*too/very*) young and learn (*quick/quickly*). But I am 59 years
9. **10.** **11.**

old, and I don't learn (*fast/fastly*). However, most of my (*mates class/classmates*) have a job, so
12. **13.**

they (*hard/hardly*) ever have time to study. Some of them have small children, so they are
14.

very (*busy/busily*). I'm not working, and my children are (*enough old/old enough*) to take care
15. **16.**

of themselves. My kids are (*proud/proudly*) of me for going to college at my age. My teacher
17.

always tells me I'm doing (*too/very*) well in her class.
18.

After learning English, I'm planning to get a (*history degree/degree history*). I am
19.

(*too/very*) interested in history. When I finish my degree, I'll be in my 60s. It will
20.

(*probable/probably*) be too (*late/lately*) for me to find a job, but I don't care. I know I'll have to
21. **22.**

study (*hard/hardly*) because history books are (*hard/hardly*) to read. But I am (*too/very*)
23. **24.** **25.**

interested, so I know I can do it. Besides, if Grandma Moses could learn to paint in her 70s

and write a book when she was 92, I can (*certain/certainly*) study history at my age. Grandma
26.

Moses is a very (*well/good*) example for me.
27.

WRITING

PART 1 Editing Advice

1. Don't make adjectives plural.

   Grandma Moses painted ~~beautifuls~~ art.
   (beautiful)

2. Put the specific noun before the general noun.

   Someone gave Anna Mary ~~materials art~~.
   (art materials)

3. Some adjectives end in *-ed*. Don't omit the *-ed*.

   Are you finish with your art project?
   (ed)

4. If the adjective ends in *-ed*, don't forget to include the verb *be*.

   Helen excited to learn to communicate.
   (was)

5. A noun modifier is always singular.

   Lilly worked for a ~~tires~~ company.
   (tire)

6. Put the adjective before the noun.

   Anne Sullivan had a childhood ~~hard~~.
   (hard)

7. Don't confuse *too* and *very*. *Too* indicates a problem.

   Helen was ~~too~~ intelligent.
   (very)

8. Don't confuse *too much* and *too*. A noun follows *too much*. An adjective or adverb follows *too*.

   You're never too ~~much~~ old to learn.

9. Put *enough* after the adjective.

   Maya was ~~enough~~ talented to win the contest.
   (enough)

10. Put *late, early, fast,* or *hard* at the end of the verb phrase.

    She ~~late~~ came home from work last night.
    (late)

11. Don't separate the verb phrase with an adverb of manner.

    Anne taught ~~patiently~~ Helen.
    (patiently)

12. Use an adverb, not an adjective, to describe a verb.

    Companies should treat men and women equal.
    (ly)

    Christina plays basketball very ~~good~~.
    (well)

PART 2 Editing Practice

Some of the shaded words and phrases have mistakes. Find the mistakes and correct them. If the shaded words are correct, write C.

       really   *C*

I ~~real~~ admire my aunt Rosa. She's very intelligent. She is marry and has three adults
  1.   **2.**   **3.**   **4.**

children. When her children became enough old to take care of themselves, she decided to go
                                    5.

back to college. She wants to study programming computer. Some people say she's too much
                                6.   **7.**

old to start a new career, but she doesn't care. She loves computers. She also works part-time
               8.

at a flowers shop. She thinks it's a job very interesting. She's very nicely to everyone, and
      9.   **10.**   **11.**

everyone loves her. Whenever I need advice, I can go to her. She listens patiently and treats
                                             12.

everyone kind.
     13.

Rosa came to the United States from Guatemala when she was 18. She had five younger

sisters and brothers. Her mother died when she was young, and she had to take care of her
                                14.

brothers and sisters. She took care of them wonderfully. She didn't speak one word of English
                         15.

when she left Guatemala. She learned quickly English, and now she speaks English very good.
                         16.   **17.**

Rosa is not only my aunt—she's a good friend.
                   18.

PART 3 Write About It

1. Write about a person you know who accomplished something at an older age or with a disability. If you research your topic, attach a copy of your sources.

2. Write about a woman whom you admire very much. You may write about a famous woman or any woman you know.

PART 4 Edit Your Writing

Reread the Summary of Lesson 10 and the editing advice. Edit your writing from Part 3.

11

Comparatives and Superlatives

**Fly Geyser, near Black
Rock Desert, Nevada**

AMERICAN
EXPERIENCES

America is not a country, it is a world.

—Oscar Wilde

Climbing Denali[1]

Read the following article. Pay special attention to the words in bold.

We often hear about people climbing Mount Everest, **the highest** mountain in the world. What about **the tallest** mountain in the United States?

The highest peak[2] in the United States is Denali in Denali National Park in Alaska. If you measure it from the base to the peak, it's actually **much higher than** Mount Everest. The base of Mount Everest is at 17,000 feet above sea level. It is 12,000 feet from the base to the top of Mount Everest. The base of Denali is at 2,000 feet above sea level. It is 18,000 feet from the base to the top of Denali.

Denali is one of **the most difficult** challenges in the Western Hemisphere for mountain climbers. Denali is **closer** to the North Pole **than** other tall mountains.

This means that the air is **thinner**, so it's **harder** for climbers to breathe. June is **the busiest** month for climbers. **The deadliest** season was May 1992, when eleven climbers died.

The first group of climbers reached the top of Denali in 1909. Two other groups were successful after that. The next group reached the top in 1947. This group included a husband and wife team, Bradford and Barbara Washburn. Barbara was the first woman to successfully climb the mountain.

The Washburns were not climbing for sport; they were explorers. In the field of mountain mapping, Bradford Washburn was one of **the best**. The Washburns mapped many mountains and the Grand Canyon. Bradford dreamed of mapping Mount Everest. Finally, in 1981, the Washburns worked on the Mount Everest project. They produced **the most detailed**[3] and **most accurate**[4] map ever made of Mount Everest.

---

[1] formerly Mount McKinley
[2] *peak*: the top of a mountain
[3] *detailed*: full of small bits of information
[4] *accurate*: exact

EVEREST
29,029 ft

DENALI
20,320 ft

Base to peak
12,000 ft

Base to peak
18,000 ft

Elevation (ft)

30,000
25,000
20,000
15,000
10,000
5,000
Sea level

A climber celebrates
reaching the top of Denali.

COMPREHENSION CHECK Based on the reading, tell if the statement is true (**T**) or false (**F**).

1. Denali is the tallest mountain in the world.

2. The first person to reach the top of Denali was a woman.

3. Between 1909 and 1947, many climbers reached the top of Denali.

11.1 Comparatives and Superlatives—An Overview

Examples	Explanation
Denali is **closer** to the North Pole than Mount Everest. Most climbers think Mount Everest is **more difficult** to climb than Denali.	We use comparatives to compare two items.
Mount Everest is the **highest** mountain in the world. The Washburns produced the **most accurate** map of Mount Everest.	We use superlatives for the number one item in a group of three or more.

EXERCISE 1 Listen to these facts about the United States. Fill in the blanks with the words you hear.

CD 2
TR 18

1. In area, the United States is the third _____ country in the world. Only Russia

   and Canada are _____.

2. In population, the United States is also the third _____ country in the world.

   Only China and India are _____.

3. The _____ city in the United States is New York. It has about 8 million people.

   It is _____ than Los Angeles.

4. New York City has the _____ cost of living in the United States. But the cost

   of living in Singapore is much _____.

5. The _____ waterfall in the United States is Yosemite Falls in California.

   But Niagara Falls is _____.

6. California is the _____ state. It has about 38 million people. There are

   _____ people in California than in New York State.

7. The _____ state is Wyoming. It is _____ than Alaska.

8. Alaska is the _____ state in area. Alaska is even _____

   than Texas.

continued

9. Phoenix, Arizona, gets the _____ sunshine. Bellingham, Washington,

   gets the _____ sunshine.

10. The _____ state is Delaware. The _____ state

   is Hawaii.

11.2 Comparatives and Superlatives—Adjective and Adverb Forms

	Simple	Comparative	Superlative
One-syllable adjectives and adverbs	tall fast	taller faster	the tallest the fastest
Two-syllable adjectives that end in -y	easy deadly	easier deadlier	the easiest the deadliest
Other two-syllable adjectives	famous active	more famous more active	the most famous the most active
Some two-syllable adjectives that have two forms*	simple quiet	simpler more simple quieter more quiet	the simplest the most simple the quietest the most quiet
Adjectives with three or more syllables	important difficult	more important more difficult	the most important the most difficult
Adjectives that end in -ed	tired worried	more tired more worried	the most tired the most worried
Adverbs that end in -ly	quickly brightly	more quickly more brightly	the most quickly the most brightly
Irregular comparatives and superlatives	good/well bad/badly far	better worse farther	the best the worst the farthest
Quantity words	little few	less fewer	the least the fewest
	a lot much many	more	the most

Language Note:

* Other two-syllable adjectives with two forms:

angry → angrier/more angry
friendly → friendlier/more friendly
gentle → gentler/more gentle
handsome → handsomer/more handsome

narrow → narrower/more narrow
polite → politer/more polite
stupid → stupider/more stupid

EXERCISE 2 Write (*C*) for comparative statements and (*S*) for superlative statements.

1. Los Angeles is smaller than New York City. _____*C*_____

2. Alaska has more snow than Wyoming. _____

3. In the United States, Denali is the most challenging mountain for climbers. _____

4. Mount Everest is farther from the North Pole than Denali. _____

5. The United States is smaller than Russia. _____

6. Canada is bigger than the United States in area. _____

7. Wyoming is the least populated state in the United States. _____

8. May 1992 was the deadliest season on Denali. _____

11.3 Short Adjectives and Adverbs—Spelling of Comparatives and Superlatives

Rule	Simple	Comparative	Superlative
For short adjectives and adverbs, add -er or -est.	tall fast	taller faster	tallest fastest
For adjectives that end in -e, add -r or -st.	nice late	nicer later	nicest latest
For adjectives that end in -y, change y to i and add -er or -est.	easy happy	easier happier	easiest happiest
For one-syllable words that end in consonant-vowel-consonant, double the final consonant and add -er or -est.*	big sad	bigger sadder	biggest saddest

Language Note:

* Do not double a final *w*:

    new—newer—newest

EXERCISE 3 Write the comparative and superlative forms of these words. There may be more than one correct answer.

	Comparative	Superlative
1. interesting	more interesting	most interesting
2. young	_____	_____
3. beautiful	_____	_____
4. good	_____	_____

continued

	Comparative	Superlative
5. quiet	_____	_____
6. thin	_____	_____
7. carefully	_____	_____
8. pretty	_____	_____
9. bad	_____	_____
10. famous	_____	_____
11. lucky	_____	_____
12. simple	_____	_____
13. high	_____	_____
14. important	_____	_____
15. far	_____	_____
16. foolishly	_____	_____

EXERCISE 4 Correct any spelling mistakes you made in Exercise 1 on pages 257–258.

11.4 Using Superlatives

Examples	Explanation
New York is **the biggest** city in the U.S. California is **the most populated** state in the U.S. China has **the largest** population in the world.	We use _the_ before superlatives. We often put a prepositional phrase at the end of a superlative sentence. _in the world_ _in my family_ _in my class_ _in the U.S._
Niagara Falls is **one of the most popular** attraction**s** in the U.S. One World Trade Center is **one of the tallest** building**s** in the world.	We often put _one of the_ before the superlative. Then we use a plural noun.

Language Note:

We omit _the_ when a possessive form precedes the superlative.

What was **your** most exciting vacation?

EXERCISE 5 Fill in the blanks with the superlative form of the words given. Include *the* before the superlative.

1. Alaska is _____ the largest _____ state in area.
                          large

2. _____ lake in the United States is Lake Superior.
            big

3. _____ river in the United States is the Missouri River.
            long

4. _____ mountain in the United States is Denali.
            high

5. The Vietnam War Memorial is one of _____ tourist
                                                         popular

   attractions in Washington, DC.

6. New York City is one of _____ cities in the United States.
                                          expensive

7. San Francisco is one of _____ American cities.
                                       beautiful

8. Harvard is one of _____ universities in the United States.
                                  good

9. Crime is one of _____ problems in big cities.
                                bad

10. Boston is one of _____ cities in the United States.
                                 old

11. _____ state to join the United States is Hawaii.
            recent

12. The state that is _____ north is Alaska.
                                far

EXERCISE 6 About You Write a true superlative sentence using the words given. You may use *one of the* + a plural noun. Then find a partner and compare your sentences.

1. long street in this city

   Western Avenue is the longest street in this city.

2. interesting place in this city

   _____

3. good restaurant in this city

   _____

4. beautiful city in the United States

   _____

5. big problem in the United States

   _____

continued

6. important invention of the last 100 years

_____

7. popular movie star in the United States

_____

8. pretty neighborhood in this city

_____

11.5 Word Order with Superlatives

Examples	Explanation
Denali is **the highest mountain** in the United States. In Boston, 2015 was one of **the worst winters**.	We put a superlative adjective before a noun.
Mount Everest is **the tallest mountain** in the world. **The tallest mountain** in the world is Mount Everest.	When the verb _be_ connects a noun to a superlative phrase, the superlative phrase can come before or after _be_.
The population of Seattle, Washington, **is increasing the most rapidly**.	We can put a superlative adverb after the verb.
It **rains the least** in Las Vegas. It **snows the most** in Alaska.	We can put _the most, the least, the best, the worst,_ and other superlative adverbs after the verb.

EXERCISE 7 Fill in the blanks by putting the words given in the correct order. Use _the_ and the superlative form of the adjectives and adverbs given.

1. Rhode Island is _____the smallest state_____ in the United States.
small/state

2. _____ in the United States is Lake Superior.
big/lake

3. _____ of Latinos is in New Mexico.
large/population

4. California has _____ .
diverse/population

5. The Asian American population in the United States _____ .
fast/is increasing

6. Latinos are _____ .
young/minority group

7. Alaska has _____ .
long/coastline

8. School children in Lakewood, Ohio, _____ .
a lot/walk

9. _____ in the world are in California.
old/trees

10. The population of Seattle, Washington, _____ .
rapidly/is growing

An Unusual Trip

Nate Damm went from Delaware to San Francisco in 2011. Did the trip take four hours? No. It took **longer**. Eight hours? No. Much **longer**. A few weeks? No. It took even **longer than** that. The trip took him over seven months. Why did it take so long? Damm walked across the United States. He walked **more than** 3,000 miles across 14 states.

Someone asked Damm, "Wouldn't it be **faster** if you just drove?" Well, arriving wasn't the point.[5] According to Damm, you learn much **more** about the United States when you're traveling at 3 miles per hour, not 500 miles per hour by plane or even 65 miles per hour by car.

Damm grew up in Maine. He never traveled **farther** west than Pennsylvania. He often thought about traveling to other countries, but then he realized he didn't know much about the United States. So he decided to walk across the country. By walking, he felt **more connected** to the people and the land.

It was hard at first, but little by little it became **easier**. In the beginning, Damm averaged about 13 miles a day. Then he started walking **longer** distances. One day in Colorado, he walked 41 miles.

At first, Damm used GPS to find his way, but the directions it gave him were often wrong. He bought a paper road map and found it was much **better**. He avoided[6] major highways; the **smaller** roads were **safer**.

Damm preferred to wear shoes, not boots. Shoes are **more comfortable**, he says. He had to cross many wet areas, and shoes dry **faster** than boots. Also, the extra weight of boots made walking **more difficult**.

Damm is not the only person to cross the United States on foot. About ten to twenty people do it every year.

---

[5] *the point*: the main goal
[6] *to avoid*: to stay away from

COMPREHENSION CHECK Based on the reading, tell if the statement is true (**T**) or false (**F**).

1. GPS helped Damm a lot in finding his way.

2. Damm preferred small roads to major highways.

3. Before traveling across America on foot, Damm traveled to other countries.

11.6 Using Comparatives

Examples	Explanation
Flying is **faster than** driving. Are shoes **more comfortable than** boots? It was **better** to use a road map **than** to use GPS.	When making a comparison between two items, we use *than* before the second item.
Damm doesn't like to walk on highways. Smaller roads are **safer**.	We don't use *than* when the second item of comparison is understood.
Flying takes **less** time than driving. In the beginning, Damm walked **fewer** miles.	The opposite of *more* is *less* or *fewer*. (Remember: we use *less* with noncount nouns and *fewer* with count nouns.)
Denali is **much taller** than Mount Everest. Walking with shoes is **a little easier** than walking with boots.	We can use *much* or *a little* before a comparative form.
FORMAL: You walk faster than **I do**. INFORMAL: You walk faster than **me**. FORMAL: He is braver than **she is**. INFORMAL: He is braver than **her**.	We use a subject pronoun (*he, she, I*, etc.) after *than*. Usually an auxiliary verb (*is, do, did, can*, etc.) follows. In informal English, we sometimes use an object pronoun (*him, her, me*, etc.) after *than*. An auxiliary verb does not follow.

EXERCISE 8 Fill in the blanks with the comparative form of the words given. Add *than*.

1. The top of Mount Everest is _____*farther*_____ above sea level _____*than*_____ Denali.

far

2. Climbing Mount Everest is _____ climbing Denali.

difficult

3. Bradford Washburn was four years _____ his wife, Barbara.

old

4. The air in the mountains is _____ the air at sea level.

thin

5. Nate Damm felt _____ to people by walking _____

connected

   by driving.

6. For Damm, it was _____ to walk in shoes _____ in boots.

easy

7. For Damm, a road map was _____ GPS.

good

8. Boots dry _____ shoes.

slowly

9. Damm says that it's _____ to walk with headphones

dangerous

   _____ without them.

Chicago

San Francisco

EXERCISE 9 Look at the information in the chart. Then fill in the blanks to make comparisons between Chicago and San Francisco. Use the words in the box and *than*.

	Chicago	San Francisco
Population	2,718,782	837,442
Average household income	$47,408	$73,802
Area	227.63 square miles	46.87 square miles
Average home cost	$247,800	$750,900
Average rent for a 2-bedroom apartment	$2,153	$3,859
Average snowfall	36.7 inches per year	0 inches per year
Average high temperature in July	83 °F	71 °F
Average low temperature in January	18.4 °F	42.4 °F
People over 65	10.3 percent	13.6 percent

(Source: 2013 U.S. Census)

bad	big	cheap	cool	expensive	large✓	old	pleasant	wealthy

1. The population of Chicago is _____ larger than _____ the population of San Francisco.

2. San Franciscans are _____ Chicagoans. The average income is higher in San Francisco.

3. In area, Chicago is _____ San Francisco.

4. Homes in San Francisco are _____ homes in Chicago.

5. A two-bedroom apartment in Chicago is _____ a two-bedroom apartment in San Francisco.

6. For people who don't like snow, winters in Chicago are _____ winters in San Francisco.

7. San Francisco is _____ Chicago in the summer.

8. For people who don't like cold weather, winters in San Francisco are _____ winters in Chicago.

9. With 13.6 percent of its population over 65, the population of San Francisco is _____ the population of Chicago.

EXERCISE 10 About You Write sentences comparing two cities you know well. Use the words given. Share your answers with a partner.

1. small _Dallas is smaller than Beijing._

2. crowded _____

3. cold _____

4. interesting _____

5. noisy _____

6. modern _____

7. sunny _____

8. beautiful _____

9. pleasant _____

10. old _____

11. amazing _____

12. confusing _____

13. expensive _____

11.7 Word Order with Comparatives

Examples	Explanation
Houses in San Francisco **are more expensive** than houses in Chicago.	We put comparative adjectives after the verb *be*.
San Francisco has **more sunshine** than Chicago. San Francisco has **less rain** than Chicago.	We put *more, less, fewer, better, worse*, and other comparative adjectives before the noun.
The Asian population **is growing more quickly** than the Latino population.	We can put comparative adverbs after the verb.
It **rains less** in San Francisco than in Chicago.	We can put *more, less, better, worse* and other comparative adverbs after the verb.

EXERCISE 11 Look at the information in the chart. Then fill in the blanks to make comparisons between Chicago and San Francisco. Use the words given and the comparative form.

	Chicago	San Francisco
People living in poverty	22.1 percent	13.2 percent
Median age	33.1 years	38.5 years
Average household size	2.57 people	2.31 people
Average travel time to work	33.5 minutes	29.9 minutes
People with a bachelor's degree or higher	33.6 percent	52 percent
People under 18	23.1 percent	13.4 percent
Foreign-born people	21.2 percent	35.7 percent
Population increase 2010–2013	0.9 percent	4 percent

1. There are _____ *more people* _____ living in poverty in Chicago than in San Francisco.

people

2. With a median age of 33 years, Chicago has a _____

young/population

than San Francisco.

3. There are _____ in a household in San Francisco.

people

4. People in Chicago _____ to get to work.

travel/far

5. Fifty-two percent of San Franciscans have a bachelor's degree or higher. There are

_____ in San Francisco.

educated people

6. Chicago has _____ than San Francisco: 23.1 percent of Chicagoans are under 18.

children

7. San Francisco has _____ than Chicago.

foreign-born people

8. The population is _____ in San Francisco than in Chicago.

increasing/fast

EXERCISE 12 About You Compare the city you live in now to another city you know. Use comparative adjectives and the words given. Share your answers with a partner.

1. public transportation _Moscow has better public transportation than Los Angeles._

2. factories _____

3. crowded _____

4. clean _____

5. tall buildings _____

6. snow _____

7. sunny _____

continued

8. traffic _____

9. beautiful _____

10. job opportunities _____

EXERCISE 13 Fill in the blanks with the comparative form of the words given. Put the words in the correct order. Add *than* where necessary.

I'm from Genoa, a small town in Illinois. Now I live in Chicago. Chicago is

_____ <u>much bigger than</u> _____ Genoa, but there are many other
1. much/big

differences. In Genoa, it's _____ to go from
2. easy

place to place because there is _____ .
3. traffic/little

So I spend _____ in my car. Parking
4. little/time

is _____ in Chicago. I also have to walk
5. expensive

_____ in Chicago to get to my destination,
6. much/far

so I get _____ . Of course, Chicago has
7. exercise

_____ Genoa.
8. good/public transportation

People in Genoa are _____ people in
9. friendly

Chicago. Neighbors talk to each other, help each other, and watch out for each other.

As a result, Genoa is _____ Chicago.
10. safe

In Chicago, there are _____ such as movies,
11. activities

concerts, plays, and sporting events. I like these activities, but I spend

_____ I do in Genoa.
12. money

The climate is the same in both places. But in winter, when there's a lot of snow, Chicago

usually clears the snow _____ . Genoa has
13. quickly

_____ and
14. little/equipment

_____ for snow removal.
15. few/workers

For me, life in Genoa is _____
16. much/comfortable

it is in Chicago. Genoa is _____ , and the town is
17. much/relaxed

_____ Chicago.
18. quiet

EXERCISE 14 Fill in the blanks with the comparative or superlative form of the word given. Add *than* or *the* where necessary.

1. August is usually _____*hotter than*_____ May in Miami.

hot

2. January is usually _____*the coldest*_____ month of the year in Minneapolis.

cold

3. Los Angeles is _____ San Francisco.

warm

4. Seattle is _____ city in Washington.

big

5. The state of Hawaii is _____ south in the United States.

far

6. New York City is _____ Los Angeles.

crowded

7. Niagara Falls is one of _____ U.S. tourist attractions.

popular

8. San Francisco is one of _____ U.S. cities.

beautiful

9. _____ mountain in the United States is in Alaska.

tall

10. _____ city in the United States is New York City.

expensive

EXERCISE 15 About You Discuss the questions with a partner.

1. What is the best thing about living in the United States? What is the worst thing?

2. In choosing where to live, what is the most important thing to consider?

3. In your opinion, which is better: life in a small town or life in a big city?

4. What is the most beautiful part of this city?

5. Do you think that it's better to own a house or rent an apartment in this city?

6. In your opinion, what is the most pleasant month in this city?

7. In your opinion, what is the worst month in this city?

8. In this city, is it easier to drive or use public transportation?

SUMMARY OF LESSON 11

Adjectives

Short Adjectives
Chicago is a **big** city.
Chicago is **bigger than** Houston.
New York is **the biggest** U.S. city.

Long Adjectives
Houston is a **populated** city.
Chicago is **more populated than** Houston.
New York is **the most populated** U.S. city.

Adverbs

Short Adverbs
He walks **fast**.
He walks **faster than** you do.
I walk **the fastest**.

-ly Adverbs
The population of Denver is increasing **rapidly**.
The population of Austin is increasing **more rapidly**.
The population of Seattle is increasing **the most rapidly**.

Comparisons with *Less* and *Fewer*

Los Angeles has **less** rain than Seattle.
Seattle has **fewer** people than Los Angeles.

Word Order

Be + Comparative/Superlative Adjective	
Comparative	Bradford Washburn **was older than** his wife. Mount Everest **is more challenging than** Denali.
Superlative	Mount Everest **is the tallest mountain** in the world. **The tallest mountain** in the world **is** Mount Everest.

Comparative/Superlative Adjective + Noun	
Comparative	Bradford Washburn had **more experience than** his wife.
Superlative	New York City has **the largest population** in the U.S.

Verb + Comparative/Superlative Adverb	
Comparative	Shoes **dry faster than** boots.
Superlative	You **travel the most frequently** in your family.

Fill in the blanks using the comparative or superlative form of the word(s) given. Put the words in the correct order. Add *than* or *the* where necessary.

A: I'm planning to visit Chicago.

B: You're going to love it. It's one of _____*the most beautiful cities*_____ in the U.S.

　　　　　　　　　　　　　　　　1. beautiful city

A: It's the second largest city, isn't it?

B: No. It's the third. Los Angeles and New York are _____

　　　　　　　　　　　　　　　　　　　　　　　　　2. big

Chicago. When you're there, you can visit the Willis Tower. It's one of

_____ in the U.S. It has 110 stories. Go on a sunny day.

　　　3. tall/building

You can see _____. When I was there, it was cloudy. I hope you

　　　　　　4. far/much

have _____ I had. When are you going?

　　　5. good /weather

A: In August.

B: Ugh! August is _____ of the summer. It's often 90 degrees or

　　　　　　　　　6. month/bad

more. If it's too hot, you can always go to the beach and cool off. Chicago is near Lake Michigan.

A: Is it big like Lake Washington?

B: It's _____ Lake Washington. In fact, it's one of

　　　　7. big/much

_____ in the U.S.

　　8. lake/large

A: Is Chicago very rainy?

B: Not in the summer. It's sunny. In fact, it's _____ Seattle.

　　　　　　　　　　　　　　　　　　　9. sunny/much

A: What do you like about Chicago?

B: The architecture downtown is amazing. The _____

　　　　　　　　　　　　　　　　　　　10. architect/good

in the U.S. designed many buildings.

A: Do I need to take taxis everywhere?

B: Taxis are so expensive! They're _____

　　　　　　　　　　　　　　　11. much/expensive

the buses and trains. Use public transportation. But be careful. It's _____ to travel

　　　　　　　　　　　　　　　　　　　　　　　12. safe

in the daytime.

A: Does Chicago have _____ Seattle?

　　　　　　　　　　13. crime/more

B: Yes. But if you're careful, you'll be OK. I'm sure you'll enjoy it. It's an interesting place. I think

it's one of _____ in the United States.

　　　　　14. interesting/city

WRITING

PART 1 Editing Advice

1. Don't use *more* and *-er* together.

    The weather in May is ~~more~~ better than the weather in January.

2. Use *than* before the second item in a comparison.

    Mount Everest is higher ~~that~~ ^{than} Denali.

3. Use *the* before a superlative form.

    China has ^{the} biggest population in the world.

4. Use a plural noun after the phrase *one of the*.

    Willis Tower is one of the tallest building^s in the United States.

5. Use the correct word order.

    People in big cities farther ~~travel~~ ^{travel} to get to work.

    There is traffic ~~less~~ ^{less} in a small town.

    Denali is the ~~mountain~~ most challenging ^{mountain} in the United States.

6. Don't use *the* with a possessive form.

    My ~~the~~ most interesting vacation was in Alaska.

7. Use correct spelling.

    Miami is ~~sunnyer~~ ^{sunnier} than Seattle.

PART 2 Editing Practice

Some of the shaded words and phrases have mistakes. Find the mistakes and correct them. If the shaded words are correct, write *C*.

I used to live in Mexico City. Now I live in St. Louis. These cities are very different. Mexico
 ~~C~~
 1.

 bigger
City is ~~more biger~~ than St. Louis. In fact, it's one of the biggest city in the world. It's certainly
 2. **3.**

the most large city in Mexico. St. Louis has no mountains. Mexico City is surrounded by tall
 4. **5.**

mountains. I think Mexico City is prettyer that St. Louis. It has beautiful parks. Mexico City is
 6. **7.**

more interesting St. Louis. It has great museums.
 8.

But Mexico City has a few serious problems: it has pollution more than St. Louis.
 9.

My the oldest brother still lives there, and he always complains about the air quality. I think it
 10.

has the worst air quality in the Americas. And I hate the subway. I think it's the subway most
 11. **12.**

crowded in the world.
 13.

No city is perfect. Each one has advantages and disadvantages. But my heart is in Mexico

City because my family and best friends live there.
 14.

PART 3 Write About It

1. Write a paragraph comparing two cities you know well.

2. In choosing where to live, what are the most important things to consider?

PART 4 Edit Your Writing

Reread the Summary of Lesson 11 and the editing advice. Edit your writing from Part 3.

Verb Review
Auxiliary Verbs with *Too* and *Either*
Auxiliary Verbs in Tag Questions

PEOPLE
ON THE
MOVE

National Geographic Explorer
Paul Salopek traveling across
Ethiopia's Afar desert

We keep moving forward, opening
new doors, and doing new things,
because we're curious and curiosity
keeps leading us down new paths.

—Walt Disney

Barrington Irving: Flying to Inspire[1]

Read the following article. Pay special attention to the words in bold.

Barrington Irving **was born** in Jamaica and moved to Miami when he was six years old. When he **was** 15, he **had** a job in his parents' bookstore. A man **came** in one day and **told** Irving that he **was** a professional pilot. Irving **said**, "I **don't think** I**'m** smart enough **to become** a pilot." The next day, the man **invited** Irving **to sit** in the cockpit[2] of his plane. Irving **knew** immediately: he **wanted to become** a pilot. He **washed** airplanes **to earn** money for flight school. He **practiced** flying skills using flight simulator[3] software.

In college, Irving **studied** aeronautical science[4] and **graduated** with honors. In 2007, at the age of 23, he **became** the youngest person **to fly** alone around the world. After 97 days and 26 stops, he **returned** to the United States.

Now Irving **wants to inspire** kids **to follow** their dreams. If you **have** a dream, he **says**, you **can do** great things. But there **is** another important thing kids **need**: powerful learning experiences. If they **have** meaningful, real-world experiences, they**'ll want to continue** their education and **start** a career.

In 2005, Irving **started** an organization called Experience Aviation. He **is developing** programs **to inspire** students **to learn** about science, technology, engineering, and math. Irving **says**, "I **want to use** aviation **to excite** and **empower**[5] a new generation **to become** scientists, engineers, and explorers."

Irving's students **are working** on different projects. Some **are building** cars; some **are building** airplanes. All of them **are gaining** confidence. He **told** a group of kids in his program, "I not only **believe** you **can build** an airplane, but I**'ll fly** it if you **do**." In just ten weeks, sixty students **built** an airplane and then **watched** Irving fly it away.

Irving **continues to fly** to locations around the world with his "Flying Classroom" project, and **to share** information about science, technology, engineering, math, geography, and history with his students on the ground.

---

1 *to inspire*: to cause to work hard or be creative
2 *cockpit*: the front of an airplane where a pilot sits
3 *simulator*: something that imitates flying
4 *aeronautical science*: the science of flight
5 *to empower*: to give someone confidence to do something

COMPREHENSION CHECK Based on the reading, tell if the statement is true (**T**) or false (**F**).

1. When Irving was a teenager, a pilot inspired him to follow his dream.

2. Irving flew the airplane that his students built.

3. Irving says that children need real-life learning experiences.

12.1 Verb Review

The Simple Present

Examples	Explanation
Children **learn** from powerful experiences. Irving always **tries** to help students. Irving **comes** from Jamaica.	We use the simple present with facts, general truths, habits, customs, regular activities, repeated actions, and a place of origin.
He **has** a lot of experience as a pilot. He **loves** to help students.	We use the simple present with nonaction verbs.
If you **give** kids fun activities, they'll want to learn. When you **finish** college, you will find a good job.	We use the simple present in future *if* clauses and time clauses.

The Present Continuous

Examples	Explanation
Look at those kids. They**'re building** a car.	We use the present continuous with actions that are happening now.
He **is sitting** in the cockpit of the airplane. He**'s wearing** a pilot's uniform.	We use the present continuous with the verbs *sit, stand, wear*, and *sleep* to describe a state or condition that we can observe now.
The kids **are gaining** confidence. Irving **is trying** to inspire kids.	We use the present continuous with longer actions that are in progress but may not be happening at this exact moment.

The Future

Examples	Explanation
Careers in technology **will grow**. Careers in math **are going to grow,** too.	We use *will* or *be going to* with simple facts or predictions about the future.
If you build an airplane, I**'ll fly** it.	We use *will* with promises.
My friend **is going to study** aeronautical science.	We use *be going to* when there is a previous plan to do something.

The Simple Past

Examples	Explanation
A pilot **invited** Irving to see his airplane. Irving **flew** around the world in 2007.	We use the simple past with short or long actions that began and ended in the past.
He **made** 26 stops on his flight around the world.	We use the simple past with repeated past actions.

continued

The Verb *Be*

Examples	Explanation
Barrington Irving **is** a pilot. He**'s** interested in helping students. His parents' store **was** in Miami.	We use *be* with classifications, descriptions, and the location of the subject.
Irving **was** 15 when he decided to become a pilot.	We use *be* with the age of the subject.
There **are** many ways to teach children.	We use *be* with *there*.
It **is** warm in Miami. When it**'s** 6:00 in Miami, it**'s** 3:00 in Los Angeles.	We use *be* to talk about weather and time. The subject is *it*.
Irving **was** born in Jamaica.	We use *be* with *born*.

Modals

Examples	Explanation
Children **can** do great things. **Could** you teach me to fly? People **should** follow their dreams. I **may** major in math. She **might** study engineering. A pilot **must** have a license.	We use modals to add more meaning to the main verb. The modals are *can* (ability, possibility, request, permission), *could* (request, permission), *should* (advice), *may* (possibility, permission), *might* (possibility), *would* (request), and *must* (necessity). After a modal, we use the base form.
Children **have to** gain confidence. They **are able to** build an airplane. They **are not allowed to** fly it.	Phrasal modals are *have to* (necessity), *be able to* (ability), and *be allowed to* (permission).

Infinitives

Examples	Explanation
Irving wants **to help** young people. It's important **to empower** children. Irving was lucky **to meet** a pilot.	We use infinitives after certain verbs, certain expressions beginning with *it*, and certain adjectives.
Irving uses aviation **to excite** students.	We can use infinitives to show purpose.

EXERCISE 1 Listen to each sentence and fill in the blanks with the verbs you hear. Then write if the verb is simple present, present continuous, simple past, future, an infinitive, or a modal.

CD 2
TR 21

1. Irving _____ to become a pilot. _____ *simple past* _____

2. Someone _____ in him. _____

3. He _____ to help young people. _____

4. He wants _____ young people. _____

5. Jobs in science and engineering _____. _____

6. Young people _____ from Irving. _____

7. Some kids _____ an airplane. _____

8. Irving _____ to fly. _____

9. Some of Irving's students _____ cars. _____

10. Teachers _____ empower students. _____

11. It's interesting _____ about Irving's life. _____

EXERCISE 2 Choose the correct word(s) to complete this essay by a college student named Lena. If both answers are correct, circle both choices.

I'm a pre-law student at Michigan State University. I'm going (*graduate*,(*to graduate*)) next
      1.

year and then (*go/going*) to law school. Last year, my counselor (*told/tell*) me about internship
      2.   **3.**

programs in Washington, DC. She said I (*might/should*) apply. I (*must/had to*) get
      4.   **5.**

recommendations from three professors. I was so excited when I (*received/receive*) my letter of
      6.

acceptance. Now my life is (*move/moving*) in a new direction.
      7.

I'm an intern at the Supreme Court this semester. Besides my work, I (*take/am taking*)
      8.

classes at Georgetown University. (*I'm gaining/I gain*) so much experience here. I
      9.

(*know/am knowing*) much more now about the law and the government. When I (*go/will go*)
      10.   **11.**

to law school next year, (*I have/I'll have*) a greater understanding of U.S. law.
      12.

(*I have/I'm having*) a roommate now. Her name is Nicole. She (*graduate/graduated*) from
      13.   **14.**

the University of California last year. Her internship is at the Department of Education.

(*She's planning/She planned*) to (*becoming/become*) a biology teacher when
      15.   **16.**

(*she'll finish/she finishes*) her internship. (*It'll be/It's going to be*) easy for her (*find/to find*) a
      17.   **18.**   **19.**

job because (*there/they*) aren't enough science teachers now.
             20.

Nicole and I are serious about our jobs and classes, but we (*like/are liking*) to
                                                               21.

(*having/have*) fun, too. Last weekend, we (*did go/went*) to the Air and Space Museum. Next
  22.   **23.**

weekend, we might (*to go/go*) to the art museum if we (*have/will have*) enough time.
                    24.   **25.**

(*There's/It's*) one thing Nicole and I don't like: we can't (*wear/to wear*) jeans to work. It's
  26.   **27.**

important (*look/to look*) very professional at our jobs.
           28.

An internship is a wonderful experience. I (*think/am thinking*) all college students should
                                            29.

(*do/to do*) an internship in preparation for their future professions.
  30.

One Man, 7 Years, 21,000 Miles

Herto Bouri, Ethiopia 2013

Tierra del Fuego, Chile 2020

MAP: RYAN MORRIS, NGM STAFF

CD 2
TR 22

Read the following article. Pay special attention to the words in bold.

Can you **imagine** walking across the world? That's what journalist Paul Salopek **is doing** right now. He **started** his journey[6] in Ethiopia in 2013. By the end of his trip, after more than seven years of walking, he**'ll be** in Tierra del Fuego, South America. Why **is** he **doing** this? How long **will** it **take** him? What **is** he **going to learn** from this experience?

Salopek's project is called "Out of Eden Walk." He **is following** the path of our distant ancestors. He **wants** to understand the story of human migration.[7] Humans **started** this movement across the planet 60,000 years ago. He estimates[8] that he **will take** 30 million footsteps to reach his destination. He **will walk** 21,000 miles.

According to Salopek, we **are** now **living** in the greatest migration of humans. Nearly a billion people **are moving** across the planet today. Things **are moving** faster than ever.

People often **ask** Salopek, "**Are** you crazy?" But Salopek **is learning** so much along the way. For example, he **learned** that water is like gold in the desert of Ethiopia.

About every 100 miles, Salopek **records** his journey in photographs and sounds. He often **interviews** local people. He **is sharing** his journey in real time[9] with people around the world.

Salopek is a journalist and National Geographic Explorer. He often **does** unusual things. Once he **rode** a mule for a year across the mountains of Mexico to write a story. Another time, he **worked** in a gas station in Chicago to write about oil. He often **puts** himself in dangerous situations. He **traveled** by canoe for several weeks down the Congo River to report on the Congo civil war. Salopek **won** the Pulitzer Prize for his Congo report—the highest award for a journalist.

---

6 *journey*: a long trip
7 *human migration*: a movement of people from one place to another
8 *to estimate*: to guess a number using your knowledge
9 *in real time*: as it happens

For more information on Paul Salopek's "Out of Eden Walk" project, go to learn.outofedenwalk.com, pz.harvard.edu, and pulitzercenter.org/projects/out-of-eden.

COMPREHENSION CHECK Based on the reading, tell if the statement is true (**T**) or false (**F**).

1. Salopek expects to finish his journey in Tierra del Fuego.

2. Salopek's canoe trip down the Congo River put him in danger.

3. Salopek will walk 60,000 miles.

12.2 Statements, Questions, and Short Answers

The Simple Present

AFFIRMATIVE STATEMENT	Barrington Irving **teaches** kids.
NEGATIVE STATEMENT	He **doesn't teach** in a school.
YES/NO QUESTION	**Does** he **teach** science?
SHORT ANSWER	Yes, he **does**.
WH- QUESTION	Where **does** he **teach**?
NEGATIVE WH- QUESTION	Why **doesn't** he **teach** in a school?
SUBJECT QUESTION	Who **teaches** in a school?

The Present Continuous

AFFIRMATIVE STATEMENT	Paul Salopek **is walking** a long distance.
NEGATIVE STATEMENT	He **isn't walking** for sport.
YES/NO QUESTION	**Is** he **walking** across the United States?
SHORT ANSWER	No, he **isn't**.
WH- QUESTION	Where **is** he **walking**?
NEGATIVE WH- QUESTION	Why **isn't** he **walking** across the United States?
SUBJECT QUESTION	Who **is walking** across the United States?

The Future with *Will*

AFFIRMATIVE STATEMENT	The students **will learn** about science.
NEGATIVE STATEMENT	They **won't learn** about sports.
YES/NO QUESTION	**Will** they **learn** about math?
SHORT ANSWER	Yes, they **will**.
WH- QUESTION	What else **will** they **learn**?
NEGATIVE WH- QUESTION	Why **won't** they **learn** about sports?
SUBJECT QUESTION	Who **will learn** about sports?

continued

The Future with *Be Going To*

AFFIRMATIVE STATEMENT	They **are going to major** in science.
NEGATIVE STATEMENT	They **aren't going to major** in math.
YES/NO QUESTION	**Are** they **going to major** in biology?
SHORT ANSWER	No, they **aren't**.
WH- QUESTION	When **are** they **going to major** in science?
NEGATIVE WH- QUESTION	Why **aren't** they **going to major** in math?
SUBJECT QUESTION	How many students **are going to major** in math?

The Simple Past

AFFIRMATIVE STATEMENT	Paul Salopek **started** his walk in Ethiopia.
NEGATIVE STATEMENT	He **didn't start** his walk in the United States.
YES/NO QUESTION	**Did** he **start** his walk this year?
SHORT ANSWER	No, he **didn't**.
WH- QUESTION	When **did** he **start** his walk?
NEGATIVE WH- QUESTION	Why **didn't** he **start** in South Africa?
SUBJECT QUESTION	Who else **started** a walk?

Modals

AFFIRMATIVE STATEMENT	I **can imagine** walking for 50 miles.
NEGATIVE STATEMENT	I **can't imagine** walking across the world.
YES/NO QUESTION	**Can** you **imagine** walking across the United States?
SHORT ANSWER	No, I **can't**.
WH- QUESTION	How far **can** you **imagine** walking?
NEGATIVE WH- QUESTION	Why **can't** you **imagine** walking across the United States?
SUBJECT QUESTION	Who **can imagine** walking across the world?

EXERCISE 3 Fill in the blanks with the negative form of the underlined verb.

1. Paul Salopek <u>is</u> a journalist. He _____ *isn't* _____ a pilot.

2. Salopek <u>started</u> his walk in Africa. He _____ his walk in Asia.

3. He<u>'ll finish</u> his walk in South America. He _____ his walk in Africa.

4. He<u>'s walking</u> to learn about human migration. He _____ for sport.

5. He<u>'s going to walk</u> across many countries. He _____ across Poland.

6. He <u>rode</u> across Mexico on a mule. He _____ on a horse.

7. He <u>sends</u> his stories to people around the world. He _____ stories every day.

8. He's brave. He _____ afraid.

9. He should be careful. He _____ foolish.

EXERCISE 4 Read each statement. If the statement is about Barrington Irving, write a question about Paul Salopek. If the statement is about Paul Salopek, write a question about Barrington Irving. Write short answers.

1. Salopek is brave.

Is Irving brave? _____

Yes, he is. _____

2. Salopek likes to teach children.

Does Irving like to teach children? _____

Yes, he does. _____

3. Salopek is walking around the world.

_____

_____

4. Salopek began his journey in Africa.

_____

_____

5. Irving flew solo around the world.

_____

_____

6. Salopek is sharing his knowledge with schoolchildren.

_____

_____

7. Irving knows a lot about the world.

_____

_____

continued

8. Irving can teach children about the world.

_____

_____

9. Salopek will finish his project in South America.

_____

_____

EXERCISE 5 Write *wh-* questions using the words given. Discuss your answers with a partner.
Answers may vary.

1. Kids need learning experiences.

   (what kind of) _What kind of learning experiences do kids need?_ _____

2. Irving's students are working on a project.

   (what kind of) _____

3. Irving washed airplanes when he was young.

   (why) _____

4. Someone created the organization "Experience Aviation."

   (who) _____

5. Teachers can inspire students.

   (how) _____

6. Irving didn't believe in himself at first.

   (why) _____

7. Salopek is going to walk to Tierra del Fuego.

   (why) _____

8. Salopek's trip is going to take a few years.

   (how many years) _____

9. Salopek will finish his walk soon.

   (when) _____

EXERCISE 6 Complete the phone conversation between Lena and her mother. Use the correct form of the word(s) given.

A: Hi, Mom. This is Lena.

B: Hi, Lena. I 'm _____ happy to _____ your voice. You
              1. be   **2.** hear

_____ . You just send short text messages.
        3. never/call

A: I'm sorry, Mom. I _____ much time.
                                4. not/have

B: Why _____ time?
              5. you/not/have

A: I have to work, go to classes, and participate in activities all day. Last weekend,

we _____ to Virginia.
        6. go

B: Who _____ ?
              7. drive

A: No one. We _____ the subway. Public transportation is really good here.
                        8. take

B: _____ enough to eat this summer? Who _____ for you?
              9. you/get   **10.** cook

A: I _____ to cook this summer. _____ surprised?
              11. learn   **12.** be/you

B: Yes, I am. When you were home, you never _____ .
                                                              13. cook

A: Nicole and I often _____ and _____ our friends for dinner
                              14. cook   **15.** invite

on the weekends.

B: Who _____ Nicole?
              16. be

A: I _____ you about Nicole in my last e-mail. She's my roommate. She
              17. tell

_____ from California.
        18. come

B: Oh, yes. Now I _____ . How _____ ? _____ it?
                          19. remember   **20.** be/your job   **21.** you/like

A: It's great! I _____ so much this summer.
                        22. learn

B: _____ enough money?
              23. you/have

A: No, I don't. I _____ most of my money. I _____
                        24. spend   **25.** need/buy

professional clothes when I arrived.

B: _____ home for a weekend? We _____ for your ticket.
              26. you/can/come   **27.** can/pay

A: I can't, Mom. We sometimes _____ activities on weekends, too.
                                            28. have

B: _____ again next week?
              29. you/call

A: If I _____ time, I _____ .
              30. have   **31.** call

EXERCISE 7 About You Write sentences about each of the topics in the chart. Use the simple present, the present continuous, the future, and the simple past. Then find a partner and compare your answers.

	School	Job	Family
Simple present			
Present continuous			
Future			
Simple past			

EXERCISE 8 Find a partner. Write questions to ask Barrington Irving and Paul Salopek. Use the simple present, the simple past, the future, modals, and infinitives.

Barrington Irving

1. _Why do you like your job?_ _____

2. _____

3. _____

4. _____

Paul Salopek

5. _____

6. _____

7. _____

8. _____

Chimene Ntakarutimana:
FROM AFRICA TO AMERICA

 Read the following essay. Pay special attention to the words in bold.

CD 2
TR 23

I was born in Africa. I'm the second of four children. Our names are Gentille, Chimene (that's me), Joseph, and Joy. When we were in Africa, our family was in great danger. We moved from country to country. I was born in Burundi, but my siblings[10] **weren't**. We were each born in a different country. Gentille was born in the Congo. Joseph was born in Zambia. It's hard to believe, **isn't it?** My parents dreamed of a better future, and we kids **did too.** You can't imagine what it's like to live in fear all the time, **can you?** But that was our life in Africa.

I was six when we came to the United States. My youngest sister, Joy, was born in the United States. She was an American citizen from birth, but the rest of us **weren't**.

At first, we lived in a small apartment in Chicago. Life was hard. We didn't speak English. My parents didn't have a job. But a refugee[11] agency[12] helped us, and an American woman **did too.** We started to call her "Grandma Sandy."

After three years in Chicago, my family moved to Kentucky. Grandma Sandy was sad when we left, and we **were too.** But she visits us often, and we always spend part of our summer vacations in Chicago. I love Chicago, and my sisters and brother **do too.**

I now speak English fluently. I don't speak my native language, Kirundi, anymore. Joseph and Joy **don't either**, but my oldest sister, Gentille, **does**. I understand it, but Joseph and Joy **don't**.

I'm now a senior in high school and am preparing to go to college. My favorite subject is history. I hope we can learn from history and that the future will be better. I'm an optimist,[13] **am I not?**

I am now sending applications to many colleges. I still don't know what I'm going to study. I don't have to make a decision yet, **do I?** One thing is for sure: I want to help other people and make a difference in the lives of others.

---

[10] *sibling*: a person's brother or sister
[11] *refugee*: a person who leaves his or her country to escape war, natural disaster, or other dangerous situations
[12] *agency*: an organization
[13] *optimist*: someone who thinks good things will happen

COMPREHENSION CHECK Based on the reading, tell if the statement is true (**T**) or false (**F**).

1. Chimene goes to high school in Chicago.

2. All four children were born in Africa.

3. Only Chimene's oldest sister still speaks the family's native language.

12.3 Auxiliary Verbs with *Too* and *Either*

We use auxiliary verbs with *too* and *either* to show similarity and to avoid repetition.

Examples	Explanation
Chimene was born in Africa. Joseph **was too**. Chimene speaks English fluently, and Joseph **does too**.	For affirmative statements, we use an auxiliary verb + *too*. It is not necessary to say: *Chimene was born in Africa. Joseph was born in Africa.*
Joy doesn't understand Kirundi, and Joseph **doesn't either**. Chimene wasn't born in the United States, and Joseph **wasn't either**.	For negative statements, we use an auxiliary verb + *not* + *either*. We usually use a contraction before *either*. It is not necessary to say: *Joy doesn't understand Kirundi, and Joseph doesn't understand Kirundi.*
A: I'm interested in Chimene's story. **B: Me too.** **A:** I don't know much about Burundi. **B: Me neither.**	In informal speech, we often say *me too* and *me neither*.
I was born in Africa. Joy **wasn't**. I can't speak Kirundi, but Gentille **can**. I **am** in high school. Joseph **isn't**.	We can use an auxiliary verb to avoid repetition in opposite statements. It is not necessary to say: *I was born in Africa. Joy wasn't born in Africa.* We sometimes connect opposite statements with *but*.

EXERCISE 9 Complete the statements about the things Chimene and her family have in common. Use an auxiliary verb + *too*.

1. Chimene was born in Africa, and Joseph _____was too_____.

2. She lives in Kentucky now, and her family _____.

3. She dreamed of a better future, and her parents _____.

4. She can understand Kirundi, and Gentille _____.

5. She is getting a good education, and her brother and sisters _____.

6. She was sad to leave Chicago. Her brother and sisters _____.

EXERCISE 10 Complete the statements about the things Chimene, her family, her friends, and her teachers have in common. Use an auxiliary verb + *either*.

1. Chimene can't speak Kirundi, and Joseph _____ *can't either* _____.

2. Joy isn't in high school. Joseph _____.

3. Chimene wasn't born in the United States, and Joseph and Gentille _____.

4. Chimene's father didn't speak English when they arrived. Her mother _____.

5. Chimene doesn't remember much about Africa, and Joseph _____.

6. Chimene's friends don't know much about Burundi. Some of her teachers _____.

EXERCISE 11 Fill in the blanks to complete the opposite statements.

1. Burundians speak Kirundi, but Zambians _____ *don't* _____.

2. Chimene doesn't speak Kirundi, but Gentille _____.

3. Gentille is in college now, but Chimene _____.

4. Chimene lives in Kentucky. Her grandmother _____.

5. The name *Gentille* is sometimes hard for Americans to say. The name *Joy* _____.

6. Joy was born in the United States, but her brother and sisters _____.

EXERCISE 12 Complete the conversation between two friends. Use an auxiliary verb and *too* or *either* when necessary.

A: I'm moving on Saturday. Maybe you and your brother can help me. Are you working on Saturday?

B: My brother is working on Saturday, but I '*m not*_____. I can help you.
       1.

A: I need a van. Do you have one?

B: I don't have one, but my brother _____. I'll ask him if we can use it. By the way, why
       2.
 are you moving?

A: There are a couple of reasons. I like my apartment, but my wife _____. She says it's
       3.
 too small for two people.

B: How many rooms does your new apartment have?

A: The old apartment has two bedrooms, and the new one _____ _____. But
       4.
 the rooms are much bigger in the new one. Also, we'd like to live downtown. We spend too

 much time traveling to work.

continued

B: I _____ _____ , but apartments downtown are so expensive.
5.

A: We found a nice apartment that isn't so expensive. Also, I'd like to own a dog, but my present

landlord doesn't permit pets.

B: Mine doesn't _____ . What kind of dog do you plan to get?
6.

A: I like big dogs. I don't like small dogs, but my wife _____ .
7.

B: I don't like small dogs _____ . They just make a lot of noise.
8.

A: Now you know my reasons for moving. Will you help me on Saturday?

B: Of course I will.

12.4 Auxiliary Verbs in Tag Questions

We use a tag question (a short question at the end of a statement) to ask if the statement is correct or if the listener agrees.

Examples	Explanation
Chimene is from Africa, **isn't she?** You lived in Zambia, **didn't you?** You speak English fluently now, **don't you?**	An affirmative statement has a negative tag question. For a negative tag question, we contract the auxiliary verb with *not* and follow with a subject pronoun.
You don't speak Kirundi, **do you?** You weren't born in the United States, **were you?** Sandy didn't move to Kentucky, **did she?**	A negative statement has an affirmative tag question. For an affirmative tag question, we use an auxiliary verb + a subject pronoun.
There are many languages in Africa, aren't **there?**	If the sentence begins with *there*, we use *there* in the tag question.
This is a long name, isn't **it?** That was an interesting story, wasn't **it?**	If the sentence begins with *this* or *that*, we use *it* in the tag question.
These aren't long questions, are **they?** Those were hard times, weren't **they?**	If the sentence begins with *these* or *those*, we use *they* in the tag question.

Language Notes:

1. In formal English, we sometimes use the full form for negative tag questions. The word order is: auxiliary verb + subject + *not*.

   FORMAL: She speaks English, **does she not?**

   INFORMAL: She speaks English, **doesn't she?**

2. *Am I not?* is a very formal tag. Informally, we usually say *aren't I?*

   FORMAL: I'm an optimist, **am I not?**

   INFORMAL: I'm an optimist, **aren't I?**

EXERCISE 13 Complete the conversation between two people at a party. Use tag questions.

A: Hi, Sam.

B: Uh, hi . . .

A: You don't remember me, _____*do you*_____?
1.

B: You look familiar, but I can't remember your name. We were in the same chemistry class

last semester, _____?
2.

A: No.

B: Then we probably met in math class, _____?
3.

A: Wrong again. I'm Nicole's brother.

B: Now I remember you. Nicole introduced us at a party last summer, _____?
4.

Your name is Max, _____?
5.

A: That's right.

B: How are you, Max? You did an internship in Washington last year, _____?
6.

A: No. Nicole did the internship.

B: So how's Nicole doing? She isn't in Washington anymore, _____?
7.

A: No. She finished her internship and started teaching.

B: I never see her anymore. She moved back to California, _____?
8.

A: No, she's still here. But she's married now.

B: Who did she marry?

A: Dan Tripton. You met him, _____?
9.

B: Yes, I think so. This is a great party, _____? There are a lot of interesting
10.

people here, _____?
11.

A: Yes, there are. But I have to leave early.

B: It was great seeing you again, Max. Say hello to Nicole when you see her.

SUMMARY OF LESSON 12

Verb Review

	Examples	Explanation
Simple present	Irving **loves** to fly. He often **helps** kids. Irving **comes** from Jamaica.	We use the simple present with facts, general truths, habits, customs, regular activities, repeated actions, and a place of origin.
Present continuous	Salopek **is walking** around the world. We **are reviewing** verbs.	We use the present continuous with actions that are happening right now, or with longer actions that are in progress but may not be happening at this exact moment.
Future	Salopek **is going to end** his trip in South America. He **will arrive** in Tierra del Fuego.	We use the future with simple facts or predictions about the future.
Simple past	Chimene's family **left** Africa in 2004. She **learned** English quickly.	We use the simple past with actions that began and ended in the past.
Be	Salopek and Irving **are** adventurous. There **are** many ways to teach kids about science. Chimene **was** born in Africa.	We use *be* with classifications, descriptions, location, age, weather, time, *there*, and *born*.
Modals	Chimene **can** speak English fluently. She **might** go to the University of Kentucky.	We use modals to add meaning to the main verb.
Infinitives	She wants **to go** to college. It's necessary **to choose** a major. She's pleased **to be** in the U.S. She's studying hard **to get** into a good college.	We use infinitives after certain verbs, certain expressions beginning with *it*, and certain adjectives. We use infinitives to show purpose.

Auxiliary Verbs

Examples	Explanation
Irving likes adventure. Salopek **does** too. I wasn't born here. You **weren't** either.	We use auxiliary verbs with *too* and *either* to avoid repetition of the same verb phrase.
Chimene can't remember her native language, but her older sister **can**. Chimene is in high school, but Joseph **isn't**.	We use auxiliary verbs to avoid repetition in opposite statements.
Irving helps kids, **doesn't** he? Salopek won't stop in France, **will** he?	We use auxiliary verbs to make tag questions.

TEST/REVIEW

PART 1 Choose the correct word(s) to complete the statements.

1. Barrington Irving (*borned/was born*) in Jamaica.

2. When he (*was/were*) 15, he (*meet/met*) a pilot.

a.
b.

3. He (*become/became*) interested in aviation.

4. He (*is loving/loves*) to fly.

5. He (*flied/flew*) around the world when he was 23.

6. He (*wants/want*) (*inspire/to inspire*) kids.

a.
b.

7. Irving's students (*working/are working*) on different projects.

8. The kids in this program (*gain/are gaining*) confidence.

9. He's going (*to fly/fly*) around the world again.

10. When (*he'll fly/he flies*) around the world again, (*he'll share/he shares*) information with schoolchildren.

a.
b.

PART 2 Write the negative form of the underlined word(s).

1. Chimene <u>was</u> born in Africa. She _____ wasn't _____ born in Congo.

2. Her last name <u>is</u> hard for Americans to say. It _____ easy to pronounce.

3. She <u>spoke</u> Kirundi when she arrived in the United States. She _____ English.

4. Her family <u>had</u> a hard time in Africa. They _____ an easy life.

5. Her family <u>lives</u> in Kentucky. Her family _____ in Chicago.

6. I <u>can imagine</u> life in another country. I _____ life in Africa.

7. Chimene <u>is preparing</u> for college. She _____ for a career yet.

8. Chimene <u>knows</u> that she wants to go to college. She _____ what to major in.

9. She <u>has to choose</u> a major. She _____ a major during her first year.

10. She<u>'ll start</u> college next year. She _____ college in the summer.

PART 3 Complete the sentences with the question form of the underlined word(s). Fill in the correct form for short answers.

1. **A:** <u>Paul Salopek isn't</u> in the United States now.

   B: Where _____ *is he* _____ now?

2. **A:** <u>Salopek will</u> travel around the world.

   B: _____ to South Africa?

   A: No, he _____ .

3. **A:** <u>He worked</u> in a gas station in Chicago.

   B: Why _____ in a gas station?

4. **A:** <u>He's writing</u> about his experiences.

   B: Why _____ about his experiences?

5. **A:** <u>He's going to walk</u> through North America.

   B: _____ through New York?

   A: No, he _____ .

6. **A:** <u>He won't walk</u> through Brazil.

   B: Why _____ through Brazil?

7. **A:** <u>He will be</u> in Tierra del Fuego, South America.

   B: When _____ in Tierra del Fuego?

8. **A:** <u>Human migration started</u> many years ago.

   B: When _____ ?

9. **A:** <u>He is sharing</u> his information on his website.

   B: _____ his information with schoolchildren?

   A: Yes, he _____ .

10. **A:** <u>He can learn</u> about the world.

    B: What _____ about the world?

PART 4 Complete the statements with the correct auxiliary verb. Add *too* or *either* when necessary.

1. Barrington Irving likes adventure. Paul Salopek _____*does too*_____.

2. Irving is interested in teaching children, and Salopek _____.

3. Irving will share his knowledge with young people. Salopek _____.

4. Irving is a pilot, but Salopek _____.

5. Chimene was born in Burundi, but her sisters and brother _____.

6. Chimene didn't speak English when she arrived in the United States, and her parents

   _____.

7. She doesn't need ESL classes anymore, and her brother _____.

8. She doesn't live in Chicago, but Grandma Sandy _____.

9. She wants to go to the University of Chicago, but her sister _____.

10. She should study hard. Her brother _____.

PART 5 Complete the sentences with a tag question. Use contractions when possible.

1. Salopek is brave, _____*isn't he?*_____

2. He started his trip in 2013, _____

3. Salopek isn't finished with his trip, _____

4. He won't go to Brazil, _____

5. There's a lot to learn about the world, _____

6. Irving comes from Miami, _____

7. Irving's students built an airplane, _____

8. They didn't believe it was possible, _____

9. This was an interesting lesson, _____

10. We should always practice verbs, _____

WRITING

PART 1 Editing Advice

1. Use the correct question formation.

   does Chimene go
   Where ~~Chimene goes~~ to school?

   did her family come
   When ~~her family came~~ to the United States?

   Barrington
   Where was born ~~Barrington~~?
   ^

2. Don't use *be* with a simple present or past verb.

   Children ~~are~~ need confidence.

   Sixty kids ~~were~~ built an airplane.

3. Use the base form after *do*, *does*, and *did*.

   speak
   She didn't ~~spoke~~ English when she arrived in the United States.

   go
   Where does she ~~goes~~ to school?

4. For the simple present, use the *-s* form when the subject is *he, she, it, family*, or a singular noun.

   s
   Lena love Washington, DC.
   ^

5. Use the correct past form for irregular verbs.

   left
   Salopek ~~leaved~~ Ethiopia in 2013.

6. Use the base form after *to*.

   study
   He wants to ~~studies~~ human migration.

7. Use the base form after a modal.

   study
   Lena should ~~studies~~ hard.

   She must ~~to~~ wear professional clothes to work.

8. Use an infinitive after some adjectives and verbs (but not after a modal).

   to   *to*
   She needs choose a major. She's not ready make a decision.
   ^   ^

9. Don't use the present continuous with nonaction verbs.

   wants
   Irving ~~is wanting~~ to inspire kids now.

10. Use the correct form of *be*.

    were
    They ~~was~~ born in Africa.

11. Don't forget to include a form of *be* in a present continuous sentence.

    are
    We learning about people on the move.
    ^

12. Don't use the future in a time clause or an *if* clause. Use the simple present.

                                   s

       When she ~~will~~ graduate from high school, she'll go to college.
                            ^

13. Don't forget *to* after certain expressions beginning with *it*.

                     to

       It's important inspire kids.
                ^

PART 2 Editing Practice

Some of the shaded words and phrases have mistakes. Find the mistakes and correct them. If the shaded words are correct, write *C*.

             C   *live*

A: Does your family ~~lives~~ in the United States?
          1.   **2.**

B: Yes, but I doesn't live with them.
                   3.

A: Why you don't live with them?
              4.

B: They live in Miami. I finded a job here, so I was moved.
          5.   **6.**   **7.**

A: When you moved here?
             8.

B: Three years ago. I don't like to be so far from my parents, but I have no choice. I didn't realized
                         9.   **10.**   **11.**

       how much I would miss them. I lonely at times, but my mom call me almost every day, so
                            12.   **13.**

       that helps.
         14.

A: I'm know how you feel. When I left home for the first time, it was very hard for me be away
          15.   **16.**   **17.**   **18.**

       from my family.

B: Where your family lives?
               19.

A: They live in Vietnam. They want visit me very much. When I will save enough money,
          20.   **21.**   **22.**

       I'm going to send them plane tickets. I'm having two jobs now, so soon I'll be have enough
           23.   **24.**   **25.**

       money for their trip.

B: How long they'll stay here?
              26.

A: My mom can to stay for 6 months. She's retired. But my dad is still working, so he can only stay
          27.   **28.**   **29.**

       for 2 weeks.

continued

B: How often do you talk to your parents?
30.

A: It's expensive talk by phone, so we usually send e-mail. Sometimes I use a phone card.
31. 32.

B: How much costs a phone card?
33.

A: It cost $10 for about 30 minutes.
34.

PART 3 Write About It

1. Write about a time you were on the move. How was your life before the move? How was your life after?

2. Write about an unusual person you know or read about. Tell what that person did or is doing.

PART 4 Edit Your Writing

Reread the Summary of Lesson 12 and the editing advice. Edit your writing from Part 3.

Vowel and Consonant Pronunciation Charts

Vowels

Symbol	Examples
ʌ	love, cup
a	father, box
æ	class, black
ə	alone, atom
ɛ	ever, well
i	eat, feet
ɪ	miss, bit
ɔ	talk, corn
ʊ	would, book
oʊ	cone, boat
u	tooth, school
eɪ	able, day
aɪ	mine, try
aʊ	about, cow
ɔɪ	join, boy

Consonants

Symbol	Examples
b	bread, cab
d	door, dude
f	form, if
g	go, flag
h	hello, behind
j	use, yellow
k	cook, hike
l	leg, meal
m	month, sum
n	never, win
ŋ	singer, walking
p	put, map
r	river, try
s	saw, parks
ʃ	show, action
ɾ	atom, lady
t	take, tent
tʃ	check, church
θ	thing, both
ð	the, either
v	voice, of
w	would, reward
z	zoo, mazes
ʒ	usual, vision
dʒ	just, edge

Make and *Do*

Some expressions use *make*. Others use *do*.

Make	Do
make a date/an appointment	do (the) homework
make a plan	do an exercise
make a decision	do the cleaning, laundry, dishes, washing
make a telephone call	do the shopping
make a meal (breakfast, lunch, dinner)	do one's best
make a mistake	do a favor
make an effort	do the right/wrong thing
make an improvement	do a job
make a promise	do business
make money	What do you do for a living? (asks about a job)
make noise	How do you do? (said when you meet someone for the first time)
make the bed	

Capitalization Rules

Rule	Examples
The first word in a sentence	**M**y friends are helpful.
The word *I*	My sister and **I** took a trip together.
Names of people	**A**braham **L**incoln; **G**eorge **W**ashington
Titles preceding names of people	**D**octor (**D**r.) **S**mith; **P**resident **L**incoln; **Q**ueen **E**lizabeth; **M**r. **R**ogers; **M**rs. **C**arter
Geographic names	the **U**nited **S**tates; **L**ake **S**uperior; **C**alifornia; the **R**ocky **M**ountains; the **M**ississippi **R**iver **Note:** The word *the* in a geographic name is not capitalized.
Street names	**P**ennsylvania **A**venue (**A**ve.); **W**all **S**treet (**S**t.); **A**bbey **R**oad (**R**d.)
Names of organizations, companies, colleges, buildings, stores, hotels	the **R**epublican **P**arty; **C**engage **L**earning; **D**artmouth **C**ollege; the **U**niversity of **W**isconsin; the **W**hite **H**ouse; **B**loomingdale's; the **H**ilton **H**otel
Nationalities and ethnic groups	**M**exicans; **C**anadians; **S**paniards; **A**mericans; **J**ews; **K**urds; **I**nuit
Languages	**E**nglish; **S**panish; **P**olish; **V**ietnamese; **R**ussian
Months	**J**anuary; **F**ebruary
Days	**S**unday; **M**onday
Holidays	**I**ndependence **D**ay; **T**hanksgiving
Important words in a title	*Grammar in Context; The Old Man and the Sea; Romeo and Juliet; The Sound of Music* **Note:** Capitalize *the* as the first word of a title.

Prepositions of Time

	Time Expression	Examples
in	in the morning in the afternoon in the evening	He eats breakfast **in** the morning. He eats lunch **in** the afternoon. He eats dinner **in** the evening.
	in the [season]	We have vacation **in** the summer. There are many flowers **in** the spring.
	in [month]	Her birthday is **in** March.
	in the ___ century	People didn't use cars **in** the 19th century.
	in [number] minutes, hours, days, weeks, months, years	We'll leave on vacation **in** three days. I will graduate **in** two weeks.
	in the past in the future	**In** the past, people didn't use computers. **In** the future, we will need more health care workers.
	in the beginning	**In** the beginning, I didn't understand the teacher at all.
at	at night	He likes to watch TV **at** night.
	at [time]	My class begins **at** 12:30.
	at present	**At** present, I'm learning French.
	at the beginning of [something] at the end of [something]	The semester starts **at** the beginning of September. The semester ends **at** the end of May.
on	on [date]	His birthday is **on** March 5.
	on [day]	I have to work **on** Saturday.
	on the weekend	I'm going to a party **on** the weekend.
from	from [time] to [time]	My class is **from** 12:30 **to** 3:30.
	from [time] until/till [time]	My class is **from** 12:30 **until** (or **till**) 3:30.
for	for [number] minutes, hours, days, weeks, months, years	She was in Mexico **for** three weeks. We lived in Paris **for** two years.
by	by [time]	Please finish your test **by** six o'clock.
until/till	until/till [time]	I slept **until** (or **till**) 9 a.m. this morning.
	until /till [event]	I lived with my parents **until** (**till**) I got married.
during	during [event]	He fell asleep **during** the meeting.
about	about [time]	The plane will arrive **about** 6 p.m.
around	around [time]	The plane will arrive **around** 6 p.m.
before	before [time, day, date]	You should finish the test **before** 9:30. You should finish the job **before** Friday.
	before [event]	Turn off the lights **before** you leave.
after	after [time, day, date]	Please don't call me **after** 10 p.m. I'll have more free time **after** next Monday.
	after [event]	Wash the dishes **after** you finish dinner.

Verbs and Adjectives Followed by a Preposition

Many verbs and adjectives are followed by a preposition.		
accuse someone of	(be) familiar with	(be) prepared for
(be) accustomed to	(be) famous for	prevent (someone) from
adjust to	(be) fond of	prohibit (someone) from
(be) afraid of	forget about	protect (someone) from
agree with	forgive someone for	(be) proud of
(be) amazed at/by	(be) glad about	recover from
(be) angry about	(be) good at	(be) related to
(be) angry at/with	(be) grateful (to someone) for	rely on/upon
apologize for	(be) guilty of	(be) responsible for
approve of	(be) happy about	(be) sad about
argue about	hear about	(be) satisfied with
argue with	hear of	(be) scared of
(be) ashamed of	hope for	(be) sick of
(be) aware of	(be) incapable of	(be) sorry about
believe in	insist on/upon	(be) sorry for
blame someone for	(be) interested in	speak about
(be) bored with/by	(be) involved in	speak to/with
(be) capable of	(be) jealous of	succeed in
care about	(be) known for	(be) sure of/about
care for	(be) lazy about	(be) surprised at
compare to/with	listen to	take care of
complain about	look at	talk about
concentrate on	look for	talk to/with
(be) concerned about	look forward to	thank (someone) for
consist of	(be) mad about	(be) thankful (to someone) for
count on	(be) mad at	think about/of
deal with	(be) made from/of	(be) tired of
decide on	(be) married to	(be) upset about
depend on/upon	object to	(be) upset with
(be) different from	(be) opposed to	(be) used to
disapprove of	participate in	wait for
(be) divorced from	plan on	warn (someone) about
dream about/of	pray for	(be) worried about
(be) engaged to	pray to	worry about
(be) excited about		

Question Formation

Main Verbs

Statement	Yes/No Question + Short Answer	Wh- Question	
She **watches** TV.	**Does** she **watch** the news? Yes, she **does**.	When **does** she **watch** TV?	
Your parents **live** in Peru.	**Do** your parents **live** in Lima? No, they **don't**.	Where **do** your parents **live**?	
You **needed** someone.	**Did** you **need** a doctor? No, I **didn't**.	Who(m) **did** you **need**?	
The janitor **found** a book.	**Did** the janitor **find** my dictionary? No, he **didn't**.	Which book **did** he **find**?	
I **copied** someone's notes.	**Did** you **copy** my notes? No, I **didn't**.	Whose notes **did** you **copy**?	
Nora **didn't go** to work.	**Did** Nora **go** to school? No, she **didn't**.	Why **didn't** Nora **go** to school?	

Statement	Subject Question	
Someone **needs** your help.	Who **needs** my help?	
Some teachers **speak** Spanish.	Which teachers **speak** Spanish?	
Some children **saw** the movie.	How many children **saw** the movie?	
Something **happened**.	What **happened**?	
Someone's tablet **broke**.	Whose tablet **broke**?	

The Verb *Be*

Statement	Yes/No Question + Short Answer	Wh- Question	
Sara **is** in California.	**Is** Sara in San Francisco? No, she **isn't**.	Where **is** Sara?	
You **are** unhappy.	**Are** you unhappy with your job? Yes, I **am**.	Why **are** you unhappy with your job?	
The boys **were** here.	**Were** the boys here yesterday? No, they **weren't**.	When **were** the boys here?	
Paco **was** born in Mexico.	**Was** Paco born in Monterrey? Yes, he **was**.	When **was** he born?	
You **weren't** at the meeting.	**Were** you at the presentation? No, I **wasn't**.	Why **weren't** you at the meeting?	

Statement	Subject Question
One student **was** late.	Which student **was** late?
Some children **are** outside.	How many children **are** outside?
Someone **is** absent.	Who **is** absent?
Someone's book **is** on the floor.	Whose book **is** on the floor?

Auxiliary Verb + Main Verb

Statement	*Yes/No* Question + Short Answer	*Wh-* Question
She **is running**.	**Is** she **running** fast? Yes, she **is**.	Why **is** she **running**?
My parents **will leave** soon.	**Will** your parents **leave** tomorrow? No, they **won't**.	When **will** your parents **leave**?
We **can invite** several people.	**Can** we **invite** our neighbors? Yes, you **can**.	How many people **can** we **invite**?
You **shouldn't drive** now.	**Should** I **drive** later? Yes, you **should**.	Why **shouldn't** I **drive** now?

Statement	Subject Question
Someone **is laughing**.	Who **is laughing**?
Some people **will come** here.	Which people **will come** here?
Someone **should help** our neighbors.	How many people **should help** our neighbors?
Someone's child **is crying**.	Whose child **is crying**?

Metric Conversion Chart

Length

When You Know	Multiply by	To Find
inches (in)	2.54	centimeters (cm)
feet (ft)	30.5	centimeters (cm)
feet (ft)	0.3	meters (m)
miles (mi)	1.6	kilometers (km)
Metric:		
centimeters (cm)	0.39	inches (in)
centimeters (cm)	0.03	feet (ft)
meters (m)	3.28	feet (ft)
kilometers (km)	0.62	miles (mi)
Note: 12 inches = 1 foot 3 feet = 36 inches = 1 yard		

Weight (Mass)

When You Know	Multiply by	To Find
ounces (oz)	28.35	grams (g)
pounds (lb)	0.45	kilograms (kg)
Metric:		
grams (g)	0.04	ounces (oz)
kilograms (kg)	2.2	pounds (lb)
Note: 1 pound = 16 ounces		

Volume

When You Know	Multiply by	To Find
fluid ounces (fl oz)	30.0	milliliters (mL)
pints (pt)	0.47	liters (L)
quarts (qt)	0.95	liters (L)
gallons (gal)	3.8	liters (L)
Metric:		
milliliters (mL)	0.03	fluid ounces (fl oz)
liters (L)	2.11	pints (pt)
liters (L)	1.05	quarts (qt)
liters (L)	0.26	gallons (gal)
Note:		
1 pint = 2 cups		
1 quart = 2 pints = 4 cups		
1 gallon = 4 quarts = 8 pints = 16 cups		

Temperature

When You Know	Do This	To Find
degrees Fahrenheit (°F)	Subtract 32, then multiply by $\frac{5}{9}$	degrees Celsius (°C)
Metric:		
degrees Celsius (°C)	Multiply by $\frac{9}{5}$, then add 32	degrees Fahrenheit (°F)
Note:		
32°F = 0°C		
212°F = 100°C		

Irregular Verb Forms

Base Form	Simple Past Form	Past Participle	Base Form	Simple Past Form	Past Participle
be	was/were	been	find	found	found
bear	bore	born/borne	fit	fit	fit
beat	beat	beaten	flee	fled	fled
become	became	become	fly	flew	flown
begin	began	begun	forbid	forbade	forbidden
bend	bent	bent	forget	forgot	forgotten
bet	bet	bet	forgive	forgave	forgiven
bid	bid	bid	freeze	froze	frozen
bind	bound	bound	get	got	gotten
bite	bit	bitten	give	gave	given
bleed	bled	bled	go	went	gone
blow	blew	blown	grind	ground	ground
break	broke	broken	grow	grew	grown
breed	bred	bred	hang	hung	hung
bring	brought	brought	have	had	had
broadcast	broadcast	broadcast	hear	heard	heard
build	built	built	hide	hid	hidden
burst	burst	burst	hit	hit	hit
buy	bought	bought	hold	held	held
cast	cast	cast	hurt	hurt	hurt
catch	caught	caught	keep	kept	kept
choose	chose	chosen	know	knew	known
cling	clung	clung	lay	laid	laid
come	came	come	lead	led	led
cost	cost	cost	leave	left	left
creep	crept	crept	lend	lent	lent
cut	cut	cut	let	let	let
deal	dealt	dealt	lie	lay	lain
dig	dug	dug	light	lit/lighted	lit/lighted
dive	dove/dived	dove/dived	lose	lost	lost
do	did	done	make	made	made
draw	drew	drawn	mean	meant	meant
drink	drank	drunk	meet	met	met
drive	drove	driven	mistake	mistook	mistaken
eat	ate	eaten	overcome	overcame	overcome
fall	fell	fallen	overdo	overdid	overdone
feed	fed	fed	overtake	overtook	overtaken
feel	felt	felt	overthrow	overthrew	overthrown
fight	fought	fought	pay	paid	paid

Base Form	Simple Past Form	Past Participle	Base Form	Simple Past Form	Past Participle
plead	pled/pleaded	pled/pleaded	sting	stung	stung
prove	proved	proven/proved	stink	stank	stunk
put	put	put	strike	struck	struck/stricken
quit	quit	quit	strive	strove	striven
read	read	read	swear	swore	sworn
ride	rode	ridden	sweep	swept	swept
ring	rang	rung	swell	swelled	swelled/swollen
rise	rose	risen	swim	swam	swum
run	ran	run	swing	swung	swung
say	said	said	take	took	taken
see	saw	seen	teach	taught	taught
seek	sought	sought	tear	tore	torn
sell	sold	sold	tell	told	told
send	sent	sent	think	thought	thought
set	set	set	throw	threw	thrown
sew	sewed	sewn/sewed	understand	understood	understood
shake	shook	shaken	uphold	upheld	upheld
shed	shed	shed	upset	upset	upset
shine	shone/shined	shone/shined	wake	woke	woken
shoot	shot	shot	wear	wore	worn
show	showed	shown/showed	weave	wove	woven
shrink	shrank/shrunk	shrunk/shrunken	wed	wedded/wed	wedded/wed
shut	shut	shut	weep	wept	wept
sing	sang	sung	win	won	won
sink	sank	sunk	wind	wound	wound
sit	sat	sat	withdraw	withdrew	withdrawn
sleep	slept	slept	withhold	withheld	withheld
slide	slid	slid	withstand	withstood	withstood
slit	slit	slit	wring	wrung	wrung
speak	spoke	spoken	write	wrote	written
speed	sped	sped			
spend	spent	spent			
spin	spun	spun			
spit	spit/spat	spit/spat			
split	split	split			
spread	spread	spread			
spring	sprang	sprung			
stand	stood	stood			
steal	stole	stolen			
stick	stuck	stuck			

Note:

The simple past and past participle of some verbs can end in *-ed* or *-t*.

burn	burned OR burnt
dream	dreamed OR dreamt
kneel	kneeled OR knelt
learn	learned OR learnt
leap	leaped OR leapt
spill	spilled OR spilt
spoil	spoiled OR spoilt

Map of the United States of America

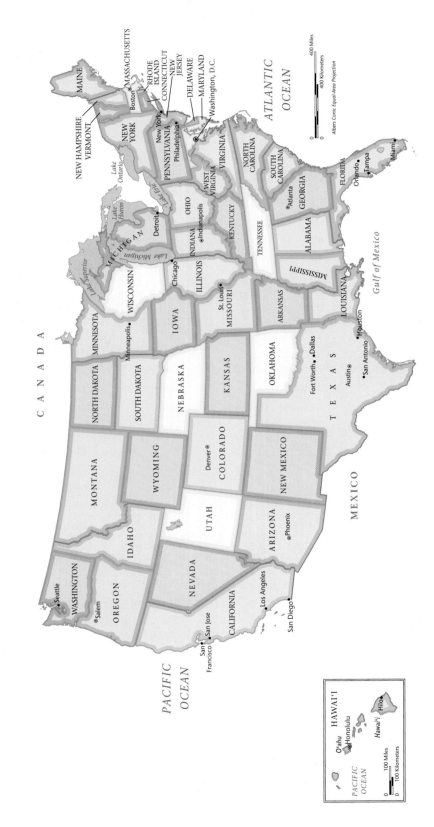

- **Adjective** An adjective gives a description of a noun.

  It's a *tall* tree. He's an *old* man. My neighbors are *nice*.

- **Adverb** An adverb describes the action of a sentence or an adjective or another adverb.

  She speaks English *fluently*. I drive *carefully*.

  She speaks English *extremely* well. She is *very* intelligent.

- **Adverb of Frequency** An adverb of frequency tells how often an action happens.

  I *never* drink coffee. They *usually* take the bus.

- **Affirmative** *Affirmative* means "yes."

  They *live* in Miami.

- **Apostrophe** ' We use the apostrophe for possession and contractions.

  My *sister's* friend is beautiful. (possession)

  Today *isn't* Sunday. (contraction)

- **Article** An article comes before a noun. It tells if the noun is definite or indefinite. The indefinite articles are *a* and *an*. The definite article is *the*.

  I have *a* cat. I ate *an* apple. *The* teacher came late.

- **Auxiliary Verb** An auxiliary verb is used in forming tense, mood, or aspect of the verb that follows it. Some verbs have two parts: an auxiliary verb and a main verb.

  You *didn't* eat lunch. He *can't* study. We *will* return.

- **Base Form** The base form of the verb has no tense. It has no ending (*-s*, *-ed*, or *-ing*): *be, go, eat, take, write.*

  I didn't *go*. We don't *know* you. He can't *drive*.

- **Capital Letter** A B C D E F G . . .

- **Clause** A clause is a group of words that has a subject and a verb. Some sentences have only one clause.

  She speaks Spanish.

  Some sentences have a **main clause** and a **dependent clause**.

MAIN CLAUSE	DEPENDENT CLAUSE (reason clause)
She found a good job	*because she has computer skills.*
MAIN CLAUSE	DEPENDENT CLAUSE (time clause)
She'll turn off the light	*before she goes to bed.*
MAIN CLAUSE	DEPENDENT CLAUSE (*if* clause)
I'll take you to the doctor	*if you don't have your car on Saturday.*

- **Colon** :

- **Comma** ,

- **Comparative** The comparative form of an adjective or adverb is used to compare two things.

  My house is *bigger* than your house.

  Her husband drives *faster* than she does.

  My children speak English *more fluently* than I do.

GLOSSARY

- **Consonant** The following letters are consonants: *b, c, d, f, g, h, j, k, l, m, n, p, q, r, s, t, v, w, x, y, z.*

  NOTE: *Y* is sometimes considered a vowel, as in the world *syllable.*

- **Contraction** A contraction is two words joined with an apostrophe.

  He's my brother.   *You're* late.   They *won't* talk to me.

  (*He's = He is*)   (*You're = You are*)   (*won't = will not*)

- **Count Noun** Count nouns are nouns that we can count. They have a singular and a plural form.

  1 *pen*–3 *pens*   1 *table*–4 *tables*

- **Dependent Clause** See **Clause**.

- **Exclamation Mark** !

- **Frequency Word** Frequency words (*always, usually, generally, often, sometimes, rarely, seldom, hardly ever, never*) tell how often an action happens.

  I *never* drink coffee.   We *always* do our homework.

- **Hyphen** -

- **Imperative** An imperative sentence gives a command or instruction. An imperative sentence omits the subject pronoun *you.*

  Come here.   *Don't be* late.   Please *help* me.

- **Infinitive** An infinitive is *to* + the base form.

  I want *to leave.*   You need *to be* here on time.

- **Linking Verb** A linking verb is a verb that links the subject to the noun, adjective, or adverb after it. Linking verbs include *be, seem, feel, smell, sound, look, appear,* and *taste.*

  She *is* a doctor.   She *looks* tired.   You *are* late.

- **Main Clause** See **Clause**.

- **Modal** The modal verbs are *can, could, shall, should, will, would, may, might,* and *must.*

  They *should* leave.   I *must* go.

- **Negative** *Negative* means "no."

  She *doesn't speak* Spanish.

- **Nonaction Verb** A nonaction verb has no action. We do not use a continuous tense (*be* + verb *-ing*) with a nonaction verb. Nonaction verbs include: *believe, cost, care, have, hear, know, like, love, matter, mean, need, own, prefer, remember, see, seem, think, understand, want,* and sense-perception verbs.

  She *has* a laptop.   We *love* our mother.   You *look* great.

- **Noncount Noun** A noncount noun is a noun that we don't count. It has no plural form.

  She drank some *water.*   He prepared some *rice.*

  Do you need any *money*?   We had a lot of *homework.*

- **Noun** A noun is a person, a place, or a thing. Nouns can be either count or noncount.

  My *brother* lives in California.   My *sisters* live in New York.

  I get *advice* from them.   I drink *coffee* every day.

- **Noun Modifier** A noun modifier makes a noun more specific.

  fire department   *Independence* Day   *can* opener

- **Noun Phrase** A noun phrase is a group of words that form the subject or object of a sentence.

  A very nice woman helped me.   I bought *a big box of cereal*.

- **Object** The object of a sentence follows the verb. It receives the action of the verb.

  He bought *a car*.   I saw *a movie*.   I met *your brother*.

- **Object Pronoun** We use object pronouns (*me, you, him, her, it, us, them*) after a verb or preposition.

  He likes *her*.   I saw the movie. Let's talk about *it*.

- **Parentheses** ( )

- **Paragraph** A paragraph is a group of sentences about one topic.

- **Period** .

- **Phrasal Modal** Phrasal modals, such as *have to* and *be able to,* are made up of two or more words.

  You *have got to* see the movie.   We *have to* take a test.

- **Phrase** A group of words that go together.

  Last month my sister came to visit.   There is a strange car *in front of my house*.

- **Plural** *Plural* means "more than one." A plural noun usually ends with -*s*.

  She has beautiful *eyes*.   My *feet* are big.

- **Possessive Form** Possessive forms show ownership or relationship.

  Mary's coat is in the closet.   *My* brother lives in Miami.

- **Preposition** A preposition is a short connecting word. Some common prepositions are: *about, above, across, after, around, as, at, away, back, before, behind, below, by, down, for, from, in, into, like, of, off, on, out, over, to, under, up,* and *with*.

  The book is *on* the table.   She studies *with* her friends.

- **Present Participle** The present participle of a verb is the base form + -*ing*.

  She is *sleeping*.   They were *laughing*.

- **Pronoun** A pronoun takes the place of a noun.

  John likes Mary, but *she* doesn't like *him*.

- **Punctuation** The use of specific marks, such as commas and periods, to make ideas within writing clear.

- **Question Mark** ?

- **Quotation Marks** " "

- **Regular Verb** A regular verb forms the simple past with -*ed*.

  He *worked* yesterday.   I *laughed* at the joke.

- **-s Form** A simple present verb that ends in *-s* or *-es*.

    He *lives* in New York.   She *watches* TV a lot.

- **Sense-Perception Verb** A sense-perception verb has no action. It describes a sense. Some common sense-perception verbs are: *look, feel, taste, sound,* and *smell.*

    She *feels* fine.   The coffee *smells* fresh.   The milk *tastes* sour.

- **Sentence** A sentence is a group of words that contains a subject and a verb and gives a complete thought.

    SENTENCE: She came home.

    NOT A SENTENCE: When she came home

- **Singular** *Singular* means "one."

    She ate a *sandwich*.   I have one *television*.

- **Subject** The subject of the sentence tells who or what the sentence is about.

    My sister got married last April. *The wedding* was beautiful.

- **Subject Pronoun** We use a subject pronoun (*I, you, he, she, it, we, you, they*) before a verb.

    They speak Japanese.   *We* speak Spanish.

- **Superlative** The superlative form of an adjective or adverb shows the number one item in a group of three or more.

    January is the *coldest* month of the year.

    My brother speaks English the *best* in my family.

- **Syllable** A syllable is a part of a word. Each syllable has only one vowel sound. (Some words have only one syllable.)

    change (one syllable)   after (af·ter = two syllables)

    look (one syllable)   responsible (re·spon·si·ble = four syllables)

- **Tag Question** A tag question is a short question at the end of a sentence. It is used in conversation.

    You speak Spanish, *don't you?*   He's not happy, *is he?*

- **Tense** Tense shows when the action of the sentence happened. Verbs have different tenses.

    SIMPLE PRESENT: She usually *works* hard.

    PRESENT CONTINUOUS: She *is working* now.

    SIMPLE PAST: She *worked* yesterday.

    FUTURE: She *will work* tomorrow.

- **Verb** A verb is the action of the sentence.

    He *runs* fast.   I *speak* English.

- **Vowel** The following letters are vowels: *a, e, i, o, u.*

    NOTE: *Y* is sometimes considered a vowel, as in the world *syllable.*

INDEX